Collecting
The Beatles

ROCK & ROLL REFERENCE SERIES

ROCK & ROLL REMEMBRANCES SERIES

**An Introduction
& Price Guide To
Fab Four Collectibles,
Records & Memorabilia**

Collecting
The Beatles

by
Barbara Fenick

**Photographs by
Rick A. Kolodziej**

pierian
press
1982

Dedication

To all the Beatle fans everywhere
who inspired me to continue,
and to The Beatles themselves,
who inspired me to begin.

Contents

continued ▶

Bubble bath containers produced in the U.S. came in Paul and Ringo models only. Another NEMS product. *Price Guide No.: 634*

Contents (continued)

The Apple Dartboard, often mentioned but rarely seen, is another promotional piece from the Beatles' own company, Apple Corps Ltd. Valued at $600! *Price Guide No.: 613*

Illustrations

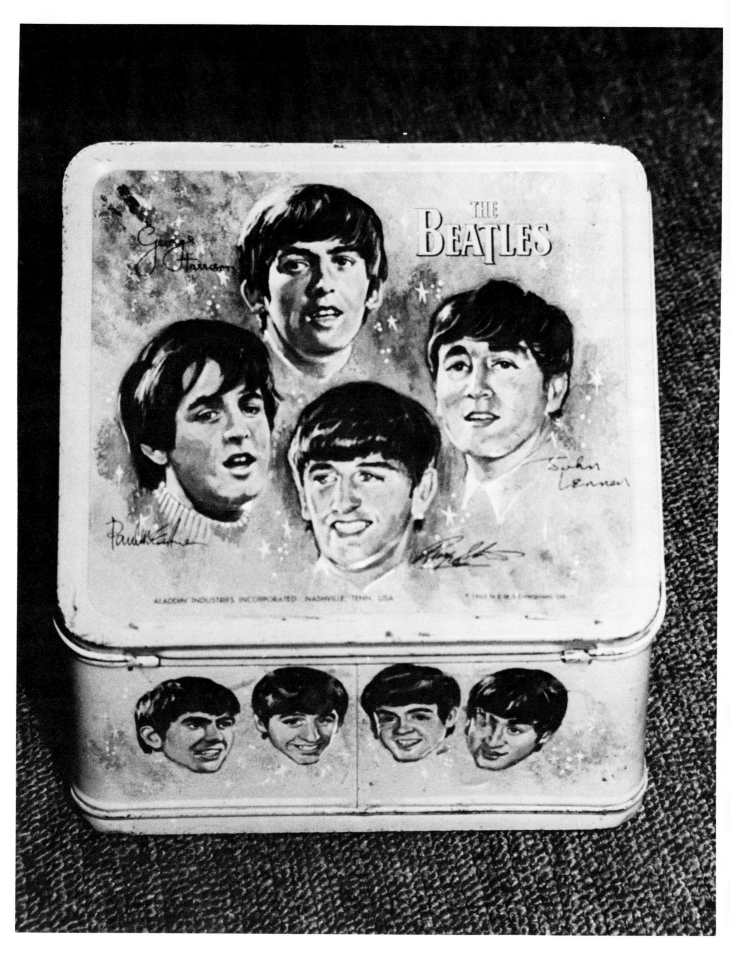

This Beatles (blue metal) lunchbox from 1965 sells for at least $40 in Very Good or Very Good+ condition.
Price Guide No.: 693

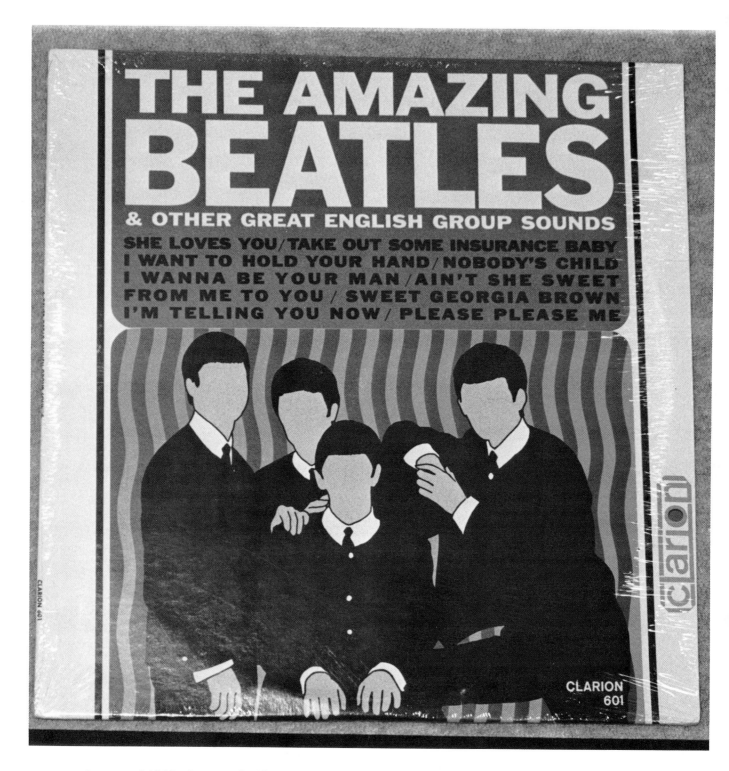

An unusual 1964 release on the Clarion label. Worth approximately $25-30 in monophonic, or $100+ still sealed (as this one is). *Price Guide No.: 3*

Preface

This book has taken over two years to research and write. Naturally, in that long a time span, the prices on the items listed in the Price Guide have had to be checked and corrected several times. Nothing stays the same these days, least of all prices, but those in this book are now as current as our publication schedule permitted, and reflect all the 1982 economic facts of life.

There are over 850 items listed in this book, with numerous variations and editions included. I'm sure there are actually thousands of Beatles records, books, and other product in existence and no one could ever hope to be complete in the first edition of a book of this type. So, I had to settle for the best that is humanly possible and include every item I could find out about, everything I've personally seen, heard about, or read about in my eighteen years of experience as a Beatle fan/collector and fan club president.

A dealer in Beatles collectibles once told me that there must be 100 or more different "Yellow Submarine" movie items alone. I haven't seen even half that many yet, and I don't know if I can ever hope to see them all in one lifetime! So, if I've failed to include some items you are contemplating buying or selling, or one you already own that you wanted to know the value of or obtain more detailed information about, please accept my apologies. But I do hope that this book is at least a useful first step in the direction of getting all the rarities and memorabilia associated with The Beatles collated and cataloged for future reference.

Perhaps succeeding editions of this book will be able to fill whatever gaps each of us might discover. You can help by alerting us to missing items, or additional variations and versions that you are aware of, and informing us of current selling prices as you see them. To this end, we have included a questionnaire page which we hope you'll make copies of, fill out, and mail to us as appropriate.

Something new is continually developing in the field of Beatles collecting. New product is still coming at us from all directions. One can barely keep up with all the new legitimate recordings, promos, magazines, and books, let alone all the newly created items like souvenirs, bootlegs, and counterfeits of valuable collectibles.

Probably no other current area needs as much vigilant monitoring as the confusing area of counterfeits. Since I wrote the chapter on that subject, a great deal of the worst sort of trickery has emerged. I should be insensitive to it by now, having seen so much of it, but some of the new schemes, cons, and tricks of the trade are just too deceitful to swallow. Counterfeiters started out, it seems to me, with the almost harmless practice of copying rare records that most of us either couldn't afford or couldn't locate, and made them available to the masses for a low price. In this way, **Family Way, Two Virgins, Beatles Christmas Album**, etc., could be enjoyed even when we were too poor to buy the originals.

Now, counterfeiting is practiced with a "buyer be damned" attitude, and they seem to take the fans for fools and suckers. The worst offense I've ever seen was at a recent Beatles convention where a counterfeit cover of the "original" art work for **Somewhere In England** was made into an LP jacket, sans record, and passed off as a genuine rarity selling for $35.00! The authentic art work for the first version of that Harrison LP is worth in the neighborhood of $100.00–$300.00, as only a few sample copies exist, the rest supposedly destroyed when the first cover was changed before commercial distribution. This counterfeit slick could legitimately be sold for $3.00–$4.00 merely as a widely distributed novelty piece, but to deliberately make it appear to be the real thing and charge such an outlandish price is pure banditry, and is typical of the types of abuses which are literally getting out of hand.

So many rare records, promos, and picture sleeves have been duplicated that even the dealers are being fooled. Unless you already have authenticated originals in your collection, it is hard to tell when a counterfeit passes your way. Often, the only clues may be in the subtle variations of colors on the label, sharpness in the picture on the sleeve or jacket, etc. I recently ended up with two expensive phonies that I won in auctions from collecting magazines. Having bid sight unseen, I believed the listings offering "rare promos"; there was no mention of bootlegs, reissues, second pressings, etc., to warn me about what I might actually end up with. I bid good prices based on current values of these rarities, and discovered in comparing them to the originals at a Beatles convention that I had actually bought fakes!

So, even a collector with years of experience can be caught in the con game without too much trouble. Had I followed some of my own advice and bought only from dealers I knew and trusted, I might have saved myself some expensive mistakes. It's a shame that a few greedy dealers must spoil the collecting hobby for all of us, but I'll be much more cautious in the future in buying records I cannot personally inspect first.

Pricing is another area which, in many cases, is experiencing ridiculously inflated increases bordering on outright deceit. There are always a few dealers who have charged far beyond the "standard," "accepted," or average price for a Beatles item. Even at a Beatles convention, where the majority of the dealers like to keep somewhat in line with each other, there are always a few who, for whatever reason, charge unusually high prices. Lately, however, I have seen items priced at not just double the norm, but at *five* or *ten times* the norm! A Beatles Christmas flexidisc, which usually sells for $100.00--$125.00 in Mint condition, was recently priced at $250.00. The paperback book *Love Me Do*, now out of print, was marked up to $80.00 in poor (water-damaged) condition. It should have been priced at around $10.00; it eventually sold for $40.00.

This kind of price gouging simply can't be attributed to inflation. Sure, many items doubled, some almost tripled in the four years between 1978 and 1982, and only a crystal ball can predict if the trend will continue at such a spiraling rate (see the list of examples below). Currently, prices are skyrocketing even between conventions, which are sometimes only three or four months apart.

SAMPLE INFLATION RATES FOR BEATLES COLLECTIBLES

ITEMS IN NEAR MINT CONDITION	1978	1980	1982
Let It Be boxed set	$75	$100	$200
Get Back (book alone)	$40	$65	$100
Can't Buy Me Love (picture sleeve)	$60-90	$100-125	$175
Dolls (Remco)	$15-20	$25-30	$35-50
In His Own Write (hardcover)	$23-26	$28-35	$35-50
Gold Records	$300	$400	$450-500
Beatles Pillow (NEMS)	$25	$50	$75
Yellow Submarine Corgi Toy	$35	$75	$100-125
Beatles Tray	$20-25	$35-50	$50-75
Tennis Shoes	$20-25	$40-60	$75-100
Two Virgins LP	$30	$50	$75
Christmas Album	$25	$50	$75
Ain't She Sweet (w/picture sleeve)	$25-30	$50	$75-80
Cold Turkey (w/picture sleeve)	$25	$35	$65-75
Gum Cards	25¢	35¢	50¢-$1.00
Gum Card Wrappers	$3	$6	$10

Fans are beginning to pass over some of the outrageously priced items, however, and I see these items packed away at the ends of many shows unsold. A book or record marked up five times higher than what it was six months before deserves to be rejected. In many cases, a dealer will dicker and eventually come down in price on an item that is still for sale at the end of a show due to it having been overpriced.

The question still remains, *when*, if ever, will the price spiral peak? Or will they just continue to climb? At what point can fans no longer afford to buy anything but remakes and bootlegs, because more desired records and memorabilia are priced ridiculously beyond their reach?

There *are* items that stay within a more conservative price range, for example:

	1978	1980	1982
I Want To Hold Your Hand (w/picture sleeve)	$15	$18	$20
I Apologise (LP)	$25	$30	$30-35
Family Way (LP)	$35	$50	$60-75
Hard Days Night (paperback)	$6	$8	$10
Real True Beatles (magazine by M. Braun)	$9	$12	$15
Buttons (original 1964 "I Love The Beatles" etc., large size)	$5-6	$6-8	$8-10

Most of the common picture sleeves (i.e., most Capitol ones) have stayed within a 25-33% price increase range. The same applies to most of the paperbacks from the sixties and magazines devoted to the Beatles. Most LPs that are out-of-print have at least doubled in price, except for the really unimpressive compilations (e.g., **The Amazing Beatles, Do It Now**), which may even drop in value as there seem to be few buyers for them. Memorabilia is one area in which almost all items are going up, up, up, and the end

The U.K. edition of the 1965 Beatles' Christmas flexi-disc with picture sleeve. This Very Good condition copy is worth approximately $85-100. *Price Guide No.: 78*

The *Please Please Me* picture sleeve is rising in value, and becoming as desirable (and expensive) as the *You Can't Do This* sleeve. With record included, it is valued at $1000 in Near Mint condition. *Price Guide No.: 109*

isn't yet in sight. The demand is so heavy, in the U.S. at least, that dealers cannot keep up. No wonder so many of them turn to selling replicas and newly made shirts, buttons, and so on.

Anyone who wants to see their collection *really* skyrocket would do well to find the best bargains and deals in original memorabilia, the rarer LPs, and the more uncommon picture sleeves. But watch out. It's not just Beatles dealers at conventions, either. People answering my want ads have been trying to make me believe that they have "rare" magazines worth $200.00. I have yet to see a Beatles magazine that sells for more than $20.00, except some rare Beatles comics or Japanese picture books. At a flea market, an antique dealer wanted $15.00 for a Beatles 8x10-inch photo which you can find as a still in many retail shops for $1.00–$3.00. "It says 'The Beatles' on it," I was told, as if that was a magic set of words which justified the overpricing.

So, it is the novice and professional alike who are charging outrageous sums for both rarities and *common* Beatles items. Fans need practical advice, tips, and some guidance, now more than ever. It's not in the least bit hard to spend a lot of money on Beatles items. Everyone selling today will gladly let you pay! But with a little extra information to steer you clear of the pitfalls, maybe you can still have fun collecting, and feel good about what you are getting. I hope this book helps out in that area. That's the reason I wrote it.

ACKNOWLEDGEMENTS

I want to especially thank Professor Peter Reed, my English professor and advisor at the University of Minnesota, for encouraging me to write in the first place, and for believing I could do it well. Special thanks also to Lorna Read at the Beatles Appreciation Society offices in England for publishing my first pieces on collecting, from which sprang the idea for a full-scale book on the subject.

I also want to thank Tom Schultheiss at Pierian Press for seeing this through with me, from outline to finished manuscript, and for his never ending patience as the project gobbled up over two years.

I want to give credit and thanks to my husband Rick, who read through all the rough first drafts, offered encouragement and served as a sounding board even though he didn't know one Beatle from the other when we met! And I want to thank him for doing such a terrific job in photographing the majority of the Beatles items for this book.

Another special thanks to the following friends and Beatles experts who lent their years of experience as collectors/dealers to read over some of the original price guide sections and offer their additions, notations, helpful hints, and useful feedback: Mitch McGeary (LPs); Rick Rann (45s); Annette Lawrence (memorabilia); and Jeff Augsburger (magazines).

I want to give credit to K.D. Peters at "The Real Fifth Beatle" for letting me make liberal use of her Beatles book list. I appreciate the research that went into that.

My thanks also to the following fans who let us photograph some of their rare collectibles: Dave Springer; Elaine and Michael Macaluso; Rick and Terry Thomas; Aixa Witkowski from *The Record Hunter*; Laurie Fiedler; and Cliff Yamasaki.

My additional thanks go out to all the following individuals, companies, stores and dealers who served (knowingly or otherwise) as sources for the prices and information given in this book:

Beatles America (Connecticut); Annette Lawrence (Queen's comics, Canada); Charles Reinhart; Tony Dawkins; New Fantasy Shop; Cliff Yamasaki (Let It Be Records); Denny's Records (New York); Sandy Andromeda; Murph; Rory Williams; Mike Sellers, Mitch McGeary (Ticket To Ryde); Liz and Jim Hughes (Cavern Mecca and Magical Mystery Store, Liverpool); Gary Shram (Blue Meanie Store, California); Colleen's Collectables (Ohio); Rick Rann; Elaine and Michael Macaluso; Record Runner (New York); Strider Records (New York); Speakeasy Antiques (New York); Wayne Rogers; Record Kingdom; Franck Leenheer (Holland); Frank Merrill (Saturday Night Records); Ken Stone; Midwest Nostalgia (Ohio); Eddie Chandler; Jeanne Cullen; David J. Smith; Felice Lipsky; Jimmy Lyford; Harold Carlton (Follies, London); Steve Derda; all the dealers at "Beatlefest" and other Beatles conventions; and the advertisers in *Goldmine, Sounds Fine*, and *Record Collector* magazines. Last, but not least, all the members of my own Beatles fan club, The Write Thing, who wrote in with tips, questions, suggestions, or who were just plain enthusiastic about collecting.

A rare Beatles phonograph which might sell for up to $500 in good playing condition. *Price Guide No.: 706*

Collecting: The New Rage

Collecting today is as much an investment as it is a hobby. Searching out Beatles items can still be just as much fun as it was ten years ago, but once a person gets hooked on building a serious collection, they can't avoid facing financial facts as well. And it is definitely "new math." Everyone is shocked the first time they realize their old 25 cent teen magazines are worth $10.00, their battered and rusty lunchbox $35.00, and that their original stereo **Introducing The Beatles** (bought for $2.98 in 1964) could fetch $100.00 in an auction.

For the last eight years particularly, the pace of collecting has escalated furiously — well past the point of innocent fun. For many, it has become a full-time business and, for the majority, it has become a confusing mess of jingo-lingo: "counterfeits," "reissues," "first state," "mint," "original," and "rare." Translating collectors' jargon into meaningful terms is the first difficult step! Anyone who wants to put Beatles items in their collection, or assess the value of what is already sitting in their record racks or on their bookshelves, needs a place to begin.

THE NEED FOR THIS GUIDE

While there have been numerous discographies and listings of record variations, no comprehensive guide, pamphlet, or booklet of helpful tips has ever been produced to aid either the novice or the experienced collector of Beatles' recordings and other memorabilia.

Several years ago, I was in England visiting the office of Beat Publications, where the monthlies *The Beatles Book* and *The Record Collector* are written. I was blithely and magnanimously giving my opinions on how their magazines should be offering collectors more in the way of tips and updates. I mentioned to the feature editor, Lorna Reed, that the letters sections were filled with questions about record values, telling counterfeits from originals, what variations existed, and so forth. But what caught my attention most were the personal ads — where fans offered to trade common records (many still for sale in record shops; e.g., **Band On The Run**) for such rarities as **Two Virgins** or the **Beatles Christmas Album**. No one was mentioning that one was worth about $8.00 and the other priced at $50.00 or more by most Beatle dealers.

I suggested that these magazines should try and educate their readers to an awareness of the current market scene and today's actual values. Lorna turned the tables on me and asked if I would write just such

an article. For her!

Put on the spot like that, I had to struggle to make sense of thirteen years as a fan club president and a participator at nearly two dozen Beatles conventions, and then somehow put that experience into perspective, describing the roots of fandom and how it grew into the collecting-mania it is today. How did five cent bubblegum cards turn into $10.00 pieces of memorabilia?

I knew the history because it was the story of my own life. I ran fan clubs in the sixties when *no one* used the word collecting, and I still run a club today and discuss values and variations as a big part of each club newsletter. I was part of the first fan conventions where the big event was the banquet and the awards and nothing was bought and sold, although a few things might have been traded. And now I travel across the United States attending conventions which feature perhaps 100 dealers, and where feverish buying and selling goes on for twelve hours a day as thousands of dollars change hands over Beatles records, books, and trinkets that once sat on shelves or in closets, totally taken for granted.

So, discussing how we got to this point was basically an easy eye-witness report. It was when I got into the current sea of confusion over intricacies of legitimate sixties era treasures versus seventies and eighties remakes that I realized the true magnitude of my undertaking.

I wanted to help fans know what was really valuable, what was merely common, what was rare, and what was a dime a dozen. But I had to pull all my knowledge, facts, and figures totally out of my own memories. There was not a single sourcebook to help me out.

In the past, when I discussed a certain record or piece of memorabilia, I had wanted so badly to reach up and grab a guidebook that would give me some background. Nothing could corroborate my own sometimes hazy recollections. Was that Beatles' pillow I saw a NEMS item? Was it blue or white background? Who made the Beatles' tennis shoes? Did such-and-such book come out in paperback, or hardcover, or both? Was this record really worth that much? Did it have a picture sleeve, etc., etc.?

The more I tried to write my comprehensive article for the *Record Collector*, the more I realized how little concrete reference information existed so far in this field. Work on an article evolved into work on a series of articles, and eventually led to my decision to expand my labors into a booklength guide. I couldn't be the only one who needed such a resource tool. Nor the only one who would be fascinated by the story behind the hundreds of items which flooded the stores in the early sixties, but which are now so scarce.

Information on all these Beatles items, from legitimate record releases and the promotional items that came along with them, to the books, magazines, and other odds and ends of Beatlemania, will not only be useful to people actively selling or collecting on a large scale, but to every fan who wants to make an occasional purchase, or who just wants to know more about their existing collection.

Beyond the practicality of such a guide, I thought it would be fun just to survey the sheer quantity of the merchandise. It's interesting to note what 17 years has done to prices, but also just to marvel at the cleverness and sentimentality evident in the mass of products which poured out in the early sixties and continues today to overwhelm us at each succeeding Beatles convention.

AN ENDLESS STREAM OF NEW "PRODUCT"

More than anything else, it was the amazing quantity of collectible Beatles-related products which fascinated me. I *lived* through that early period and I was not aware of more than a fraction of it at the time and have encountered the rest of it only gradually and through extensive searching, questioning, and research. When you think that the Beatles were only a group for seven years, the amount of memorabilia (most of which is from 1964 anyway) is staggering. Not to mention the records which they have released, or have had released about them, around them or because of them, the books written, the magazines published, and the concerts, films, plays, etc., produced and staged because of them. It adds up to a remarkable achievement for a Pop group originally considered merely another "teenage fad" by the critics and business community.

I had only imagined finding 300 to 400 different items, but by the time my research was complete (a year and a half later) I had found double that number and realized that the figures were practically infinite. New "product" (sort of a generic term used by dealers and collectors to refer to all manufactured goods associated with the Beatles) continues to be made, new promotional items come out to plug a new single by one of The Four, and so forth. There are lulls, then there are periods when there seems to be a rebirth of interest: 1974 — Beatles' ten year U.S. anniversary; 1976 — Paul toured Europe and the U.S.; 1977 — "Beatlemania" stage show began; 1979 — "Birth of the Beatles" on TV; 1980–81 — Aftermath of John Lennon's murder.

Each new rebirth of public interest and fresh media attention brings a new wave of books, magazines, and recordings. The Beatles, as a recording group, continue to seem like a viable and current entity, not something musty and finished and of a different age. New product seems always (even today, eighteen years later) to be in demand.

I knew that no matter how thorough I was, I would never be able to identify everything that exists and is collected by Beatles fans. I had pledged to keep trying until I could locate about 500 different items. But as that figure got closer, I realized that I had only scratched the surface and that a more practical figure might be closer to 1,000.

Not only does new product continue to be manufactured monthly, but tracking down every piece of memorabilia from the sixties is a task for a super-sleuth. The Beatles' picture was apparently plastered on every conceivable item on the face of the earth — it was even on edibles like the "Ringo Roll" or "Beatlenut Icecream." Some items were plentiful and show up at almost every Beatles convention, like the Remco Beatles dolls, the lunchboxes, the Beatles wigs and tennis shoes. Some are a little more unique and surface only occasionally, like the Beatles phonograph, the NEMS pillow, or the Beatles hummer. Some are so obscure, at least in this country, that they are more often talked about than seen, showing up perhaps in a Beatles museum, and are rarely for sale (e.g., the Beatles tea set, curtains, rug, etc.).

TAKING STOCK

In the end, I had to settle for being as thorough as possible. I began to write down on separate index cards each and every item available from a variety of sources. I attended at least four Beatles conventions a year, where 100 dealers' tables were stocked with memorabilia, magazines, books, and rare records. I subscribe to a dozen Beatles fanzines, all of which run ads trading and selling in Beatles items. I received dozens of dealers' lists from all over the world. I also read record collecting magazines featuring auction lists and sales lists of rare items. *Goldmine* and *Record Collector* not only let me know what was currently being offered and what the minimum bids were, but also allowed my participation in actually making bids on these items.

I learned quite a bit from my own mistakes. I learned how to read the small print! Once, I bid on a **Life With The Lions** LP only to end up paying $17.00 for the cover only!! I learned from months of bidding, seeing which bids won, and which were not high enough. I asked dealers for feedback on winning prices. I found out which items were in demand, which ones people considered rare and valuable, and what price they were willing to pay. Finally, I learned how to make wise purchases and to know when I was getting something for a good price, an average price, or was needlessly paying top dollar.

By the time I had collated over 700 different

This NEMS item from the U.K. is called the Beatles hummer, sort of a hum amplifier with which you could hum along with your favorite Beatles song! *Price Guide No.: 681*

items, I felt ready to begin typing an inventory list from my cards. These eighty pages of notes were then shown to the most knowledgeable dealers and collectors I knew. For each different section, I sought out an expert in the field, someone who personally collected these items. They double-checked all my descriptive details, offered additions to my list, and volunteered information about items so obscure I'd never seen them for sale. I was shown rarities so I could get a better idea of what I was talking about. With the help of people who both bought and sold, and who really understood the market, I was able to fill in most of my blanks. Fans from all over the world contributed information about the gems in their own collections.

My number of items soon rose to over 800. More importantly, I had compiled details on each item from more than one source. Ideally, I wanted to have at least half a dozen different sources for prices. Without allowing my own personal opinion and judgment to enter into it, I marked down, without prejudice, the condition, any special variations, and the price of every item I saw or read about. My cards were kept alphabetized in twelve different sections. After an eighteen month period, I was running out of new items to add and knew it was time to start making sense of this mountain of trivia.

PRICES: THE "GOING RATE"

I wanted a *range* of the most typical prices a given item was selling for, not just one (perhaps) unrepresentative sample price. Thus, from approximately six different prices I had seen placed on an item, I could sensibly compute an average, disregarding the outrageously high or the abnormally low.

If one dealer sold a hardcover copy of Hunter Davies' Beatles biography for $50.00, and four dealers sold it for $25.00, and a sixth for $10.00, I would write that the book was worth $25.00, and disregard the other prices. If the dealers were divided thus: one $10.00; two $15.00; two $25.00; one $50.00, I would mark it as having a $15.00–$25.00 price range. I didn't just mathematically run an average on $10.00–$50.00, which in some cases would give a completely unrealistic figure, but instead chose the *common range*. I wanted to let people know what items were really, *literally* selling for — not what I thought they should sell for, but what was the practice.

The prices I have listed in this book are on the high side, not the low. These prices came from the most knowledgeable of Beatles dealers and are thus top dollar asking prices. The dealers who you encounter at Beatles conventions and through mail order are actually the last step on the price ladder. (A separate chapter is devoted to how to avoid paying these higher prices by doing just as the dealers

do, searching out the original sources, secondary sources, and so on.)

It has been suggested to me that by printing these prices, I influence what dealers will charge and only help to drive good bargains away. This is the major fear of most collectors. The dealers especially worry that they in turn won't be able to buy cheaply from anyone else. Such complications can be avoided if people don't misuse this information by taking it as gospel. I am not seeking to dictate prices, merely to report on what they are in today's marketplace.

It is commonly accepted that dealers offer to purchase at only 50 to 60 percent of the total value on an item. So, if *In His Own Write* is valued at $30.00–40.00, a dealer will offer to buy it from a source for about $15.00–18.00. A higher priced item like a Butcher cover (Yesterday And Today) worth about $100.00–125.00 would bring a dealer offer of $50.00–75.00. Sometimes a dealer will offer 75 percent of the value on a particularly rare item, or one in high demand that they know they can resell quickly. Likewise, they might offer less (perhaps 25 percent of the value) for something which might not sell quickly. The prices in this book don't have to be detrimental to dealers as long as both they and their customers realize that they are merely typical "going rate" figures, not absolutes.

These prices are the facts, they are the current selling prices, and I felt this information should be shared to make better informed buyers out of all collectors. How can you know if you bought wisely when you have no basis for comparison? When I used to pick up a Beatles magazine for $4.00 at a swap meet, or flea market, I didn't know what its "real" value should be and could not tell how my purchase price fit into the scheme of things. I also didn't know what to value it at if I wanted to resell it, or to trade it. Now, by looking at the figures I've been able to compile, I can see at a glance that its average value is $10.00–12.00. If I had bought it at a Beatles convention for $10.00 I'd know that I got a fair deal. If I got carried away and had paid $18.00 for it in an auction, I'd know I was a chump. Only by documenting these averages, common ranges, and actual selling prices can anyone, myself included, know how they stand on a purchase. So, rather than seeming to indicate that a particular magazine, book, record, etc., can *only* be worth $10.00 — I would like prices in this guide to provide the much needed basis for comparison mentioned above. If you encounter prices that are below those listed, then you can probably be assured of a bargain. If you see prices extremely beyond these, taking inflation into account, then you might question the purchase.

Prices are bound to increase and, if the current trend is anything to judge by, they'll continue to increase drastically. The prices listed here are those prevailing during 1980–82. Even during this time period, I recorded increased price changes at least once on many items, while some items changed prices two or three times, escalating wildly from convention to convention. The Remco Beatles dolls used to be $14.00 as a standard price when I bought them in 1978. They were $25.00 in 1980, $30.00 at the beginning of 1981 and, by the August '81 Beatles convention, they were an astronomical $50.00 apiece! On the other hand, many magazines, paperbacks, and most records stayed within the range already noted at the beginning of 1980. Some increased $2.00–4.00, but still stayed close to the range. Singles picture sleeves held steadily at one value, except for the rarest sleeves in demand like *Can't Buy Me Love, Cold Turkey*, or *Ain't She Sweet*. These skyrocketed in price, and can be expected to continue on that upwards path.

When you look at any prices, take inflation into consideration. If you see a dealer offering a Beatles pillow or game for $75.00, but this book says the selling price is usually around $50.00, the higher price can still be reputable if the standard has risen that much. A clue will be the extent to which dealers have priced their other items. Have all their items increased to the same degree above the values reported in this book? How do the new prices compare with other dealers' prices?

Common items are holding their own pretty decently: picture sleeves, books, magazines, etc. Other memorabilia, on the other hand, continues to be in such high demand among collectors in America, and is so extremely hard to locate, especially in fine condition, that it just continues to increase in value at a rate of 25 percent or so a year. Consider such factors as you compare the prices you see against those in this book. The rarer the item, the more likely it is to have increased in value.

THE IMPORTANCE OF CONDITION

Prices in this guide are all for *Near Mint* condition copies. I collated prices for all conditions, but included principally those prices for items in top grade condition. These figures can therefore serve as the starting point of what to expect in the way of costs for the finest example of an item.

Near Mint is the usual top-of-the-line condition for items circulating in the collecting business. *Mint* would be something never handled by the public, never sold, never owned, never opened, still sealed, never read, never played. After eighteen years, most early Beatles items are unlikely to still be Mint, unless preserved by a hard-core collector. So, Near Mint is considered the best most people will encounter. Near Mint is just that; the closest thing to being perfect, but still circulated in the retail business. It may have been played minimally, read without defacing,

and it will have been opened and unsealed.

If an item should turn up that is legitimately in Mint condition, perhaps still sealed in the original wrapper and guaranteed original, then it is of course worth much more than the Near Mint prices listed in this book. You can add an additional 50 percent at least to the price. Some rare records can fetch 100 percent more. A perfect Mint copy of an already rare collectors item is such a find that the final price comes down to negotiation. The prices for the Near Mint items listed in this book can serve as a guideline to know where to begin bidding for Mint items.

Most of the time, the items you will see will not even be in Near Mint condition. For picture sleeves and albums, this is usually the case. Beatles fans, of course, *played* their records often! And picture sleeves and jackets tend to show age more quickly than, say, books or magazines. I have given the price of Very Good for most of the records, but not as often in other sections. A *Very Good* item is anything that is showing its age. There may be ring wear on a picture sleeve, visible marks or surface noise on a record, scuffs, tape marks, staples, etc. If there is writing, it should be very minimal to qualify as Very Good. The item will not be defaced, it will just be a step down from a nearly perfect Near Mint item. Thus, its value can be expected to take a drastic drop.

A collector (especially the hard core or the one investing for the future) wants to secure the very best example of an item. He or she is willing to pay the higher price for a Near Mint condition item rather than a lesser price for a lower condition copy. The Very Good item can go begging, the Near Mint at a higher price will probably be scooped up immediately.

A not uncommon example would be the picture sleeve for *She Loves You*. A dealer could sell a Near Mint, almost perfect copy, for $22.00–25.00. That same dealer might price a Very Good copy at $18.00-20.00 and end up holding on to it a lot longer. Meanwhile, a Good copy, one showing lots of wear, perhaps with a tear, split seam, some writing, water marks, lots of old tape, or a beat up looking record, might be priced at a cheap $10.00–12.00 and not find a buyer at all.

Condition is one of the most important factors in collecting. This cannot be overly stressed. So often, Beatles fans overlook the condition an item is in when they start questioning the price. Why is this copy worth more than that one? How can one dealer be selling it for $20.00 and the person at the next table be selling the same thing for $25.00? Answer: it could be that the item varies in quality from Very Good to Near Mint. A closer inspection of both items might show the difference.

So, when comparing what you want to buy or sell against the prices in this book, take into account

THE RECORD THAT STARTED "BEATLEMANIA"

ENGLAND'S SENSATIONS

JUST DID

JACK PAAR SHOW
(JAN. 3)

COMING UP

ED SULLIVAN
(FEB. 9 & FEB. 16)

FEATURED IN TIME, LIFE,
NEWSWEEK

THIS IS THE RECORD
THAT STARTED IT ALL

PLEASE, PLEASE ME
AND
FROM ME TO YOU
BY
THE BEATLES

VEE-JAY RECORDS

VJ-581

(PROMOTION COPY)

A rare promo single from Vee-Jay Records, with a picture sleeve. Extremely rare (especially the sleeve), it might

Examples of Differing Price Ranges
in the Condition Grading System for Collectibles

ALBUMS	Poor	Good	Very Good	Near Mint	Mint	Still Sealed
LIFE WITH THE LIONS	$10	$18-20	$25-35	$35-50	$50-60	$100-125
TWO VIRGINS (*w/brown cover) (**w/brown cover & original sealing tab)	$10	$30-35	$50-75	$75-100	$100-125*	$150**
MEET THE BEATLES (Original first pressing)	$5	$8-10	$15	$20	$30	$40
MY BONNIE (MGM)	$10	$18-20	$25-30	$30-35	$35-40	$70

SINGLES	Poor	Good	Very Good	Near Mint	Mint	Promo (record only)
AINT SHE SWEET (w/picture sleeve)	$10	$25	$50-60	$75	$85-100	$80
AND I LOVE HER (w/picture sleeve)	$0-3	$10	$12-15	$20	$25	$40
CANT BUY ME LOVE (w/picture sleeve)	$50--	$80-100	$150	$165-175	$200	$40
I WANT TO HOLD YOUR HAND (w/picture sleeve)	$5	$12-15	$15-18	$20-22	$22-25	$40
PLEASE PLEASE ME (VJ) (w/picture sleeve)	$10	$25--	$50-60	$65-75	$80-85	$65-80

BOOKS & MAGAZINES	Good	Very Good	Near Mint	Mint
IN HIS OWN WRITE (Price may also vary by printings; first printing higher priced than twelfth printing, although all are part of the "first edition").	$25-30	$35	$40	$50
THE BEATLES by Hunter Davies (Hardcover; must have dustjacket to be V.G.-Mint)	$15	$18-22	$25-30	$30-35
BEATLES 'ROUND THE WORLD (Magazine)	$5-8	$10	$12	$15
LIFE (Beatles on cover 8-24-64)	$8	$10-12	$15	$18

MEMORABILIA	Good	Very Good	Near Mint	Mint
FLIP YOUR WIG GAME	$35-45	$50-65	$75-85	$100
LUNCHBOX	$50-60	$65-75	$75-80	$100
COLORING BOOK	$10	$15	$18-20	$25
MODEL (Revell) (*Still in box, sealed)	$20-25	$25-35	$35-40	$45-50*
DOLLS (Remco) (*In box w/instruments)	$20-25	$35	$40	$50-60*

the condition your item is in. How close to Near Mint is it? If perfect, then it is worth a price similar to that listed. If defaced in any way (a name written in a book, a page missing from a magazine, rust on an old Beatles lunchbox, a part missing from a Beatles doll) the value is markedly less. Anywhere from 25 percent to 50 percent less!

A WORD ON VARIATIONS

Variations are always a consideration as well. Any differences in the item that might make one copy different in value from another are noted in my description of each item. If a picture sleeve originally came with an insert, the price for that variation is listed. Books are designated hardcover or paperback with prices for both. An LP such as VJ's **Introducing The Beatles**, with a dozen plus different variations of label, song order, jacket, etc., are all described. Variations involved are just as important a factor as the condition an item is in. It is meaningless to tell someone you have **Introducing The Beatles** without describing which variation, as each one has a totally different value, ranging from the most common reissue at $3.00--5.00 to the rarest promotional versions at $400.00.

In a chapter introducing the Price Guide, I've discussed a few more of the particulars involved in collecting items within the different categories. There are different things to be aware of and notice for records as opposed to books or other memorabilia.

THE NEXT STEP

Even a cursory glance at these pages will reveal how much more there is to the subject than most of us casual collectors ever realized. There are so many intricacies to the ins and outs of collecting that only the professional dealer can be aware of them, and even they may not be equally knowledgeable in *all* the different areas. But for anyone interested in trading, buying, or selling Beatles items, I hope these two years' worth of notes on prices and descriptive information will be useful. I also hope it takes some of the mystery out of collecting, so that everyone can know *exactly* what they are getting and have a lot more fun while getting it. For me, the most important thing to come out of my efforts would be that a deeper understanding is gained about the entire field of "Collecting the Beatles."

Happy hunting!

2.

The History of Collecting

My biggest Beatles fantasy is a time machine set for 1964. My mind has been fixated by one particular destination all these years: Woolworth's! No, not the Woolworth's of little old ladies with gray hair and immense paper shopping bags, nor the Woolworth's of cheap cosmetics and costume jewelry — but a 1964 Woolworth's filled with nearly endless rows of Beatle toys, trinkets, and tempting memorabilia. Now *that* would be a sight for sore eyes!

After eight years of attending nearly every Beatles convention in the U.S. (twenty-five at my last count), "jaded" would be too mild an adjective to describe my current state of mind. How refreshing to be transported back to a simpler, more innocent time when Beatles merchandise literally surrounded you, and all of it sold for just a few dollars. We didn't even have to worry if it was "mint," "still sealed," or what "woc" meant (dealer jargon for "writing on cover") — because it was *all* pristine and gleaming, brand-new, and for sale. One didn't have to bid on it and then, caught up in the enthusiasm of the moment, spend every last dime, bus token, and good luck piece you had to acquire it.

In 1964, Woolworth's had to be Ali Baba's cave. But we didn't know it at the time. Any Beatle fan could walk in right off the street (imagine, no admission charge!) and purchase any of four Remco Beatles dolls, instruments and all, for under $3.00; Beatles coloring books were only 59 cents, and all kinds of gaudy necklaces, bracelets, and pins with The Lads' lovely faces on them were piled high and going cheap. Lunchboxes, thermoses included, would cost you no more than any other lunchbox in the store. The singles' racks were full of the latest releases, each only 88 cents, picture sleeve and all. Nearly every magazine in the winter of '64 headlined enticing secrets about the Beatles, their love lives, and their "lonely nights." *Sixteen* magazine came in every month, right on its announced date (circled in red on my calendar), as did *Teen Screen, Teen Life, Teen Talk,* and others — all with pictures of the Beatles plastered on the front, the back, and most of the insides as well.

That we had to pick and choose was the ultimate cruelty. We only had one hardship in those days . . . poverty! No plaguing doubts about authenticity, no question of getting a better deal somewhere else — everything in Woolworth's was the real McCoy, straight from the manufacturer to the retail outlet. But to a kid on an allowance, even 25 cents for a magazine might blow the whole wad! So, I don't want to venture back merely to relive my past; I want

to do it up one better: I'd like to go back with a few big bills and my years of honed experience . . . and then pounce on those tables like a starving man at a smorgasbord!

The truth is we just didn't know we had it so good. Perhaps that was for the best, since our limited budget hardly stretched farther than bus fare and lunch money. As it was, we could hardly afford more than one single at a time, and had to save for weeks to get their new album. We were spared the further torture of knowing what the next sixteen years would bring, and that the Beatle dolls we passed up would be worth at least five times their original value a decade and a half later.

Now, all a fan can do is dream about going back in time, and there, with magical foresight, buy not just one of everything — but ten, twenty, or 100 of everything! At today's collectors' prices it would be almost as good as investing in gold!

THE MASS MARKET

Of course, one of the biggest reasons Beatles paraphernalia was so cheap then (and is so outrageously expensive now) is the first law of economics: supply and demand. There was plenty of everything in 1964, more than enough to go around considering the average wealth of the pre-teen Beatle fan of the day.

Every manufacturing company in the Western world panted for a piece of the action. With Beatles albums going gold, and the top five singles on the *Billboard* charts all by the Beatles, no businessman alive wanted to miss the opportunity for a cash-in if he could help it. After all, the hysteria might be short-lived, just another passing fancy for capricious youth. Licensing rights were hastily secured (or just as hastily circumvented) to numerous odds and ends. Everyone envisioned a quick fortune just from pasting a Beatles picture on their item, no matter how gimmicky or gauche, or how unrelated it was to either music or youth. Thus, we ended up with Beatles talcum powder, Beatles bow ties, Beatles lampshades, bubblebath, banks, and bamboo trays from Taiwan.

Legally, everything had to have permission from NEMS Enterprises Ltd., which was the company name Brian Epstein gave to his business when it became more than just four lads playing in a cellar for a few quid. Brian derived the name from North End Music Stores, the Epstein family business in Liverpool where he had been employed until his mentoring

An original art cell from the "Yellow Submarine" film. Thousands exist, but few feature one of the Beatles of the Beatles took up 100 percent of his time.

When you look on the bottom or backside of many original items you will see the words "c. NEMS ent. 1964" (or "1965," "1966"); many, in addition, will have: "m. by SELTAEB, inc.," the latter being the name (Beatles, spelled backward) of the licensor of all U.S. product. Dozens of equally old Beatles items do not have this seal of authenticity, but are just as original and valuable (although anything carrying the NEMS trademark obviously acquires some sentimental value as well). Many of the un-marked items seem to have been made in Hong Kong, Taiwan, or elsewhere outside the United States.

Authorized or not, hundreds of different gim-micks found their way into the market. How well they might have sold has never been determined. At the time, it seemed like every kid on the block had at least *some* memento to show off. Beatle tennis shoes, on the other hand, must have been real clinkers: a warehouse full of them (in Mint condition) was re-cently discovered, creating visions of what must have been mass returns by disillusioned shopkeepers.

Despite all the wealth that must have been gener-ated by Beatles product, both Brian Epstein and the Beatles commented to the press on several occasions that most of their "cut" of this lucrative sideline never made it across the Atlantic.

The yearly Beatles tours of 1964--66 kept alive some of the merchandising dreams built on corporate greed. "Ringo for President" buttons gave way to "I *Still* Love the Beatles" buttons. Many of these were unauthorized and "unofficial," and were hawked at concerts by shady types much in the way back-alley programs, posters, and t-shirts are ped-dled today.

Gum cards changed from black-and-white to colored "diary" cards with quotes from each of the Beatles on the flip sides. And a few more practical souvenirs, like the Beatles "disk-go-case" (NEMS 1966), were produced. Memorabilia hadn't yet come of age, but at least Beatle wigs and "bug" jewelry were finally passe.

Surrounded by so much of everything, the Beatle fan of the time was blithely unaware of the impermanence of it all. We only bought exactly what we intended to use with no thought of how hard it might be to obtain the rest of it later on. Hundreds of currently valuable items were passed up in those days as we, naively, couldn't imagine a day when it wouldn't all be sitting there on the shelves.

It came as a rude awakening when the Beatles stopped touring, began a long, secluded recording session, grew beards, and grew up. Beatles memora-bilia seemed to dry up and disappear, too. Without all the hype of concerts, press conferences, Ed Sullivan appearances, and films, merchandising minds turned to other hot new "fads" to fill the void: The Monkees, for one. "I Love Mickey" buttons, Monkee

gum cards, puzzles, and paperbacks drove the old Beatles paraphernalia out of the stores, at least tem-porarily.

A second round was begun anew when King Features (Suba Films) licensed dozens of companies to put out product with a "Yellow Submarine" theme to help hype the movie. By late 1968, just in time for the Christmas rush, U.S. stores were once again well stocked with a new line of lunchboxes, picture puzzles, and everything you could possibly think of that could accommodate a picture of a "Yellow Submarine" character. There were "Yellow Submarine" coasters, light switch plates, key chains, stationery, greeting cards, calendars, toys, paint sets, mobiles, and much, much more.

Probably the nicest, most meaningful items of all were the authentic animation cells from the film it-self. These were being sold in department stores for a mere $35.00. We thought it was a lot back then, mainly because we still didn't have that much money, not to mention foresight, so once again we passed it by. Today, a little piece of the film without even a single Beatle or any other recognizable "Yellow Submarine" character pictured in it is going for near-ly that much, so the choicest ones, with a Beatle or Blue Meanie in it, must be worth at least $150.00 and, in an open-bidding situation, perhaps a lot more.

Most of the items seemed geared to young chil-dren: the games and toys and coloring sets, so we teenagers barely gave it a second glance. We "older" fans were picking up Beatles "Yellow Submarine" photo albums, scrapbooks, and the like, which we could actually put to some use. I remember admiring the "Yellow Submarine" toy put out by Corgi Co., thinking how cute it was, but wondering (at eighteen) what I would do with a toy? Now, that little gimmick is worth a hefty $75.00 at least, but is rarely offered for sale.

The third phase in the manufacture of original collectibles came shortly after the "Yellow Sub-marine" craze started to fade. The Beatles set up their own record label, and a new merchandising enterprise replaced NEMS. After Brian's death in 1967, the Beatles floundered in that area, no one else came in either to "exploit" or hype the "Sgt. Pep-per" era, and the merchandising aspect lay dormant until the Beatles' own Apple Productions got into the game.

Most of the items that proceeded to flow out of the company over the next half dozen years were just promotional pieces, not designed for mass retail sales. This fact makes them all the more valuable to-day, since their numbers are so much more limited. Whereas the 1964 to 1966 souvenirs are valuable for the sentimentality of the era, their originality, and their age, the Apple items, like DJ promotional materials, are valuable today because of their exclu-siveness. More than other items, they have an almost

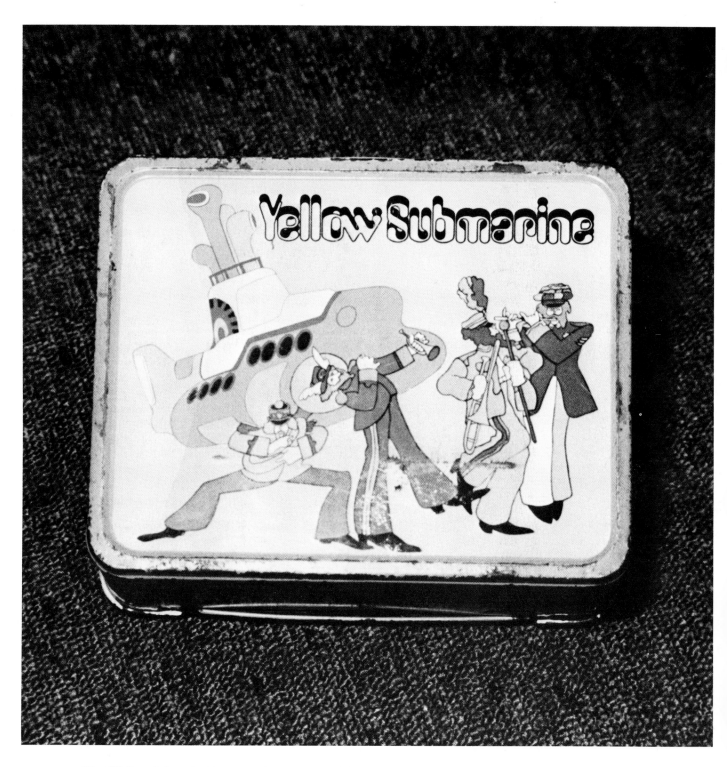

The "Yellow Submarine" version of a Beatles lunchbox sells for approximately $35, even in this rusted condition.
Price Guide No.: 760

"holy" aura about them — something straight from the Boys, not from the tycoons of big business. An Apple promo item is considered as close as one can ever get to a personal memento.

Thus, the most expensive mass-produced "memorabilia" (if you can even call it that) today are Apple promo items: the watch (square with a picture of an apple on the dial) is highly coveted, but rarely seen. One fan was offered $800.00 for his! Also, the set of four matchbooks, packaged together and inscribed "Merry Christmas from Apple" (estimated value today is $25.00 each, or $100.00 for an unopened package); the key chain with a big red and green apple on it ($25.00), Apple stationery, even a promo Apple dartboard, are all extremely prized pieces now.

VALUES

Not every single item with the Beatles' names on it is worthy of the tag "collectible," nor the high price usually attached to such things. This assumption is the commonest misconception held by non-fans and novice fans alike. If selling, they want to make an instant fortune on every single Beatles record, book, and magazine; when buying, they often get carried away and forget to be discriminating and careful about an item's real value, or potential value.

To correctly approach the market and its values, first ask yourself: "How hard is it to get this item?" Why is the LP, **Discotheque In Astrosound** on Clarion going for about $50.00 on dealers' lists today, for example? Certainly not because it is such a great album; in fact, it was so lousy that nobody bought it when it came out (1964), and thus it has become one of those obscure items a collector will pay a high price for solely because of its rarity. On the other hand, **Meet The Beatles**, a classic, sold millions. It is still available brand new in the record stores, although, like all Beatles albums, it has undergone several label changes through the last eighteen years. Most fans are content to pick up the store copy for list price, but a collector wants the original first pressing with the original Capitol Rainbow label, and is willing to pay $15+ for a Very Good condition copy. An equally old original copy in any lesser condition has very little value and may not even be able to find a buyer. If you want the *music*, you buy it brand new. If you want a *collectible*, which will increase in value, then you look for perfection or come as close to it as you can get.

Many long-time fans already have a complete collection of the Beatles' releases (at least all the common Capitol ones), but their copies may be worn out, warped, written on, or otherwise far from Mint. Combined with all the new fans just discovering the Beatles, that adds up to quite a multitude of people searching for the *finest* examples of every Beatle record and souvenir.

So, when it comes to selling and buying, condition is one factor, but scarcity is an equal factor. All the Beatles albums from the earliest period (1964--1966) have a market. Most of the newer releases do not, nor do the solo LPs. (Picture discs, colored vinyl, etc., are completely different matters.) Today's million sellers are far too common to be overly concerned about, although, with the lesson of how "common" mid-sixties items have now become so valuable, picking up at least one of today's "common" items usually can't be avoided, if only for future reference.

I have run ads in local papers looking for Beatles merchandise, records, and books, and 75 percent of my calls offer me common Capitol LPs, usually in the same poor shape as my own eighteen year old collection. When the caller starts out with "I bet I have something you don't have," I know it will be **Meet The Beatles, Introducing The Beatles**, or the "White Album." One caller even wanted me to believe that his "White Album" (stereo, mind you) was worth $65.00! He told me he'd found that figure in a library book (*Fantasy Island*, perhaps?).

Today's collector is looking for those 1964 albums that managed to surface in the first heady days of Beatlemania before Capitol got their act together and realized what a goldmine they were letting slip through their grasp by not putting a quick halt to every release but their own. For a few short months though, we had record stores full of strange looking Beatles albums put out by Atco, Clarion, MGM, Savage, VeeJay, United Artists, as well as singles from most of the above, plus Swan and Tollie. The majority of these were hasty cash-ins, mostly full of Tony Sheridan material and very little Beatles. Their demise from the scene can, in most cases, hardly be lamented. The best material (e.g., all the cuts from **Introducing The Beatles**), was transferred to Capitol's own **Early Beatles** album, so at least it isn't lost to us.

Because this non-Capitol material was so short-lived, its value today as a collectible far outweighs its purely artistic merit! Its scarcity certainly adds challenge to the "sport" of collecting. The search and bagging of some of these obscurities — **Songs, Pictures And Stories, Beatles And Frank Ifield, Ain't She Sweet**, and **Amazing Beatles** — is part of the excitement of the collecting scene.

Prior to the disappearance of non-Capitol product from the record bins of the early Beatlemania period, some of the LPs went through a complicated series of label and jacket variations in the short period of time just before Capitol wiped them out completely.

Introducing The Beatles has at least a dozen different configurations. The VJ symbol was changed from an oval, to brackets, to standing alone. The song

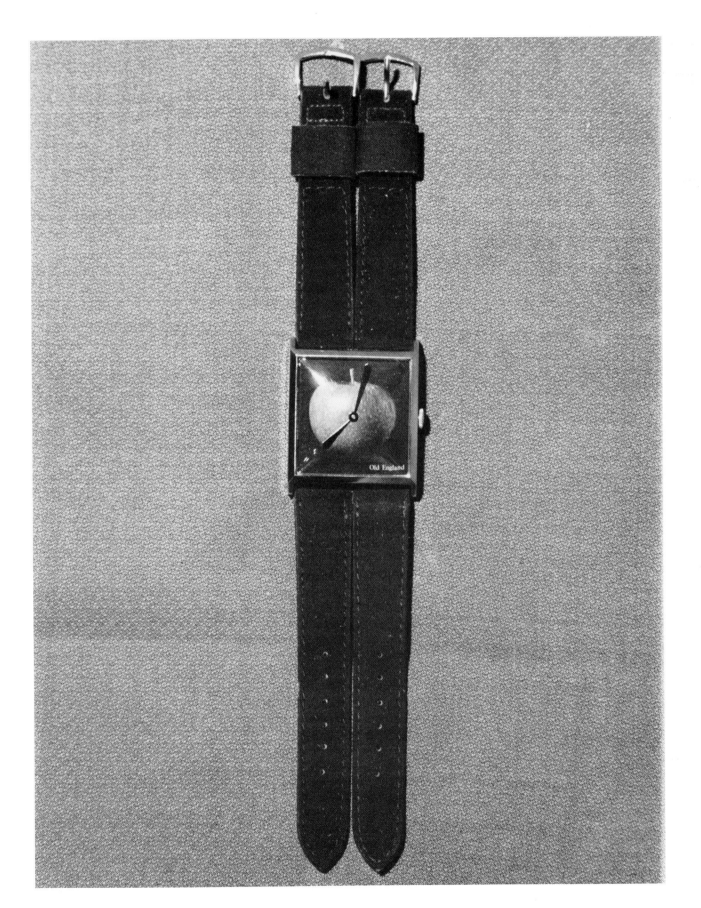

The Apple Watch, a promotional item from Apple Corps Ltd. (the watch band is not the original). Very rare,
as only a limited quantity were made. Valued at $200-500. Price Guide No. 612

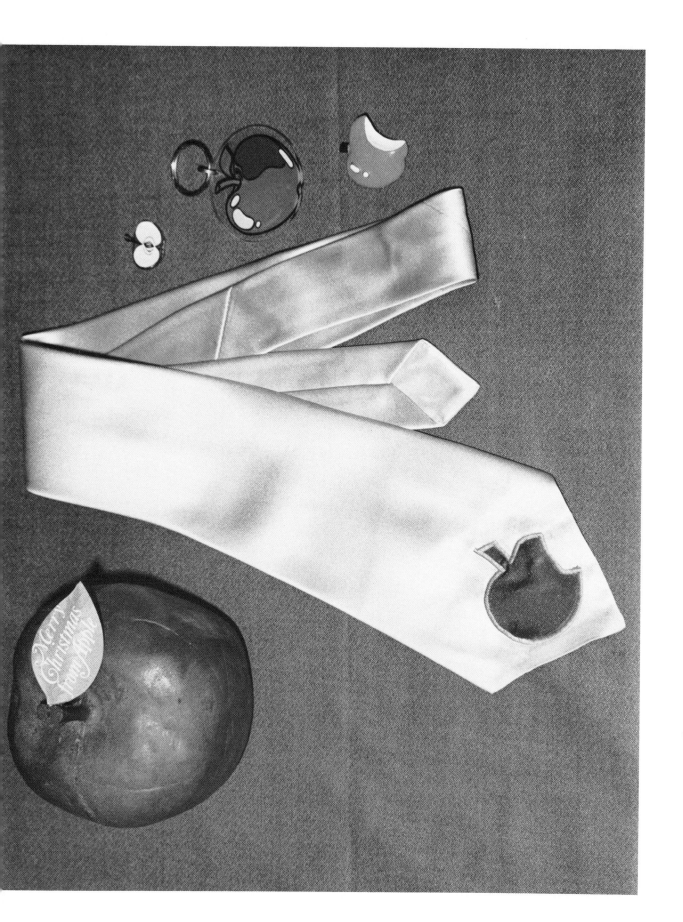

A collection of rare Apple promo items: a display apple (upper left), an Apple tie, Apple key chain, and two Apple pins. These are extremely valuable, and rarely seen offered for sale. *Price Guide No.: 614*

listing went from *Love Me Do/P.S. I Love You* to *Please Please Me/Ask Me Why*. There are monophonic versions and stereophonic versions. The back covers differ from a listing of twenty-five various VJ records to a completly blank back, and all the combinations seem endlessly mixed. Many of these variations have different values based on the particular rarity of each.

PACKAGING

Jackets, labels, and picture sleeves often dictate the value of records. The records themselves seem of lesser importance. Maybe that is because almost all Beatles material is available today in Mint condition in brand new editions — either on re-pressed Capitol LPs, the new compilation LPs, or the boxed sets of a couple years ago. The collector has every cut the Beatles left for posterity, and many they never intended to leave us (rejects, culled from wastebaskets, which ended up on bootlegs!). So, now the hunt extends to the original packaging, both for its obscurity and its sentimental value as a piece of the Beatles' past.

If most of us treated our records roughly (playing them on old monophonic phonographs with cheap needles, storing them haphazardly, etc.), we were doubly negligent with the picture sleeves our singles came in. Many of us stored singles in round holders not made for sleeves. The sleeves we did save ended up with pinholes or tape marks from being pasted on walls or in scrapbooks.

Collecting picture sleeves is today an area unto itself. They have wildly different values, assigned by age and/or original number pressed. Some, like *Can't Buy Me Love*'s sleeve, were marketed so minimally that the price tag on that one alone is nearly $200.00 for a Near Mint copy. Others, equally as old, like *I Want To Hold Your Hand*, are going for a more modest $15.00--20.00 in that condition. The most uncommon are non-Capitol 1964 sleeves, such as Atco's *Ain't She Sweet* (now selling for $50.00--70.00); MGM's *Why* (about $50.00), or Tollie's *Love Me Do* ($25.00). All 1964 sleeves bring respectably high figures for Good, Very Good, and Near Mint copies. Almost every sleeve has a value exceeding its original selling price by a substantial amount. Even solo sleeves (the ex-Beatles post-1970 recordings) are valued by collectors, although mostly in the $2.00--5.00 range. There are many exceptions though, such as the sought after sleeves for *Cold Turkey, Instant Karma*, and *Mary Had A Little Lamb* (with B-side title listed additionally), to name just a few.

There is a reason for every item having a high value, be it in the limited pressing, the variations, the short shelf life it had, or its original limited availability (perhaps only marketed in one area of the country, or only one country).

Many items are being sought after today as replacements for the broken and beat-up remnants of our childhood mementos. Even if we did have the funds to buy memorabilia then, we rarely saved its packaging. An eighteen year old item with its box, bag, or wrapper still intact (perhaps even unopened) is the ultimate find.

Most original memorabilia doubles in price when it comes still boxed or sealed. The Remco Beatle dolls usually sell for $30--40.00, but dealers ask $50.00 when still mint and packaged. Gum cards sell for only 25--50 cents apiece, but anyone who had the fortitude and grit to leave five cents worth of gum unopened and unchewed would now have a $7.00--10.00 collectible!

Books with dust jackets are worth more than those standing naked. First printings are slightly more sought after than later printings (especially in the case of *In His Own Write*). Anything still containing original 1964 advertising, inserts, accompanying loose photos, posters, etc., is several times more highly priced today than picked clean versions.

The story on every single Beatles collectible is the same: the selling price is not fixed, it caroms widely across the board, dependent on many curious and confusing variables. It is not enough that it says "BEATLES" all over it and looks old. A serious and sincere collector needs a lot more than that to go on.

Collecting as a hobby is a lot of fun, but the real satisfaction comes from knowing all the factors involved in appraising items, ascertaining their *real* value, noting the degree of their obscurity, knowing all the variations, and building a collection which you can really be proud to own.

3.

The Rebirth

Beatles merchandising in the sixties was dominated by the financial dictates of big business. Fans themselves had no control, other than to buy or not to buy. We were given what some enterprising tycoon *thought* we wanted, not necessarily what we may really have desired. The Beatles' pictures were stamped on anything and everything without discrimination or regard for taste or usefulness. A Beatles bow tie, for instance?

The shelves of dime stores were overflowing with memorabilia (i.e., junk) during that first crazy spring of '64. But after the Beatles' touring years were over, the business world retreated, counted up their dollars, and went on to new teenage crazes.

Maybe our numbers had dwindled from the millions to the thousands — but the fans who were left were definitely the *hard core*. And we weren't quite ready to go cold turkey yet! Just when the majority of us were moving into the age group of part-time employment, where we might have some disposable income for the first time, the items we wanted to spend it on were disappearing from sight. By 1969, the business world had declared the Beatles passe. Despite the fact that **Abbey Road** sold over five million copies that year, no souvenirs or tie-ins appeared on the market. Beatlemania was no longer "in."

Collecting *could have* died in the seventies, but it didn't. All the signs were bad as the decade began: The Four were battling in the courts, they were argumentative and negative, and everyone else was brought down by their wrangling. Even their official fan club, Beatles USA Ltd., disbanded at the beginning of 1971. My own independent club, Beatles Rule, gave in to the bad vibes about the same time. There was too little positive coming out of the Beatles scene to make continuing worthwhile. With the virtual end of fan publications, last links for fans, the last bonds of communication, were snapped.

While in England, in 1972, I asked for McCartney posters on Carnaby St. Only three years previous, it had overflowed with such Beatles kitch and swinging London hype. Now I was told: "No one cares about Paul McCartney anymore." The Beatles were now beyond passe; they were pronounced dead and buried.

For the first four years of the new decade, it looked like it was all over. It seemed to each of us, in our own isolation, that no one really cared any longer and that we fans would not again have a way to give expression to our sublimated interests.

While we did continue to buy any new official releases, "head" shops in major cities began to stock a new phenomenon: the plain white-sleeved bootleg albums containing unreleased outtakes, rehearsals, and interviews. The records were called "underground" LPs, as it was all done rather clandestinely; such records never appeared in major chain record stores, and circulated without advertising or publicity. News about the latest "rare record" was spread by word-of-mouth.

Bootlegs were the first fan-initiated Beatles business that really prospered, outside of fan club newsletters. In those quiet days of the early seventies, they were the only source of excitement a Beatle fan really had to look forward to; the only "collecting" that was being done involved building up a bootleg collection. They came out one after another with irrelevant and very often misleading titles pulled out of thin air; tracks were of poor quality and were often repackaged again and again in new ways. It was very unsophisticated, but at least it provided the beginnings for a new hobby that gave new life to fandom.

In the sixties we had all been fans *first* — we didn't even think in terms of collecting. You didn't "collect" Beatle items, you merely bought what you could afford and use. Most of us didn't have the money to think of being systematic about it. We bought what we really wanted personally, without even a clue that it might have potential value beyond its personal sentimental worth. Or that it might become a sought-after rarity. We didn't buy to impress, or to invest, or to make a collection complete. We were blithely and blissfully unaware of how Beatle fandom would evolve in the seventies.

When collecting finally became an alternative to being "just" a fan, it was because the merchandise was no longer so readily available. It became a real job and art to find anything in good condition, and because things were hard to find and demand became greater than availability, prices started to rise. Once they did, they just continued upward at a staggering rate. The inflation rate for Beatle items makes even that for gasoline prices look reasonable. Gum cards, originally five for five cents, are now 25--50 cents apiece, and an old *16 Magazine* that used to be 25 cents is now $15.00 — that beats the hell out of any other rate of appreciation around!

People today tend to be *both* collectors and fans, and don't appear to prefer one label above the other. They see both roles as complementary, not conflicting. So far, I have never run into anyone who thought of themselves only as a collector, to the exclusion of also being a fan. In today's fan scene, one almost has to start thinking in terms of "collecting" as opposed to merely buying. Items are so scarce, and also so expensive, that it takes much more skill to locate them than it ever did before.

A NEW ERA BEGINS

A series of different events in 1974 gave the new era its start; fans began to pick up the pieces, shake off the doldrums, and revive the enthusiasm they once had for the Beatles.

For the tenth anniversary of the start of Beatlemania in the U.S., Capitol Records decided to launch a new promotional campaign to promote some of the Beatle product they still held rights to. They issued t-shirts, posters, and wall hangings, and sparked a resurgence of interest in the Beatles' recordings by the media. At the same time, the four ex-Beatles were putting out some high quality solo music as well. Ringo released his biggest hit of all, **Ringo**; Paul had his career revitalized with **Band On The Run**; John was in the papers with **Walls & Bridges**, and doing promo tours; and George was doing concerts in the U.S. on his first major solo tour, and celebrating the release of **Dark Horse** and the initiation of his new label. It was one of the busiest years for new material since 1964, and radio and the press were full of the Beatles' names and news once again. It was a perfect time to spread the Beatles' message to the public in a new effort to add life to an otherwise moribund Beatles fan scene.

It was, just maybe, beginning to look like being a die-hard Beatles fan (or at least admitting to it) didn't have to be such a big dark secret anymore.

With no claim on being psychic, it was in January of 1974 that I reorganized and brought back to life our independent Beatles fan club, this time under the name The Write Thing. I had no pretentions of it being anything more than a hobby for myself, a club for friends and peers to air their own interests and activities, to keep in touch and to share with each other.

As it turned out, it was the prime time to get re-involved with the Beatles fan scene. In 1974, we were all like caterpillars who had been wrapped in a deep sleep for a couple of years and were only now shaking out our wings, and taking off on our own power — bigger and better than ever. And we weren't dictated to by the corporate scene, not regimented and controlled by "official" hierarchies like Beatles USA Ltd., which had become mired in its own bylaws and red tape and had died forever three years earlier.

Fans really came into their own that summer of '74. The first Beatles fans convention since 1964 (on a scale bigger than the neighborhood, the school, or with more than just a quorum present) took place in Boston in July of 1974 at Joe Pope's "Magical Mystery Tour" fan gathering. Beatle people (over a thousand of them) from *all* over the United States and Canada attended. I met fans from New Orleans, Cleveland, Richmond, San Francisco, Charlotte and Chicago. It was an incredible feeling of discovery. It was literally like a minority group coming out of the closet and liberating themselves in a new-found group identity. Being a fan had almost become something you didn't discuss anymore. In Boston, you were surrounded by your peers; sixties' teenyboppers were now young adults (the average age span at this convention was 17--25), and could unself-consciously drape themselves in Beatle t-shirts and buttons galore, and, with pride, show off personal mementos, photos, autographs, and prized rare Butcher covers.

During the all-night films, these college students, career people, and parents (with their babies in miniature Beatle t-shirts) all cheered and sang along at the top of their lungs in a vocal outpouring of their relief that, finally, they could express themselves without inhibitions, surrounded only by their own kind!

Conventions (Cons) took off after that, with two more summer "Magical Mystery Tour"'s in Boston, and the first "Beatlefest," which was held in New York City. Conventions sprang up in Chicago, Los Angeles, and a few other one-time locations. Now there have been Cons in Minneapolis, Connecticut, Cleveland, England, France, Germany, and Holland. I have personally attended over twenty-five different ones in the last eight years.

These mass gatherings gave the necessary stamp of legitimacy to being a fan. At least once a year you could put your devotion on display, and do it among sympathetic fellow fans, without worrying about raised eyebrows and questions of possible insanity.

In 1968, Beatles USA Ltd. made a tally of at least 200 different independent Beatles fan clubs in the United States alone. Most of them were forced into becoming branch clubs of that official organ, while many others folded. Only a few survived all the re-organizing and, on top of that, the Beatles' break-up. Some changed hands: The Harrison Alliance and McCartney Observer were passed on to others with more time and enthusiasm to continue. Some area secretaries, like Pat Simmons of Ohio, began their own club (With A Little Help From My Friends), and Joe Pope made Strawberry Fields Forever a powerful example in the art of newsletter writing, introducing the word "fanzine" to the Beatles fan scene. Clubs started popping up all over in 1974; most of them, however, lasted a year or less and then disbanded or went bankrupt. Some, like The Write Thing and Beatlefan (begun in 1978), had better luck, involved themselves totally in the new excitement, and drew in fans from all corners of the world, making fandom an international participatory event instead of a national phenomenon alone. Soon, thousands of fans in every country where Beatles music is heard were feeling

An example of a "peeled" monophonic Butcher Cover. Still covered with the glue from the back of the super-imposed "trunk cover," this one is considered in Very Good condition and worth about $150-200. A stereo copy in Near Mint condition might be worth $250-$300. *Price Guide No.: 67*

like they had kin, some for the first time.

FANS BECOME COLLECTORS

The clubs and the Cons were also the cohesive force that made collecting more than a solitary activity. With these outlets for expression and the sharing of knowledge and opinions, a new understanding was beginning to emerge. A new lingo developed: "cons" for conventions, "fanzine" for newsletters, "boots" for underground records, "collectibles," "memorabilia," "rarities," "limited editions," "first state" — all became the new banter.

Prices on Beatles items began to be determined in more than a merely arbitrary manner. After several national Beatles conventions, discussion of their values in clubs, and the appearance of lists put out by new entrepreneurs seeking to buy or sell, Beatles items entered into the ranks of true collectibles. They became a hobby for many and practically a vocation for some.

At the first conventions, people merely assigned an arbitrary price to the items they offered for sale — no standards were set, no price guides existed. You made deals on the basis of whatever you thought was right, or whatever you thought you could get. A Beatles pen and desk set made by NEMS in 1964 went for a mere $8.00. Butcher covers were thought so rare than even the most ragged one might fetch $300.00 or more. But gradually, as the same people continued to hawk their merchandise from convention to convention, they grew wiser about the relative rarity of different items. It became apparent what was really *rare*, and also what was the most in demand.

Now, a desk set like the above sells for at least $20.00, and sometimes up to $35.00. Butcher covers seem to keep appearing with such regularity that price is determined more by actual *condition* than it is by mere existence. A shoddy job of peeling off the second cover (the "trunk cover," as the picture of the Beatles sitting in an old trunk is called) which

has marred in any way the original cover showing the Beatles, dressed as butchers and draped with hunks of meat and various "baby" (doll) parts, would probably reduce the price to $100.00 or less. As condition improves, so does the price. For one in Mint condition, $300.00 *might* easily be the asking price. If it had never been covered by the second "trunk" cover (i.e., "first state"), its value could climb to an astronomical $1,500.00--2,000.00, as supposedly only a handful (maybe as few as two) stereophonic first state Butcher cover jackets ever existed.

Prices are not literally "fixed" on any Beatles items, though. It is still a matter of discretion for each individual seller. But common ranges have developed over the years and, despite the upward trends of inflationary living, still serve as rules of thumb for both dealers and customers. At least at conventions and among the most well-known Beatles mail-order dealers, some degree of uniformity is evident. Perhaps because of the grapevine — the interrelating friendships, partnerships, and cooperation among dealers — it serves their best interests to price items alike. Rather than undersell or overprice, dealers may watch each other and intentionally maintain similar prices.

Beatles dealers you meet today are the very fans who supported the group all through the tumultuous times of the sixties. By mid-1974, many had so much Beatles merchandise stored up that their collections were devouring their living space, taking over whole rooms in their homes. While the older fans had almost too much, new fans, many just born the year the Beatles broke in to the U.S. charts, were looking for some part of the wealth of material produced in the past decade, and were willing to pay prices significantly beyond the prices it originally sold for.

Bringing these two elements together was the impetus for such things as the dealers' room at Beatles Cons, mail-order Beatle businesses, new fanzines and collectors magazines, all of which flourished rapidly in the process, and have continued to do so for the last eight years.

4.

The Counterfeit Controversy

Beatle fans are greedy. They want the *real* thing, not a reasonable facsimile. In the last seven years, knowledgeable and active shoppers have managed to substantially deplete the available resources of *genuine* collectibles. So, when recent Beatle conventions have rolled around, other fans loudly complained about the lack of original 1964 memorabilia, rare records, and first edition books. What they found instead was table after table piled high with remakes, bootlegs, counterfeits, and reproductions. Looking just like the real McCoy, these "incredible simulations" have created widespread confusion and are the biggest boondoggles in the entire collecting field.

During the first three or four years of conventions (which began in 1974), there was still quite an abundance of originals; in fact, these early cons were literally treasure troves of *real* finds. Memorabilia, authentic promos, and first pressings were coming out of dusty attics, basements, and closets for the first time, and the mad scramble was on to purchase it all while it was still "hot" and the getting was good.

I remember the key word at the 1974 Boston "Magical Mystery Tour" convention was "deals." Everyone was "doing a deal," making fantastic purchases, and trading their own rare items for something else they wanted even more. Collections were built up at prices that would be a steal today, if you could even get your hands on the stuff at all. And that has become the major problem in today's collectors' scene.

The same dealers have been doing conventions three to five times a year for eight years now. The places they went to for their own stock have been picked clean by this time. And new sources are few and far between. The news media has aggravated the problem by reporting on these trends. In discussing the current vogue for collectibles and concentrating on the value of these old Beatles items, they have developed an *aware* public. Now, it is hard to find *anyone* who is unaware of potential values and still naive enough to part with anything for a bargain price. All of which means that dealers have to dig deeper, expend more valuable time, and pay a keener price for anything they do manage to locate. The result — price inflation — is passed right along to the customer.

Just as the items become harder and harder to find, it seems the demand for them continues to increase. New people are becoming attracted to the Beatles every day, and they want a little piece of the past to hold on to just as much as old time fans who want to add to their own collections. Also, more

people are becoming aware of just what a good investment collectors' items can be. Since the price doubles every year or two, collecting beats a savings account for earning "interest" on your money. I have found the majority of collectors to be genuine Beatle fans themselves, indulging in a hobby that is of great personal interest as well as being monetarily profitable but, all the same, it is quite a different scene from the sixties, when we were all "just" fans and only bought what we really intended to use. Back then, only a handful of us bought a Beatles lunchbox without actually using it, or a scrapbook without writing in it. And all our Beatles records were to play. Now, a lunchbox, a note book, and the records and their sleeves are status symbols, investments. For many, items are displayed in all their glory, but rarely used. The thrill of ownership is perhaps no less, but it has without a doubt changed and broadened the scope of the whole Beatles' business.

THE BIRTH OF NEW "MEMORABILIA"

Dealers have obviously done all right for themselves as a result of all this competition and growing interest in their wares. But what do they do when they find themselves hard-pressed for more and more merchandise? After a sellout show in New York City in February, how can they manage to restock satisfactorily to meet the demand for the Chicago convention in August, and the big Los Angeles "Beatlefest" coming close on its heels in November? And, in the meantime, they have put out a mailing list of items for sale to satisfy their hungry mail-order customers all over the rest of the world! The impossible starts to loom large. Everyone wants the real thing and they are willing to pay for it . . . but the real thing just happens to be eleven to eighteen years old and getting older and rarer every day.

Something had to fill the void. Dealers were faced with the nightmare of paying $100.00+ for a table at "Beatlefest," only to have thousands of fans with money to burn descend on their *empty* tables! They could still display all the rare records, sleeves, books, and memorabilia they could locate, but it just wouldn't be enough. Those would sell out within the first few hours of opening day. They had no choice but to turn to their own inventiveness and start creating *new* product.

This practice has become a mixed blessing. Dealers started to put the Beatles' pictures on every conceivable surface — from ashtrays to t-shirts, from wall plaques to serving trays, on belt buckles, playing cards, and even dollar bills. Since these could all be mass-produced, the quantity alone assured relatively low prices on these goods, although today's high costs in manufacturing, labor, and overhead means that new product can never be produced as cheaply as the original memorabilia once was. But still, the opportunity to purchase some inexpensive paraphernalia — like Beatles stationery, and tote bags — is a positive way to show off one's fandom without draining the pocketbook.

Criticisms grew only as all this new consumer merchandise began to take over and *dominate* the dealers' room. After saving all year in order to buy up those elusive and legendary 1960's valuables, it can be a supreme letdown to be bombarded instead with counterfeits, remakes, bootlegs, and a lot of funfair-like souvenirs.

The most disgusting and discouraging are the counterfeits, especially to the new collector. A counterfeit is anything that has been remade without authorization to look as much like the original item as possible.

I was notified by a perturbed dealer at a New York Beatles convention recently that the word "counterfeit" is a misnomer and an unfair label to place on their newly made product. They prefer "reproduction." A counterfeit, they say, tries to pass as the real thing; their admitted remakes, which look like exact duplications to me, are priced at very "reasonable" figures, and a knowledgeable fan *should* realize, I was told, that a $9.00 Beatles pouch is a remake, since the 1964 original (which comes in many different colors, including blue, red, black, gold, aqua, olive green) sells for $25.00–40.00. The repro comes in red only and omits the NEMS trademark logo, and is "obviously" not pretending to be anything but a new souvenir. This fine splitting of hairs over terminology just illuminates how confused and tangled in verbiage this area is, especially for the novice collector.

Take the area of counterfeit recordings, for example. Since the counterfeiter strives to produce as exact a duplicate as is possible of the original first pressing, the resulting confusion for the collector is enormous. The Beatles' **Christmas Album, Roots, The Family Way,** and **Two Virgins (Unfinished Music, No. 1)** are just a few samples of recent LP counterfeits. All are deleted, out-of-print albums that can't be purchased new from any record store and are increasingly difficult to locate even in used condition. So, what harm can there be in counterfeiting them? In many ways, it is argued, counterfeits serve as "noble" a purpose as do bootlegs: they preserve particular material that would otherwise be lost. As very rare and much sought after items, the originals of these LPs were bringing in $40.00–75.00 on dealers' lists and at convention auctions. The copies, priced at only $10.00–15.00, were exact enough to satisfy fans who wanted the record for the sake of its contents or cover.

Bootleg records, on the other hand, while just as unauthorized, present material that has never been officially released and which therefore can't be "passed off" as the real thing. When one buys a bootleg, one usually knows it. The recent **Collector's Items** boot is an exception. Its masterful reproduction of Capitol's own label, trademarks, and other features confuses even very savvy collectors into mistaking it for a new "official" release. The recent **Decca Tapes** boot had such excellent liner notes and great sound quality that it could have and *should* have been a legitimate release! But the majority are distinctively bootlegs and nothing else and, while collecting them is fraught with problems galore, determining their authenticity is not one of them.

As long as the person buying the record or other counterfeit knows exactly what he or she is receiving, there doesn't seem to be any harm done. To put together a good Beatles collection without going bankrupt, it helps to know if you are getting the bargain of a lifetime, or the biggest ripoff. When I see any of the above mentioned counterfeit LPs with a price tag in the intermediate range of $18.00–25.00, my thoughts begin to turn to the second of those two alternatives.

SPOTTING AND AVOIDING COUNTERFEITS

Price is the first and sometimes, the only indicator you may get to help you know whether you are being offered an original or a copy. Mail order shopping can be the quickest and most convenient method of collecting, but also the most disappointing. Without being able to see the items, you must base your decision on the dealer's credibility, previous service, or recommendation. On a set sale list, price is the only variable you can bet they'll tell you about, and going by that alone can definitely be buying blind. Best advice is to write first and probe for further details.

The condition and the quantity available should also be the useful tipoffs to reproductions. If the price is reasonable, the condition Mint or still sealed, and the dealer is sitting on a pile of them, you are probably staring at a counterfeit. Whether or not the dealer knows it or wants to admit it, any such pile of *Mint condition rare records* (and that includes all the above), even if marked deceptively high, should still shout "copy" good and loud to you.

Mint copies of these rarities do surface occasionally, but hardly ever in quantity. Finding a rare ten to eighteen year old record still sealed or flawless is a major accomplishment, and any record dealer alive will reward such a prize with a suitably high price. Those who are confused about what they themselves have just picked up may try to pass that confusion on to you by pricing a record in that gray area between

This pouch is actually a pencil case (not to be confused with a similar item called the Beatles purse). The originals come in many colors — black, red, gold, aqua, olive green — and sell for $30-40. *Price Guide No.: 713*

cheap copy and expensive collectors' item. Don't fall for it. The least you deserve is to *know* what you are getting. If you want an unauthorized copy, you'll be able to find it easily enough and, with a little more diligent shopping, more cheaply as well. But if you must have an original, be willing to pay for it.

The place you buy and the person you buy from are equally important factors for collectors to be sensitive about. Purchase opportunities are really quite numerous: Beatle conventions, Beatle specialists who sell by mail order, record swap meets, flea markets, antique stores, used record shops, and magazines like *Goldmine* and *Trouser Press* which run ads placed by record dealers, both pro and novice.

The opportunities are the greatest, of course, at the specifically Beatles-oriented conventions, with up to 100 tables full of items, 90 percent of them manned by people who deal only in Beatles merchandise. But the odds are against your coming upon anything ridiculously underpriced at one of these. Most dealers at a convention are regulars by now, and they know the prices too intimately to give anything unique or rare away.

The unpleasant facts are that all the best bargains are scooped up by the dealers themselves during the two to three hour setting-up period before the convention even begins! Anyone who "dares" to set reasonable prices on his goods will find them disappearing very quickly into the hands of his fellows, the more unscrupulous of whom might have enough nerve to mark up the price drastically and offer it for resale at his *own* table. I've seen it done at every convention I've attended.

By the time the majority of the fans enter the dealers' room, then, the concern should be less about price, and more about whether you are paying for what you really want, or think you are getting. Is that **Christmas Album** in Very Good condition for $30.00 the original 1970 release, or just the now out-of-print counterfeit marked up to meet the demand?

Usually the only significant giveaway upon inspection is the clarity of the jacket or label. The picture, the print, the colors may be exactly the same as the original, but slightly faded, a bit grainier, or lacking in sharpness in the counterfeit. The difference becomes a little more obvious when the original can be held up next to a counterfeit for comparison. If that isn't possible, then I hope you have good eyes, because the variance is quite negligible in most cases.

When visual inspection is possible, then check to see that the ink color used on the label is what it should be. The copying process often loses something in the tones and hues; perhaps the right shade just wasn't available. I recently got stuck with a fake copy of the *Penny Lane* promo 45. The label, I soon discovered at a Beatles convention, should have been *pea*

green instead of the yellow of my otherwise exact reproduction. In a mail-order purchase, I also received what was supposed to be the promo copy of *She Loves You*. In this case, the ink color was a reddish-purple, but a true promo copy should be a bright and vivid pure red. Also, the tell-tale wax markings were scratched on instead of being stamped on professionally. I paid about $50.00 for these two records; the real value of these counterfeits is only $3.00 a piece.

The Beatles' **The World's Best** was released by the German Record Club in limited quantity. These rare LPs have been priced at $35.00–50.00 by reputable dealers in the U.S. Last year, the counterfeits were plentiful at cons for only $8.00–10.00. The color cover of the copy was very poorly reproduced. It must have been hard to pick up those tricky reds and oranges. The original is very distinct and colorful. Look closely; if the colors seem to bleed into one another, then it is the counterfeit.

Beatles In Italy, issued in 1965 on the Parlophone label, pictures the Beatles on its open-out cover in their famous pouring champagne pose. Dealers have tagged this item at anywhere from $60.00 to $125.00 and up. There was a legitimate second pressing, but the cover did not open. This version is worth only about $15.00. The counterfeit doesn't open up either, and you shouldn't have to pay more than $10.00 for that. The newly reissued (by EMI-Holland) copy has a different cover photo. VeeJay's **Songs, Pictures & Stories** album from 1964 is a similar case. If you've found a used or cheap cutout copy in a record store for $5.00 or less, and if it doesn't open out, it is the common repressing and not the rare original which is now worth $35.00–40.00 in monophonic form, and and incredible $150.00+ for the even rarer stereophonic version. Also, the reissue is called only **Songs & Pictures**. It has no stories.

The original Ed Rudy **American Tour** interview albums from Radio Pulsebeat News came with a thirty-four page booklet and promotional stickers. I have seen Mint, still sealed copies of this advertised for $40.00, and even up to $100.00. The counterfeits do not have the extras. This was also bootlegged with a completely different paste-on cover, and was also recently (1981) reissued by Ed Rudy himself.

With many of the other counterfeits, covers and labels are exact down to the last detail. However, since the maker didn't have the original photographic negatives to work with, he had to copy from the already printed covers. As with any photo recopied in this manner, the edges tend to blur, or lose just the slightest amount of contrast between the blacks and whites.

New items are counterfeited every month, so it is impossible to list them all or even keep up with it. Suffice it to say that anything with a high price tag is a likely prospect for future copying. Collectors need more than just sharp eyes and lots of knowledge, because you can't always see what you're buying. Mail-order catalogs offer a wealth of items, but descriptions are often vague, incomplete, even false.

IMPROVING YOUR CHANCES

The best way to eliminate much of the confusion is to *know your dealers*. Whether dealing in person or by mail, the best possible advice is to buy from someone you trust.

The dealers you choose should be able to give you straight answers on just "why" the price is what it is. Many factors can affect how the dealers decide to price their merchandise: where they bought it themselves, how rare they feel it is, how they judge the condition, how much demand for it they have currently witnessed, etc. There is no reason why the customer cannot know the factors that have gone into the price decision. An honest appraisal of the situation will take some of the mystery out of seemingly overpriced items. As long as the customer has the chance to be informed and is an aware buyer, instead of a duped one, bootlegs and counterfeits can be a bonus instead of a scam.

If you are buying at a convention, a few friendly faces in that big room can be invaluable. A knowledgeable and completely straight dealer will be able to steer you to the worthwhile buys and away from the overpriced fakes. In fact, if you know some of them well enough, they will probably let you borrow the original version of something they have if you need it to check out a cheaper competitive offer across the room.

Knowing the dealer is even more crucial when buying through mail-order catalogs, for sale and auction lists. All you have to go on in such a circumstance is a brief description of the item and the credibility of the dealer. If you have never ordered from them before and want some assurances, look to see if they offer any guarantees, money-back-if-not-satisfied statements, and return privileges. The best dealers will give just that kind of safeguard, and will stand by their assessments of an item's originality and the grading they have given to its condition. You can feel a little more at ease about buying sight unseen if you have the assurance of a refund should something prove unsatisfactory.

I have encountered incredible variations in prices even among regular dealers at conventions, so you can expect no less from the record-selling public at large. The only fact that is a certainty concerning prices at present is that they are climbing.

Even counterfeit copies will be costing you more in the months to come. Recent government crackdowns (and raids) have eliminated much of the supply. Any dealers with stock left of such LPs as **Two Virgins**, **Family Way**, **Christmas Album**, etc., have raised that old $10.00 price tag to a heftier $14.00–

17.00 one.

HIGHER PRICES AND MORE PROBLEMS

Counterfeits are by no means restricted to albums and picture sleeves. The imagination of the counterfeiter knows no such bounds. But the record business is much more lucrative than the minimum markup possible on Beatle buttons, for instance. All the old collectable 1964 buttons have been reproduced: from "In Case of Emergency, Call Paul" to "I'm a Beattles Booster" (misspelling and all, ala the original). When the real thing sells for $5.00 and the copy for $2.00–3.00, it is difficult to get too overwrought about it. Telling the difference between counterfeits and originals of buttons is a science I haven't mastered yet, although I have seen examples of both. They have been reproduced in exact detail: size, color, markings, etc. — all identical. In this area, it all comes down to knowing your dealer. Many dealers *only* sell original items and will guarantee their product. Others "specialize" in repros, and usually will admit same, but may have some special original items for sale as well. The list of remade buttons grows monthly, so a current accounting is impossible. Any button which sold well in its original form, from '64 booster pins to recent promotional buttons marking a solo LP, are all targets — so nothing is safe!

Another item recently remade are *arcade cards*. These used to be sold in vending machines, along with movie stars cards. The backs had interesting facts and biographical notes on the person pictured. These cards sell for $3.00–5.00 each if original. The fakes do not have the writing on the back (at least so far!), and the pictures are grainier, less finely detailed, etc.

Assorted promotional items have been redone in the past couple of years in another attempt to give dealers more merchandise to hawk at cons and through their mail-order catalogs. Everything from promo t-shirts to the little extra giveaway items (combs, pins, stickers, etc.) have been duplicated. Buy with your eyes open these days — it's no sin to buy the remake when the real thing is just not around, as long as you know that that is what you are getting.

Since some of the unscrupulous dealers (a minority, I'm sure) will go to any length to provide the outward appearance of authenticity to their replicas, knowing a reputable dealer is of utmost importance. There was a time you could rely on your eyesight to tell you what was old enough to be genuine and what was newly minted. These days, you will encounter some items that were purposely made to *look* old — left in the rain to rust, smeared with dirt, etc. It seems far-fetched, I know, but I've heard even worse horror stories than that, so I put nothing past *some* dealers.

Lately, countless paperbacks and magazines about

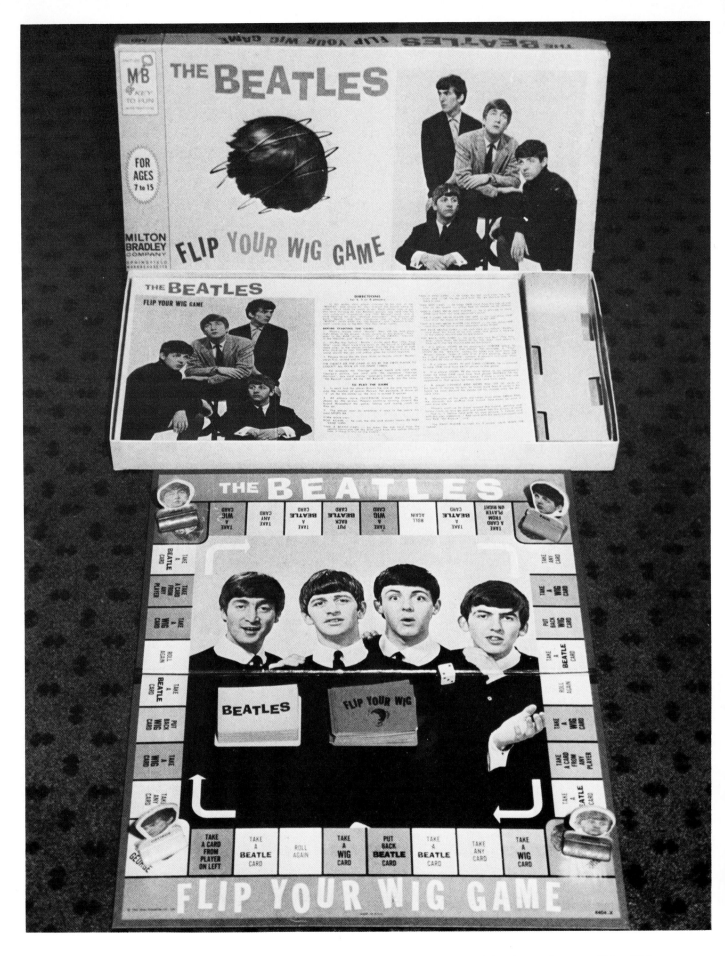

A "Flip Your Wig Game," with all its pieces and in Very Good condition (like this one), may sell for $75 or more. *Price Guide No.: 668*

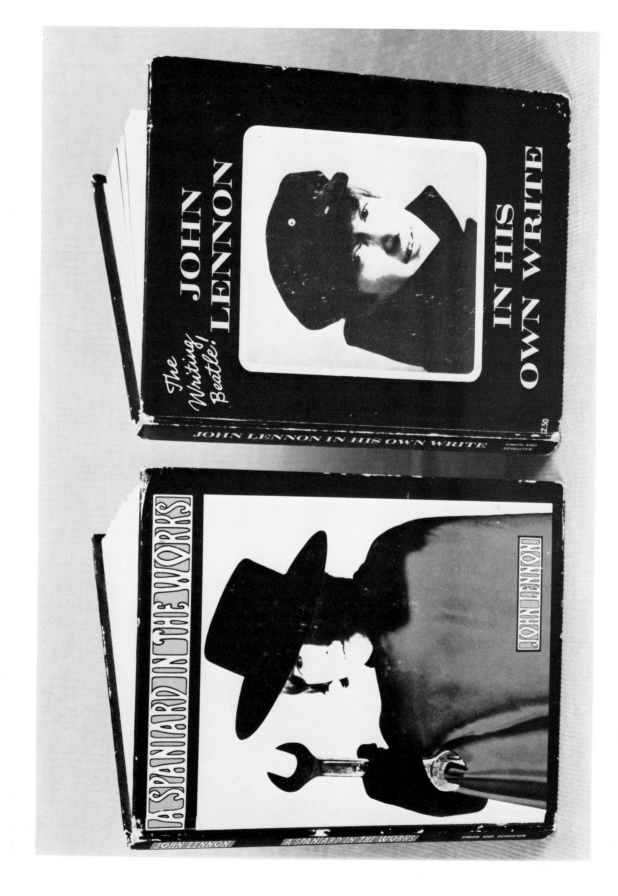

Hardcover editions of John Lennon's books from 1965 and 1964 (left to right). Depending on how early they were printed, these would each be worth $35-50 in Mint condition. These copies, in Very Good condition, are worth about $30 each. *Price Guide Nos.: 425, 455*

the Beatles have been reappearing as well, but for the most part these are not strictly counterfeits, but legitimate reprintings by their original publishers or by the firm with rights to the material. When such items are remade to look almost exactly like the valuable old originals, collecting them becomes a matter for some caution on the part of collectors. You don't want to pay $10.00 for a reissued magazine which you should be able to pick up for $2.00–3.00. If in doubt, the quality of the pictures will often by a dead giveaway, those in the remakes having an inferior, fuzzy graininess due to the fact that the paper is of thinner and cheaper stock. The newly reprinted *Beatles Book* monthlies are a good case in point. A dishonest dealer may remove the new cover and extra wrap-around pages, leaving only the reprint of the *Beatles Book* issue which, redone from its own plates, is nearly indistinguishable from the original. But extremely close scrutiny reveals just the slightest bit of graininess and lack of contrast in the photos — the blacks are grayer, with an overall rather mottled effect. Also, the color inks on the reprints are different in hue from the originals (reddish pink is now reddish orange, and the royal blues now peacock blue, and so on). All rather trivial perhaps, but with this in mind it could save you from spending $10.00 on a newly printed copy worth only $2.50–$3.00.

In most cases, paperback books which have been republished are worth nearly as much as their '64 counterparts. The U.K. imports of *A Hard Day's Night* and *Help!* sell for approximately $5.00–6.00, with a fine condition original bringing up to $10.00 (but usually less). *A Cellarful Of Noise* has just been counterfeited, as well as reprinted, allowing fans to pick up Brian's interesting biography for only $4.00-5.00, instead of scrounging for the really rare $10.00 paperback or even scarcer hardcover.

Hardcovers of Brian's book and John Lennon's two volumes of poetry and stories are now priced in the $25.00–40.00 range, and so far the ability to reproduce such editions has eluded the canny counterfeiters. Manufacturing costs for hardcover reproductions are probably too prohibitive for them to bother.

For that same reason, the *majority* of memorabilia has escaped this desecration. At latest count, the following memorabilia has been remade, some of it an almost exact reproduction of the original authentic piece of Beatle history, while others are noticeably different: Beatles scarf (fakes sell for $8.00–10.00 and have no fringe); pouch (fakes in red only); desk set pen holder (new ones are cubes instead of flat rectangular); beach towel (printing job not as intricate and professional); Beatles megaphone (bugle) in yellow (originals were white). Something new usually turns up at each convention, so it is impossible to keep tabs on them all. You can still safely look for lunchboxes, Beatle dolls, and the "Flip You Wig" game without bringing a microscope to inspect the grain content, or a color chart to note the various hues or the amount of bleed. But nothing, absolutely nothing, would surprise me in the future.

The dealers expect *you* to bear the burden of knowledge. They figure if you want to pay $8.00 for a remade scarf instead of $35.00–40.00 for the real '64 item, they should oblige you. And why not? You may *want* to wear a Beatles scarf, put your pencils in the new pouches, decorate your clothes with tons of buttons, etc., all without having to take out a loan from the bank. As long as you *know* exactly what it is that you are getting when you pay for it, then there is little harm in the proliferation of all these new counterfeits, replicas, "reproductions," or whatever dealers choose to call them next year.

5.

The very first Beatles bootleg was probably part of a TV offer made during the sixties, with promoters trying to pass it off as a legitimate recording. Capitol Records soon put a halt to anyone else's fanciful wishes to achieve wealth through selling such highly commercialized bootlegs. The Alpha-Omega boxed set of Beatles hits was one such attempt whose time had not really arrived yet. Today, these four LP sets have a collectors' value of $30.00+ based on their limited availability and current rarity.

A few quasi-bootlegs were put out as cash-ins during the height of Beatlemania, with look-alike covers and deceiving titles like **Meet The Beetles**; these were also unauthorized and quickly quashed by Capitol as well. Tons of novelty records mimicking, spoofing, or praising the Beatles also poured out during the mid-sixties, but as long as they didn't pretend to actually *be* the Beatles, they were tolerated by record company executives.

BOOTLEG BEGINNINGS

By the later sixties, imaginative fans were starting to get creative bootleg ideas of their own. One of the first Beatles bootlegs with a wide circulation, and the first one I was ever aware of, was the now famous **Kum Back**. It had a plain white cover, no liner notes, but had beautiful (to my own uncultivated ear) sound, and the first outtakes we'd ever been able to have of an actual recording session. Included was the long version of *Teddy Boy*, left off the final **Let It Be** album and abbreviated in its official release on the **McCartney LP**. **Kum Back** was a popular success and widely discussed, as it came out a good year before we ever saw the film "Let It Be" or the legitimate Capitol album. Once **Let It Be** was released, however, it had been so overdubbed by Phil Spector ("Spector-ized") that this bootleg became and remains a classic in its simplicity. It may not have A+ sound, but it was the unadulterated purity of the Beatles' voices and the feeling of "being there" that made it such a favorite.

I wasn't aware of bootlegs again for several more years and, when they did resurface, they showed only slight improvement in packaging. Between the white jackets and the shrink wrap were printed inserts. These monotone inserts usually had the album's title, a picture of the Beatles, and sometimes (not always) a play listing of the LP's cuts. The insert was sometimes pasted on the jacket, and sometimes merely slipped in loosely under the shrink wrap.

Titles started to multiply like jack rabbits during the mid-seventies as mail-order business in boots became a flourishing industry. Catalogs were put out and albums were graded for sound on a scale from A to D. These letters are still in use today, but the standards for assigning them seem higher. It is an amazing experience to go back and listen to old bootlegs and hear how poor the sound quality actually was on most of them. I can't remember now how they were graded at the time, but I suspect not as strictly as they would be today when compared to some of the fine examples of bootleg recordings which have been produced in just the last few years.

Yellow Matter Custard (As Sweet As You Are) is another well-known LP, as it was one of the first to bring out material that hadn't yet been heard by the vast majority of fans. Most of the songs were done live by the boys in November of 1962 on a BBC radio show. Unfortunately, this LP *sounds* as if the material was recorded off the radio!

Most succeeding albums — **Abbey Road Revisited, EMI Outtakes, Rare Beatles**, for example — still had plain white labels, and we counted ourselves fortunate if one turned up which indicated things like side one or side two on them. A few appeared with track listings on the labels at this time, but even today this is a rare feature on boots. A sophisticated job, like that done on **Hollywood Bowl**, has a picture and track listings actually printed *on* the jacket and not just on an insert — a unique idea for the mid-seventies.

George Harrison's 1974 tour initiated a whole spate of albums with the following unimaginative titles: **Chicago, Dallas, Excerpts From Three Major Concerts (NY), Fort Worth, Live In Calgary** (presumed from the Vancouver show), **Long Beach**, and others all with the same material.

For some reason, McCartney's '76 tour inspired a little bit more creativity in the LP titles, as we saw the following emerge: **Encore, Flash Bomb, Fly South, Laser Beams, Light As A Feather, Liquid Paper, 9mm Automatic, Ride A Killer Bird, Wings From The Wings**, among others. All but the last one were short-lived, limited production efforts, while **Wings From The Wings** reportedly sold in the tens of thousands due to excellent sound quality, good packaging, and wide distribution.

Up through the mid-seventies, single disc bootleg albums sold for only $4.00–5.00 apiece. When the double albums, like **Sweet Apple Trax**, came out, they were priced at a mere $8.00. Those prices have at least doubled today.

Sweet Apple Trax had many different configur-

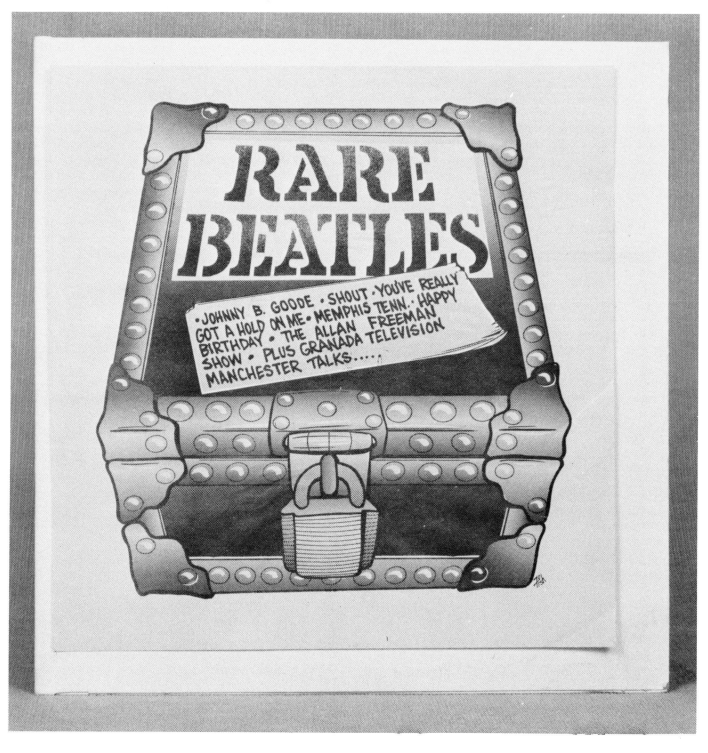

A typical Beatles bootleg from the mid-seventies, with paste-on cover over plain white jacket. Today's value: only $8-10. *Price Guide No.: 339*

ations (e.g., **Hahst Az Son, Hot As Sun**), and also appeared as a two-album, two-volume set with a 1970 picture of the Beatles on the insert, and in the New Sound version, which sported the picture from the Revolution promo. All the material is exactly the same and is all from the **Let It Be** sessions: outtakes that never made it on any authorized LPs, including practice versions of *Get Back*. (Without these boots, we never would have known that that song originated as a white power song complete with salute to Enoch Powell!)

Over the last six years, this album has become practically a legend. It is probably the best known and most instantly recognizable bootleg album of all. In a survey I did among 2,000 members of The Write Thing fan club, **Sweet Apple Trax** came out miles ahead on the list of *most wanted* bootleg albums. Probably in response to all these demands for the product, this LP was remade in 1981, this time under the title **The Black Album**. In style and appearance a take-off of the Beatles' "White Album," it is complete with brand new poster, with song titles identical to the original **Sweet Apple Trax** boot. The album had a rather limited circulation, but was extremely popular to all the new collectors of boots who missed **Sweet Apple Trax** the first time around.

CURRENT TRENDS IN BEATLES BOOTLEGS

The trend in bootlegs for the eighties seems to be pointing in the direction of remakes. Not that remakes are a new phenomenon, but packaging has become a little slicker these days. All through the seventies, one of the biggest complaints about boots was that so many of them were mere reissuings of the same old material redone under different titles. There is only so much in the way of different Beatles' outtakes, interviews, and live material preserved from the short time period when they were a group; thus, innovative bootleggers have had to find ways of stretching what they have their hands on and making that go around . . . and around and around.

Bootleggers used to have a bad habit of renaming a song, so it appeared to be something new on an album, and selling it under that false premise. Today, they merely take all the same material and repackage the whole LP using a new name and cover. Because there are so many new collectors every year, they can sell the same album in just as large quantities as they did originally. The **Beatles Vs. Don Ho** from the late seventies was a fairly good seller, and it sold just as well entitled **Beatles Silver Lining** in 1981! Many collectors will buy the album knowing it is the same thing, just to have the different jacket. Bootleggers, knowing that, go so far as to make label and jacket variations within a single series of bootleg pressings — just to sell the same album to the same people twice!

Reissues are not the total story on boots in the eighties, though. Actually, some all new *classics* have been discovered in tape vaults and who-knows-where by the canny bootleggers, and they've made their way into the light of day in the last couple of years. The most reknowned are **The Decca Tapes, The Beatles Broadcasts**, and **Collectors Items**. The first two made available to the fans and collectors material the Beatles did on historic occasions, such as their first audition for Decca, a session all fans were overly anxious to hear for themselves. Although many other previous boots have purported to be the Decca sessions (one even entitled **Decca Sessions**), they were usually radio broadcasts and usually had the same material as **Yellow Matter Custard**. But **Decca Tapes** was the first time the real sessions actually got out to the public on an LP, collected in one place after being issued previously on colored vinyl bootleg singles. **Broadcasts** contained live material the Beatles did on BBC radio shows in the early sixties, the most exciting aspect of this album being that the sound quality was vastly superior to the average boot and far above the broadcasts collected on the **Yellow Matter Custard** LP. Versions of *Clarabella* and *Soldier Of Love* on the **Broadcasts** LP are so magnificent, they rate as equal to anything the Beatles ever released legitimately and their appearance on this boot should be commended as a public (Beatle fans, at least!) service.

Collectors Items has a history all its own: it preceded the legitimate **Rarities** album by Capitol by a few months, but contained much of the same material and, more importantly, was far superior in packaging. The cover was a color montage of rare Beatles collectibles, records, and memorabilia against a background of rare Beatles wallpaper. Measured against the big name record company's puny visual offering: a gray background with a little wallet-sized picture of the Beatles looking bored, **Collectors Items** got rave reviews from all fans. Today, it is a collectors item in its own right and sells for $20.00–30.00. It is also an example of a jacket change (*Paperback Writer* was exchanged for *I'm Down*, and the code numbers were changed between pressings). Both versions are highly collectible, the first one being slightly more valuable than the second.

Bootlegs all began as plain LPs with plain sleeves, but the genre has expanded into all forms of recordings. The 10-inch EP size became the rage in the later seventies. A whole series was released under the Tobe Milo label which spoofed not only other bootlegs but legitimate Beatles product as well. The most memorable of these was **Life With The Lennons**, a take-off on **Life With The Lions**, filled with your wildest nightmare *outtakes* of Yoko and John's screaming.

These 10-inchers started the trend toward numbered copies. Usually, only 500–1,000 copies were made

THE BEATLES

Visit To Minneapolis

Melvin Records MMEP001A

A bootleg 45 of the Beatles' Minneapolis press conference, together with some other live material from their 1965 U.S. tour. Now out-of-print, and valued at $5-7. *Price Guide No.: 339*

in total, and numbers were stamped on each one to show the exclusiveness of these limited editions.

Bootleg singles also became the new rage, complete with the colorful picture sleeves and (usually) colored vinyl pressings. Every color in the rainbow, including a clear wax and a marbled one, were introduced. Some collectors felt they had to get every version of a record, so this embellishment was definitely a boon to the manufacturers and sellers!

Just recently, there was a short-lived trend for bootleg picture discs. These were hot items at first, and picture discs of **Decca Tapes** and **Casualties** were fast sellers. By the time the market was flooded with legitimate picture discs plus the dozens of versions of bootlegs and counterfeit discs, the fans had lost much of their initial enthusiasm for the product and duds, such as **Timeless**, died along side gems like **Listen To This Picture Record**. The former had a few interesting moments of Beatles interviews, but the material has all appeared before, and since the rest of the recording – the "outtakes" – were actually sung by amateurs and not the Beatles at all, this album got a bad reputation. On the other hand, **Listen To This Picture Record** featured John as a disc jockey in New York in 1974 and was really great fun to hear. The time was no longer ripe for such discs, however, which only sold if the price was lowered down from $15.00--20.00 to a more reasonable $11.00--12.00. The days of the $25.00 picture discs seemed to be over.

BOOTLEG VALUES

Most bootlegs *are* priced reasonably. They usually follow the trend set by legitimate commercial recordings; currently such LPs are selling for $8.99 and up. Single bootleg albums, therefore, are now running $7.00--10.00; normally $8.00 is the going rate, unless the LP is something extra special like **Collectors Items** which, even new, sold for $12.00--25.00. Double bootleg albums run from $12.00--15.00, and triple sets usually $17.00--20.00, very similar to what the record industry recommends for their own product. Singles (45s) or EPs usually cost twice as much (or more) as you might expect to pay in stores but, with their colorful picture sleeves and colored vinyl, bootleggers can get away with a $3.00--5.00 price tag. You are buying the exclusiveness of the product, and its limited availability.

The values I've been discussing are the current prices for *available* bootleg recordings. Anything out-of-print is a whole 'nother story. Bootlegs have a short "shelf life," so to speak. Their pressings are always limited, usually to just 1,000. Some bolder bootleggers expand their production to two to three thousand. The majority never go over a 5,000 copy pressing. Obviously, this is not going to allow for a very wide distribution of product. A few dealers scattered across the country will get 100 to 200 copies or so, and perhaps a few well-placed record shops in major cities (e.g., New York, Chicago, Los Angeles, San Francisco, Detroit, etc.) might get a few dozen or less. Most only last as a current selling item for a year or so. Some of the popular records with very low pressings may last only a couple of months. **Collectors Items** seemed to be wiped out as a stock item in under two months. The follow-up LP, **Casualties**, with its gorgeous butcher cover, was available only about three months. The price on both records rose steadily during the limited time they were still in stock, because the demand was so much greater than the known availability of the album. Those who wanted it had to pay the asking price; it was a seller's market, as collectors knew they wouldn't have the opportunity to shop around at their leisure.

As soon as an album does go out-of-print, it can become a collectible. As you recall, my definition of a collectible includes anything that sells for more than its original selling price. Some bootlegs were never that exciting to the public in the first place, and they are worth today (even out-of-print) just what they were going for originally, give or take a dollar or two. On the other hand, some albums, singles, etc., are so much in demand that a dealer can get away with charging quite a few extra dollars. This great increase in price is much more the exception than the rule but, even though I have heard it said that bootlegs do not have a collectible value, I know from personal experience (and a survey of fans all over the world) that this is not true.

Copies of **Sweet Apple Trax** (before the recent release of **The Black Album**) were fetching $15.00 apiece. **Casualties** was bringing $20.00. **Five Nights In A Judo Arena** (with the color jacket) was going for $15.00. And **Wings Live At The LA Forum** (**Wings From The Wings**), the three-record boxed set with red, white, and blue vinyl records, was getting up to $30.00 in auctions and at Beatles conventions. These records were in high demand and the supply on them was pathetically low. They could demand and receive even higher prices in future.

Some discs can bring a higher price today because of the *number* originally stamped on them. If they have this proof of their limited pressing and show a low number, they might go for an extra couple of dollars. It was an old joke among collectors (and even more between dealers) that some unscrupulous types make 1,000 copies of bootleg records, but stamp the first 500 with the number "one." That is probably an exaggeration of a genuine practice; just be aware that low numbers on your bootlegs are not always a definite guarantee of anything!

Very old Beatles bootlegs, the ones with inserts (printed Beatles pictures on one-color paper, glued on plain white covers or merely left loose between the shrink wrap), are currently selling for $8.00–12.00 at auctions and conventions. Some of the live material (**Hollywood Bowl, Tokyo, Live In Munich**, etc.) sell quickly. Others can sit around unwanted, especially if the title is unknown to today's buyer. Their simpleness contrasts sharply to the elaborate jackets currently popular.

BOOTLEG BUYERS & SELLERS

The most obvious reason why fans want to own bootlegs when they can buy all the legitimate recordings of the Beatles they want (which is a heck of a lot easier, too) is the desire to own material that is just unavailable in any *legal* form. It's the unreleased tracks: the Beatles rehearsing, jamming, or appearing live on stage, on the radio, on TV, etc., that intrigues the hard core Beatles fan/collector. This breed of fan is simply not satisfied with just what the record companies have to offer, although they naturally buy every official offering as soon as it appears anyway, as a matter of course. Pure and simple, they just want every single piece of Beatles trivia that they can manage to own. No matter that the Beatles themselves never intended it to be preserved on wax, or that they never thought anyone would even hear it outside of themselves. To the fans, these recordings are history and therefore *must* be preserved.

When asked what bothers them the most about bootlegs, a few fans mention the idea of their illegality, their "unethicalness." The fact is that neither the artist nor the record company have given their approval for the release of these recordings, and will receive no royalties from their sales. Only the bootlegger, and the dealers selling the albums, will make any profits from them. The thought of this, however, bothers only a third as many collectors as the number who are much more concerned about the low quality of the records themselves. The fans buying these records care a great deal more about *what* they are getting for their money than *where* their money goes.

Buying bootlegs can be a tricky business. In a recent survey I did, Beatles fans answered two to one that they had never been ripped off in a bootleg purchase. But they did add postscripts referring to some near-misses, potential catastrophes, and names of dealers to be avoided. Some of the problems or incidents which did occur are common pitfalls in the bootleg business. As earlier explained, some old bootlegs do not even list the contents on either the jacket or the label. Another disturbing practice is the frequent use of what appears to be any old label the manufacturers has in good supply, no matter how unrelated it is to the records' actual contents, on a Beatles bootleg. Actually, as a result of record industry pressures and crackdowns at commercial pressing plants, bootleggers frequently supply bogus labels which pressing plant operators (who may have been specifically warned to stop stamping out easily identifiable Beatles bootlegs) can apply to "limited edition records" which apparently have nothing to do with the Beatles. The recent **Je Suis Le Plus Mieux** "jazzersize" LP label, and the nondescript label for **Johnny And The Moondogs Silver Days** album are cases in point. You'll notice that nowhere on either of these albums are the words "The Beatles," or their personal names. Who can be blamed if pressing plant workers and printers simply "fail to recognize" the Beatles' pictures or snatches of their songs? All their office files show is a two-sided "jazzersize" record featuring two versions of something called *Boogaloo At Thirty-Two*, and what has that got to do with the Beatles? After all, not everybody in the world knows who Dr. Winston O'Boogie or the Moondogs really are! Unfortunately, a buyer will oftentimes look at the bogus label and want a refund, when in fact it *really* is the Beatles and not the "Sunshine Boys."

At the other extreme, what I've often experienced in buying a bootleg whose label reads Beatles, or Wings, or whatever, is having it play something like Lawrence Welk music when put on a turntable! Not only the inside label may give a buyer problems; I have seen record jackets that claimed to contain an album of Beatles material, only to be nothing of the sort when played. Many respondents in our survey cited incidents such as these happening to them, along with many other variations of the kind, such as finding one side of an album completely blank. Sometimes a two or three record set with blank labels can end up being two or three copies of the *same* record, while the other sides which were supposed to have been included are missing altogether. Of course, a lot of this type of thing grows out of just plain poor quality control, and not out of intentional fraud. I sincerely believe a ripoff wasn't intended in the majority of cases. After all, even a bootlegger doesn't usually just take the money and run; most of them try to operate some sort of continuing business and want repeat customers as much as any businessman. But this is an industry without any double-check system, one where return policies may be questionable and the guarantees few and far between.

It has therefore become obvious to me — and believe me I have learned the hard way along with many other collectors — just how essential it is to *know your dealer*. I have discussed the same topic as part of my advice on buying original collectibles and avoiding getting stuck with an unwanted counterfeit, but this advice is equally pertinent when it comes to collecting bootlegs.

First of all, buy from someone who will give you straight answers about contents, and especially about sound quality. And secondly, buy only from those who offer complete refunds and/or exchanges if not absolutely satisfied. When I bought what I thought was the **Christmas Album** from an anonymous dealer at a convention, someone I hadn't seen before and someone whose name I didn't ask for, I discovered too late that the record inside was not the Beatles. In fact, it wasn't even rock-and-roll! By the time I played the disc I was miles away from the convention and had no recourse. In a happier case, I bought a Wings bootleg with a jacket that said Wings and a label that said Wings, but which played an unmistakable Bob Dylan. I had won this LP in an auction through a record collectors magazine, and in rereading the original ad I saw a "full refund if not satisfied" claim and took advantage of it. My money was returned with an apology. This has happened to me on other occasions when I've bought from reputable dealers, even through mail-order. Sometimes you cannot be one hundred percent certain about what you're getting when you bid on an item sight unseen. Thinking an auctioned copy of **Two Virgins** was an original, I offered a fair price to a dealer and won. The LP turned out to be the common counterfeit (the colors on the jacket were a faded brown rather than a sharp black). When I wrote the dealer, he was glad to give a partial refund, and he let me keep the copy and was very grateful for the information I supplied on how to spot fakes.

Many record collectors dislike bootlegs; the majority cite the oftentimes poor sound quality involved. At least this is a remark I've often heard. In my own listening opinion, bootlegs range across the entire quality spectrum: everything from "unplayable," to mixed (some decent tracks, some only fair, and at least one very good cut), all the way to the impeccable excellence of **Decca Tapes, Broadcasts**, and **Wings Fly South** (one of my favorite live recordings). It is not fair to lump them all into one category but, rather, wise collectors should simply be forewarned about possible disasters, and should become as knowledgeable as possible on what exactly they want to get from a record (be it an investment, an addition to a collection, or a listening experience).

My survey elicited more than a dozen good reasons why the fans *do* like bootlegs and revealed fully the positive side of the coin. Aside from the obvious argument that bootlegs give us the "extra" material no other source seeks to provide, many people noted the historic value of these recordings, and the feeling that their preservation is more than worthwhile. Most fans enjoy the feeling of closeness to the Beatles they get from hearing the boys doing the original versions, the raw, unpolished first versions. Also, everyone enjoys the spontaneity of live concerts, interviews, and off-the-cuff remarks captured by some microphones and now available for all of us. Many feel as if they are getting to know what the Beatles are *really* like, not just what they or their record company might want us to believe. Fans like to follow a song's progression and gain a deeper insight into the musical workings of the group. Also, younger fans mention that the bootlegs featuring old TV shows, radio programs, etc., are priceless to them, since they missed all the hoopla the first time around. For us older fans who didn't happen to have sophisticated taping or video equipment back then, having a recording of these old memories is just as desirable.

Bootleg recordings exist today because they fill all these fan needs. The demand was there and someone enterprising enough to fill it stepped in. As the number of Beatles conventions, record swap meets, and mail-order record dealers (especially ones specializing in Beatles items) continues to multiply yearly, the need for greater and greater quantities of Beatles products likewise escalates. As I mentioned in my discussion of counterfeits and reproductions, bootlegs keep being churned out because dealers need something new to sell. There are only so many original copies of collectibles out there, and few dealers are going to be able to furnish the quantity necessary to keep up with the overwhelming demand. A Beatles convention attended by over five thousand fans is too choice a market to lose. Dealers feel a little more comforted when they at least have *something* in stock, and bootlegs, being as popular as they currently are, will be with us as long as fans continue to buy them.

As long as bootleggers enjoy the challenge of competition with each other over new ideas in packaging and material, they will continue to surprise and delight us. Bootleggers have incredible egos, and they like nothing better than seeing one of their "creations" becoming a talked about sensation in the underground world of collecting. They will continue to try for bigger and better things, so we all have something to look forward to as fan and collectors (at least for as long as bootlegging lasts, record companies and law enforcement agencies willing!).

A limited edition 12-inch single from the U.K. with color picture sleeve which sold out quickly. *Price Guide No.: 158*

6

Exactly what is it you want to collect? Anything with the Beatles' names on it, no matter what, or only the true collectibles? The market place is filled with Beatles product; knowing which of it you want is the most logical beginning.

I define the term "collectible" as any item you cannot currently buy *new* off the shelf and, at the same time, one that is now worth more than it *originally* sold for.

TIPS ON BUYING NEW PRODUCT

Of course, the majority of fans buy *all* the new Beatles items anyway. Eventually, today's magazines, books, and records will be old, scarce, and thus possibly of an increased value as well. So, most of us start naturally in the retail stores, combing the shelves for every new release and publication. However, most items bought in the last few years haven't *yet* entered collectible status, and whatever inflation there has been in their values has so far been slight. Even so, fans, by very definition, are not going to pass up the opportunity to acquire the latest releases. At the same time, it is a mistake to think that solely because something features the Beatles' voices, faces, or logo, that it is instantly valuable. *Potentially*, it may be, but it is not currently in the same category as the items priced and described in this book.

Records such as **Love Songs, Live At The Star Club**, most of the solo LPs, most of the current singles and picture sleeves are all too common right now to be worth any amount above their original selling price. Many, as *used* records, are in fact worth much less. Almost all the books released in the latter half of the seventies, such as *Man Who Gave The Beatles Away, Beatles Forever, Shout*, etc., are still for sale in most stores and are not collectibles. Magazines from the seventies may only be worth an extra dollar or two, as most fans and collectors picked them up when they were still for sale. Those few collectors who missed certain ones may be willing to pay a little above cover price for them, but not to the same degree they'd pay out for an early sixties all-Beatles magazine.

Newly available items like the above confuse non-collectors and beginners. The experienced collector, however, knows not to second-guess the market, and that buying every new item is the only way to secure potential rarities when they do chance by. An example would be the recent picture sleeve to *Love Comes To Everyone*. It was pressed in a limited quantity (1,000), and when word spread of its limited availability it became an instant collectible, now selling for $50.00--100.00. Every once and a while, this happens with a new picture sleeve. Paul's *Waterfalls* sleeve was distributed in only a few areas of this country. Minnesota got them, while most of Chicago did not. In only a few weeks, it was selling for $5.00, and a few months later it was a $10.00 item. On the other hand, if you think every single with a picture sleeve will duplicate this profit-making performance, you'll be sorely disappointed. The majority of current sleeves (John's **Double Fantasy** ones included) are currently worth no more than their first sticker price.

All of this is part of the fun and challenge of collecting, and the reason some of us get hooked on it. It's all such a guessing game sometimes! The best advice is just to get what new items you can afford, keep your ears cocked for rumors, and if you hear the slightest noise about something not being available somewhere, *then* scramble to get as many as you possibly can!

Whenever a new item is released in only one country, it becomes immediately desirable every place else. New releases like **Scouse The Mouse**, Ringo's soundtrack LP from a U.K. TV production, never reached the U.S. and is already deleted even in England. Anyone with the foresight to pick it up at the time it first appeared in the stores now owns an item valued at $100.00–$150.00 in the U.S. Lots of B-sides to singles appear only in the U.K. as well, songs that never come out officially on singles in the U.S. (such as Paul's *Zoo Gang*), and that makes them significantly collectible. Conversely, since many U.S. items are never released beyond our shores, it is just as advantageous to pick up all U.S. Beatles products with an eye to an eventual resale abroad. So, even though an item may have no extra value at the time you buy it, or in the country where you got it, that does not mean that it will never have added value in the future, or in another area of the world.

Surprisingly, it is sometimes the "shlockiest" stuff that becomes the most valuable over the years. Look at what sells for the highest prices today. It's not the Beatles best albums: **Meet The Beatles** or **Abbey Road** for instance, but junk like **Beatles In Astrosound**, or **Jolly What! The Beatles And Frank Ifield**. Precisely because it was "junk," no one bothered to buy it in 1964, and today it is a rarity. And what's rare is what's valuable! Records that have curiosity value today, but were not considered good music (i.e., commercial) when they were released, such as **Two Virgins, Life With The Lions,**

Wonderwall, Electronic Sounds, etc., are much sought after today. So, perhaps the least likely, least attractive, least advertised and promoted new items will be the highest priced collectibles in 1990. These are all reasons why hard-core collectors/fans buy every new Beatles product, no matter how useless, unlistenable or obscure it seems at the time. When the century turns, they will either be sitting on a pile of riches or the biggest bunch of junk you ever saw.

Almost every Beatles item produced in the sixties is a collectors' item today. True, that's a basic starting point, but some important differences which distinguish the new from the old sometimes confuse the novice collectors. To begin with, all the Beatles major Capitol Records albums are still being (re) pressed today. Thus, **Meet The Beatles**, even though it was originally recorded in 1963 in England, is still a current release. For $8.99 (or whatever your local record shop charges for new albums), anyone can pick up the current copy of this old album. It won't be the original pressing, of course, and is therefore not a collectible. It's the *original* pressings which are in demand and have collectible value. Even though it is the same album, the pressing date makes all the difference in the world. A first pressing in Near Mint condition is worth about $15.00--20.00, double the price of a brand new unplayed current copy. On the other hand, since collectors want only the finest specimens for their collections, *a poor condition copy of the same original pressing is almost worthless.*

Furthermore, many of the original albums are becoming even more attractive to collectors recently because of new cost cutting policies in packaging. Record companies reason that new fans won't know the difference if they eliminate the original inserts, or make fancy covers plainer. So, all frills and extras, even those the Beatles once considered artistically essential, are gone. (The posters and 8x10-inch photos of each Beatle which were part of the "White Album" concept are a notable example.) Also missing from current copies of **Sgt. Pepper** are the original freebie cutouts. The panels that opened up on **Walls And Bridges** are gone, and of course all picture books (for **Magical Mystery Tour, Ringo**, etc.) are no longer being printed. These albums (many of which were already being collected for the original rainbow label, or as record club editions, etc.) are now being sought out for their original packaging as well. Rule No. 1: If you can't get it in the store today, it is most probably a collectible.

SEARCHING FOR TRUE COLLECTIBLES

A collector always wants every item as close to its original presentation as they can possibly get. They may buy a newer stereo version of an album to play for the sound, but they want the original monophonic version to preserve as a collectible. Many collectors' goals are to have one copy of every variation in existence — label changes, cover changes, mix changes, whatever. Even if differences in the value of such versions is negligible, increased value lies in the existence of the *complete* collection, the sum being worth more than the parts. Collecting every release, alternate version, and variation can be an unending process, but then Beatles fans don't really ever want to run out of items to collect anyway!

After you've examined the "mainstream" stores for all currently available Beatles items and you still want to plunge into the quicksand of collecting, you have to begin to readjusting your thinking. The very way you go about shopping has to be altered. So far, we've just bought everything with B-E-A-T-L-E-S emblazoned on it. To be a collector, you have to be a lot more discriminating, knowledgeable, and careful.

You first need to know the whys, the whats, the hows, and particularly the wheres. In the History of Collecting chapter, we delved into the "whys", and the "what" is detailed in the Price Guide section. So, now we're left with the real nitty-gritty: the how to and where to of collecting. Surprises are always inevitable, both good and bad, but at least armed with the facts, you'll know the difference between a foolish buy, a grab-it-and-run miracle, and/or a merely expensive fact of life.

The novice collector is at a severe disadvantage from the very outset. Their vulnerability due to lack of basic facts makes them easy prey. Naivete can be expensive, frustrating, and counter-productive. But knowledge of the marketplace (what's available and at what prices, along with where best to find it), plus an awareness of all the latest schemes and scams (counterfeitings, remakes, etc.) will increase one's chances of successful finds and fair purchases. At least you'll be receiving value for your money.

The prices in this guide are the current top market value on each item. This is what a dealer making a living in the business might charge, and what you might expect to pay if you buy from these professionals. You may choose to start with the pros and save yourself a lot of time. But if you're like a lot of us these days, money is less plentiful than time, and alternate avenues might seem worth the investment of your own efforts.

Dealers themselves have to start someplace, too, and they usually begin with what I call the original source, or the bottom line. The first owner of an item is the prime original source. My number two fantasy as a collector (after a time trip back to Woolworth's) is to meet a *former fan*, someone who idolized the Beatles in 1964-66, bought everything that came out, and then put it in storage. After preserving it for sixteen or seventeen years, they now want to unload it all . . . and I'd be on hand and more than happy to oblige! Most likely these fans might now be pressed for funds and decide to part with some sentimental memories for cold hard cash. In other cases, they are moving and figure they can trade a pile of "junk" to someone who will give it a good home.

THE VALUE OF ADVERTISING

Unfortunately, dreams like these are more myth than reality! But if it can happen, here's how: *Advertise*. Check out the classified rates in your city newspaper, or newspapers in several nearby towns. Also, try the rates in neighborhood monthly or bi-weekly tabloids. Especially check on all underground or alternative publications in your area. These latter are sometimes free, and oftentimes ad rates are very reasonable. Just make it simple: WANTED: RARE BEATLES ITEMS. CASH PAID, and list your phone number. Maybe add a list of a few such rarities to give them the general idea: "memorabilia, picture sleeves, sixties albums, books, magazines, etc." If you are looking for something specific, like a Butcher cover or gum cards, mention that as well. It is best to make your ad as general as possible, however, because you never know what surprise calls you might receive.

When people answer such an ad, they are already seeing dollar signs before their eyes. I'm afraid the days when non-fans were blithely ignorant of the values of rare Beatles items has long since passed. Ten dollars used to sound like a lot of money for an old, dust-covered Beatles relic, but today the whole world seems to assume that anything that says Beatles, and I mean *anything*, no matter what, is worth its weight in gold. A lot of publicity has been created on the subject by the media in the last couple of years. Articles have appeared in magazines and newspapers, and TV has even covered conventions. Collecting is no longer a well-kept secret exclusive to the hard-core fans alone. What is really a misfortune is that these non-fans are holding on to your heart's desire and they often want a small fortune for it!

A caller will describe the item they have for sale, and usually expect you to come up with an offer. Or you may (*calmly*) want to ask them how much *they* had in mind. If you don't like their figures, you may want to make a counteroffer; if they don't like yours, you may need to do some reasoning, and negotiating. The rule of thumb is supposed to be: offer what it is worth to you. Of course, something may be *worth* a million dollars to you, but if you can only *afford* $20.00, then stick to that. I'd say make an offer based on a fair figure determined from the prices in this guide. If you want to add it to your personal collection, then you may want to offer (and pay) the going book rate. If you can afford it. If you want to buy it for resale (as a dealer would), then you would offer 50 to 60 percent

of the book value, or of the resale price you think you can finally get. As memorabilia and the more obscure records become harder and harder to get a hold of (most of them already seem to be in the hands of hard core collectors), dealers are finding it necessary to offer 75 percent of the value they will eventually resell for. If they don't want to take a cut in profits, then obviously the customer ultimately ends up paying higher and higher prices for these rarities.

Not all items have a concrete and tangible price base. Memorabilia does not have many variations, outside of packaging and condition, and is an easy type of item to discuss with a caller on the phone. However, if you are being offered something as nebulous as the Beatles' autographs, or a supposedly "exclusive" photograph, a caution sign should flash on for you and a lot of very *specific* questions need to be asked.

Autographs are virtually worthless unless you have some proof they are genuine. Ask the caller if (and how) they can verify authenticity, and indicate you'd probably want them to sign a statement to that effect. Everyone knows that the Beatles' associates and secretaries scribbled many a fake Beatles signature during the sixties. Also, a yearly photograph with signatures was sent to members of the official Beatles fan club; these "autographs" look real, but were actually stamped on, not personally signed. Anything known to be genuine can be used to compare a questionable autograph to, so ask the caller to send you a picture or a photocopy of their offered signature before you put any valuable money into anything so potentially dubious.

One caller told me she got their autographs from a pen pal in South Africa, who obtained them "when the Beatles visited there." The Beatles, of course, *never* went to South Africa!

A picture of the Beatles actually signing the autograph in question is one guarantee. Knowing the source from which the signature was obtained is also important, in both verification and determination of value. An autograph which comes direct from a close friend, family member, or associate of the Beatles, is more legitimate and therefore more valuable than a name scrawled on a nondescript piece of plain paper from an unknown former fan. A picture of John from the Cavern days (yellowed with age) signed by John, Paul, George and Pete Best, which came from an old Liverpool crony of the Boys, sold for $175.00 several years ago.

Another high risk item can be the photograph. You will get a lot of calls offering you "rare, unpublished" photos. Often times, they turn out to be Instamatic shots of the TV screen when the Beatles appeared on the Ed Sullivan show! Not exactly a rare collectible. But, for some reason, a gem to the non-fan. I was once even offered one of my own photos (stolen from the photo processing lab, I assume), which had been sold to an antique dealer. From my cross-examination on the phone, I figured out I could buy my own picture, worth about fifty cents, for $10.00!

Are there photographs that really are worth large sums of money and have collectibility? There are, but they are usually few and far between and rarely come the way of the average collector. They have to be sought out from much more esoteric sources. Most photos you'll encounter have been printed somewhere by somebody in some quantity, and are copies of the originals. Even if they come from your own negatives, they still are not that much more valuable then any other picture. After all, *thousands* of fans have personal photos of the Lads taken at concerts, off the TV, even at their homes in England, at press conferences, at hotel doors or stage entrances, or on vacations in different parts of the world, and so on. These photos range in quality from the most typical Instamatic, red-eye shot, to 35mm close-ups by semipros. Still, they all sell for reasonable figures of $1.00--2.00 each at Beatles conventions and through mail order. Anyone wanting or expecting more than that for a standard size 3 x 5 is just not being realistic. Some people have an exaggerated conception of what their own personal photos should be worth, just because they mean so much to *them*.

A truly valuable photograph would be something unpublished from an historic photo session, such as those for the Butcher cover or the cover of **Abbey Road**, or early Hamburg or Cavern Club pictures. They must be original photos, printed from the original negatives or slides, not pictures of pictures, familiar magazine pictures, or anything substandard or common. A collection of rare pictures taken by personal friends of the Beatles or members of their families would also bring a collector's price, which is not a concrete figure, but rather one that would have to be negotiated. The cost of a photo or collection of photos that unique would not be determinable in advance.

The most serious collectors in this area go right to the source. They look up the original photographers, usually in England, and somehow — trade, buy, wheel-and-deal — end up with some exclusive original shots that no one else is ever even likely to see. These outtakes, never published but taken by "name" photographers, are among the most prized of any collector's possessions.

Most of your calls from an ad, however, are going to be about records. The more copies of a record that originally sold, the more times you can bet someone will call about it. Unless you are looking for 100 copies of **Meet The Beatles**, these calls are pretty worthless. It always seems to be the caller who begins, "I bet I have something you don't have

. . . ," that always has the most common items of all.

In many cases, a record may be valuable only in a certain variation, so a lot of questions need to be asked if you want to save yourself some unnecessary expense and trips around town. If they offer you **Introducing The Beatles**, for example, realize that of the dozen plus variations in existence, only a couple are especially rare, and some are almost worthless. They may have the $400.00 promo, but on the other hand they more than likely have the common '64 monophonic version with *Please Please Me*, or even the 1970s reprint worth only a couple of dollars.

You always have to be careful to ask enough of the right questions to pinpoint exactly the version, variation, and of course quality of the offered item. I also always ask, whenever there is a possibility of the caller having a counterfeit copy, bootleg, or recent remake, just exactly *when* they bought the album or where they originally got it from. Having it in their collection for seventeen years is one matter, but if they just picked it up in a store then there is reason for skepticism. And if they should say they have a couple, and they are all still sealed, then I'm particularly leery about making any investment until I'm positive the item is the genuine article.

Hear The Beatles Tell All on VJ was once rare and valuable, until the counterfeit edition came out and flooded the market. The original was in mono, but a new edition in stereo has just been legitimately released by VJ. The new ones are the only stereo copies, so do not be fooled by them. They are worth only $8.00, as opposed to at least $35.00 for a Near Mint copy of the original mono. The latter once sold for $75.00, which illustrates how demand can change when counterfeits and repressings destroy uniqueness.

Many times, unless you have the original in front of you, it is hard to identify a good reproduction job. Since many jackets and sleeves are photo copies of the original, just having it described on the phone may not be good enough. You would need to examine it yourself and check carefully for picture quality: graininess, fuzzy picture or writing, bleed and off-color reproduction . . . all the minute details that can give away a fake to the sharp and practiced eye. For example, an original **Two Virgins** is distinctly black and white, the counterfeit is a brownish tone. The picture on authentic **Introducing The Beatles'** jackets is so sharp you can even read the time on their watches, while the copies are washed-out looking. (Also, a counterfeit "stereo" copy does not in fact play true stereo, so sometimes if you cannot *see* the difference, you can *hear* it!)

Many non-fans are misinformed about the *real* rarity of their possessions. I tell my callers the whole story behind an item, its "history," so to speak. I explain the variations, and how condition plays an important role in value, too. It is all a matter of reason and negotiation in arriving at a fair buying and selling price.

One caller told me a disc jockey had estimated the value of her *She Loves You* picture sleeve at $75.00. Actually, it sells for $18.00--22.00 (in Very Good to Near Mint condition) at most conventions. I explained that, and offered $10.00 for her Very Good copy. I also suggested perhaps the DJ was referring to copies that *they* receive at the radio station, which are called *promo* copies. The only *She Loves You* picture sleeve worth that much are rare label variations and promos. My caller had the common version, and decided to sell for $10.00 after I told her these facts. Making purchases is not always this easy because, even though most people believe me when I tell them the facts behind their items, they still hold out for a higher price because they've often overpaid for it to begin with, imagining riches upon resale.

I get a lot of calls from antique dealers who see my ads and, being in the business of collectibles themselves, understand when I make an offer of 60 percent of value for an item. The people who seem to think I'm trying to cheat them are usually the ones with the least attractive items available for the highest prices!

A different slant on advertising (for the more enterprising collectors) is to answer other people's ads. The want ads sections of newspapers, especially garage sale ads, are the best starting places. Rarely does an ad state specifically that there are Beatles items for sale, but it may refer to sixties records, or just plain "used records" for sale. It can be worthwhile, if you can manage the time, to check out all such ads. One collector I know always manages to casually bring up the Beatles while sifting the dust from the dregs of beat-up wax, just to see if perhaps something more valuable is still in storage. Finding the U.K. version of **Let It Be**, he asked about the box set it originally came with. The owner produced the *Get Back* book and, thinking it worthless, accepted my friend's offer of $1.00 for it! So, rather than just waiting for your own phone to ring, the best buys may come from those so unaware they wouldn't even think to call you about it in the first place.

GARAGE SALES, FLEA MARKETS, RUMMAGE SALES

Most record aficionados already know the glories of the *garage sale*. During the nicer months of the year, one can become addicted to checking out the listings in the ads pages, mapping out a route and/or cruising up and down some prime streets looking for impromptu sales. It's my favorite summertime sport! Once in a blue moon, an ad will even indicate that there are old Beatles items for sale. In that case, you can be sure these people already recognize the potential value of the items and have probably priced

them above ordinary garage sale junk. Still, if you get to such sales early enough, you may be able to pick up unique items for less than dealers' prices. Most garage sale ads, however, merely state "much misc.," and you'll have to sift through a lot of bizarre belongings, unidentifiable rubbish, and pure trash if you continue in this arena.

Garage sales, however, can be the best primary source of all. Chances are good that the prices will be very minimal, as people usually try to clean house with a sale like this and everything not sold is earmarked for the Goodwill or the garbage anyway. Unfortunately, the number of Beatles items turning up these days has diminished steadily over the years. When I first began, I managed to find something almost every trip out. In the mid-seventies, it seemed people were just beginning to clear out the memorabilia of their teenage years. Now I find it necessary to ask after Beatles items. After a quick once-over reveals nothing in the Beatles line, I ask, just to be safe, if they might have something on the Beatles I haven't noticed (or that they haven't put out).

If something does catch my eye, I try to stay calm and pay for it first before indicating I'm interested in more of the same. I don't want my source to turn greedy just because of overenthusiasm on my part.

But lately, as items become scarcer and gas prices continue to rise, it no longer seems quite as financially viable to spend a day in the car going from one sale to another in hopes of finding a $10.00 paperback for a dime. To minimize costs, then, I select only the sales along one circular route, with stops for any unadvertised sales along the way, of course. The best ones to hit are the *block* sales, where several families are participating and you can walk between them all.

Real garage sale-aholics get up at the crack of dawn (practically) and begin hitting the first ones while the people are still in their pajamas! For this reason, people are now stating "no pre-sales" in their ads. But it is still wise to be the first one to check out a potentially good sale. If they start on Thursday, be sure and be there then, because by Saturday or Sunday everything will be completely picked over.

I have learned how to tell at a mere glance if the people have anything worth searching through. Head for the books, and look for the *type* and *period* they come from. If anything catches your eye from the sixties in the pop/youth genre, then you need to look closer. If they are *all* gothics, or *all* westerns, or *all* from 1940, then you needn't strain your eyes over every single one. The same with records; a quick shuffle through the pile will clue you in. If something stands out from the sixties, you should check more carefully than if everything is Lawrence Welk or Frank Sinatra.

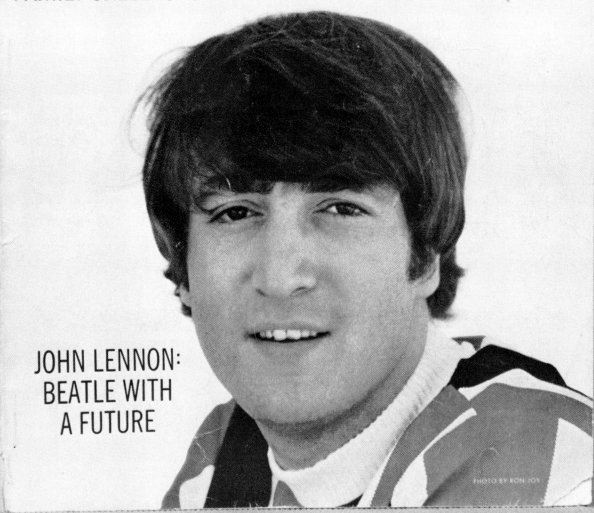

DECEMBER, 1964 ● 35¢

COSMOPOLITAN

DO RELIGIOUS SCHOOLS TEACH PREJUDICE?

THE USELESS SEX
EXCERPTS FROM THE STARTLING BOOK BY EUROPE'S MOST CONTROVERSIAL JOURNALIST ORIANA FALLACI

SPECIAL REPORT: OUR UNADOPTABLE CHILDREN

FAMILY SKELETONS: MYSTERY NOVEL BY PATRICK QUENTIN

JOHN LENNON:
BEATLE WITH
A FUTURE

PHOTO BY RON JOY

An early *Cosmopolitan* magazine with an article on John Lennon by one Gloria Steinem (!). A Near Mint copy would go for $18-20; this Very Good- copy might bring $12-15. *Price Guide No.: 541*

Bigger and better than garage sales, or as an alternative, are *flea markets* and *rummage sales*. Here, you get a crack at dozens of different people's goods all in one spot, or under one roof. Such sales seem to be proliferating these days. You find them held anywhere from drive-in theatre lots, to shopping centers, to churches and community centers.

You quickly learn how to best utilize your time at sales like these, and size up a table as swiftly as you did a garage or back-yard sale. I do eyeball carefully all knickknack displays for the occasional Beatles doll or other small piece of memorabilia. I check out games and toys for Beatles puzzles, "Flip Your Wig" games or Beatles lunch boxes. Even though most gum cards are sports oriented, I do find Beatles cards once in a great while, and even an original Beatles gum card box at one flea market.

I look over every stack of magazines, first for the time period; if there are any sixties' issues, I look a lot closer. I've found many a Beatles cover on *Post, Life, Look,* even the rare *Newsweek* cover at such sales — all for usually $1.00 or less. If they have a stack of *Playboy*s, I swallow my pride and check hastily for the February 1965 issue, which featured the Beatles as interview subjects and is worth $12.00–15.00 today.

If something is not obviously marked for price, do not show too much excitement when inquiring about it. If you give away your interest you may up a 50 cent magazine to a $2.00--5.00 one. You have to learn how to be blase and only mildly interested. And if you bring along a friend or family member, be sure and coach them first on their reactions or they may unwittingly ruin a good deal for you with overenthusiasm about their rare find.

I've found everything from Remco Beatles dolls to Zapple albums, Beatles jukebox EPs, and old paperbacks at flea markets, and what is especially nice is that I was able to look at hundreds of tables at once, instead of putting miles and miles on my car.

You may even want to go so far as to take a table at one of these events yourself. Usually you can set up for a minimal fee ($5.00 or less) and sell your own old junk. The advantage is that you will be there when the other people are just setting up and you'll be sure to get first chance at anything special.

Items at flea markets, as at garage sales, are most often personal items being discarded. So, you can usually feel confident that whatever you find there is the real thing. Of course, some people make a living out of selling things at these sales and you see them there week after week, but they buy their merchandise at other garage sales, estate sales, and so on, so they are just as likely to have original items, even if the price is a bit more than that set by someone merely doing housecleaning.

Condition may be the biggest consideration here. A 25 cent record is really no bargain if it is warped, cracked and completely unplayable. You have to check for damage from sun, water, mildew, and so on. I once found a *promo* copy of *Sie Liebt Dich*, but it was cracked right through. It might have been worth $85.00 or more in Mint condition, but in the poor shape I found it in, only a few dollars. Sometimes the dust is so thick it obscures the true quality of an item, and a good record cleaner may bring up the original luster. Many people leave all their records for sale right out in the hot sun to warp into a new shape; if you can get there in the early morning, at least you may get a chance to pick through them before they're destroyed.

One last thing to be on the lookout for: just because the jacket says **Two Virgins**, that doesn't mean the insides can't be Lawrence Welk! Check everything out thoroughly before you spend your money. Thumb through magazines for cuts and writing, books for pages missing, etc. Lots of roughly handled merchandise ends up at such sales, so be careful!

FORMER FANS, OLD FRIENDS & OTHERS

One other primary source often overlooked is *contacting former fans*. This ingenious method was described to me by a fellow collector who occasionally thumbed through the penpal sections of such hard-core Beatle magazines as the monthly *Beatles Book*. Anyone who read that magazine during the sixties was likely to have also bought other Beatles items. Since he lived in one of the largest cities in the U.S., it was easier for him than for most of us to look through the names and addresses, pick out those in his own area, and make a local call to any still in the phone book. He would then inquire about their current interest in the Beatles and whether they might be interested in selling any of their old Beatles magazines or other memorabilia.

Perhaps you grew up with a few fans who are no longer as interested in the Beatles as you still are. In 1964, *everyone* (or so it seemed) was a fan, and many young people bought everything in sight dealing with the Beatles, as much for status and competition as for any true desire to own the item. It might now be languishing on some shelf, only preserved for sentimental reasons. The offer of cold, hard cash might be persuasive enough to wrest a few of these precious keepsakes from their former owners. I have had many a former fan, once a close acquaintance of mine, call me and ask if I'd like to buy their old collection. The more well-known your "hobby" is, the more likely you'll get called. But you can always call *them*! Anyone who has kept such things this long may suspect that their treasures have some commercial value, they may not be willing to just give them away, even for old-times sake, but a fair offer is often accepted. Unless they plan on selling them themselves

eye

Sep./68 50¢

**101 Hours With
John Lennon &
Paul McCartney**

**Tom Wolfe
Takes You Through the
Noonday Underground**

**10 Student Rebels
Explain Their Cause**

**A New Study
Where Should You Touch—
Mother, Father,
Friend, Lover?**

**Up in Flames
With Arthur Brown!**

**Are Your Parents
Making You Drop Out?**

**Bob Dylan
Returns—
On EYE'S Giant Poster Page**

ICD

A rare copy of *Eye* magazine. The color cover picture of John Lennon was photographed by Linda McCartney. A short-lived magazine, this issue is worth **$18-25.** *Price Guide No.: 544*

through mail order or at a local convention, they will come out ahead by selling it to you even at 50--60 percent of what it might bring at top market resale.

The more people around you that know about your affliction and all consuming interest, the better for you. The word will spread and items are bound to turn up. Your own parents may have friends or business acquaintances with children of the sixties' generation who may have left Beatles records, magazines, scrapbooks, or memorabilia in their parents' basements, garages, and attics. I have gotten full boxes, even trunk loads of collectibles from friends of my parents who just wanted to clean house! These are the people who have no conception of what these items are worth, and you are doing them a favor by helping them to be rid of it.

There is a lot of ground to cover single-handedly, so why not have a dozen people searching for you instead of just one? Even local record shop owners, when told about your interest in other things besides records, will send customers your way once in a while. Or, they may allow you to pin up a notice in their store of items wanted. Someone selling used records may see that you are also interested (and will pay for) other related Beatles items: books, magazines, promotional displays, and so on.

It pays to have *contacts in the record business*. If you want to successfully collect the rare promotional pieces, displays, posters, etc., you not only have to know the right people, you also have to be aggressive about it. The collectors who come up with the most merchandise are those who know how to be in the right place at the right time, and are the most persistent about it.

When new promo pieces come into a record store, you have to alert the owner that you want one. Often they start a list of those interested, or write names on the back of the larger pieces. If you keep coming back for it, you may end up with it just because they want to get rid of you! Sometimes, they may just give you a new promo record or item they don't plan to use, especially if you are a good customer. But never take for granted that someone will automatically save something for you; they may be getting dozens of requests, so always call and remind them.

Professional dealers who do the best at conventions and through mail order, often know plenty of the "right people" (those who work for the record companies, DJs, record store owners, etc.). They manage to "score" such gems as: original cover art work for jackets and sleeves, promo copies of records (some that never even make it out officially), test copies, and all promotional pieces that might be manufactured to huckster a new solo Beatles item. Even book stores get advance literature about new Beatles books, or posters for them from the bigger publishing houses. The posters for recent books like *Shout!*, and *I Me Mine* were selling for $5.00 each at recent conventions, but book stores just gave them away when they were through with them. Often, they never use these things at all and might give them to you if you ask.

Contacts with old friends of the Beatles, former associates, even members of their families can be the most rewarding. A few of the biggest Beatles collectors have cultivated these sources and ended up with gems too precious to even price. The people who used to work as secretaries, gophers, roadies, etc., for the Beatles and their former companies (EMI, NEMS, Apple, etc.) might still possess original letters, demos, tapes of rehearsals, alternate versions, back stage passes, promo pins, stage clothes, photos, autographs, memos, and so on. Only your own good judgment can put a value on such mementos. But if you knew the right people you could end up with a collection that would make even one of the Beatles green with envy!

The majority of us, though, are never going to be on a friendship basis with anyone that close to John, Paul, George, or Ringo. For the average fan, more realistic goals need to be settled on. Not all of us can travel to Hamburg to meet their old cronies there, or track down former girlfriends in Liverpool, or ex-secretaries in London. Most of us have to consider ourselves lucky if we can just meet a former fan from 1964 with a box of old memorabilia anxious for a new home!

the
lennon
factor

by Paul Young

A rare book still on a lot of want lists, this Lennon-inspired work of poetry is valued at $35-50 in Near Mint condition (published in hard-cover only). *Price Guide No.: 457*

Once you have exhausted all possibilities of locating material from its original owners, the next step is to check the retail outlets that have already done the legwork for you. One step up the rung in the market place are second-hand shops of every kind and description. Here people make a living selling other people's rejects. Unfortunately, you now have a middleman involved who has to make a profit over and above the investment he's already made by purchasing the item in the first place. Still, the majority of these people are not Beatles experts by a long shot, or even aficionados of the pop/sixties scene, so they may undervalue many prized Beatles collectibles. If you are lucky, that is! There are four basic types of second-hand shops to be aware of and to check out: Used books shops; Used record shops; Antique shops; and Junk shops.

SEARCHING FOR BOOKS

Shopping in used book shops is easy, painless, and frequently rewarding. A new idea called Paperback Exchange is catching on around the country and making this type of outlet even more common. Books in such places are usually filed by author (for fiction), so it helps to carry a list of the authors (rather than just the more familiar book titles) of the books you are searching for. Without such a list, you may spend hours scanning the titles of over 1,000 books. In the fiction department alone, you may find the film-novel paperbacks for "Candy," "How I Won The War," "Magic Christian," "Alfie," "A Hard Day's Night," and "Help." So far, I have always found these movie titles under the heading Fiction, never under Film. The Biography section may yield Hunter Davies' *The Beatles, Body Count* (rarely), *The Paul McCartney Story, The John Lennon Story, Lennon Remembers*, etc. A section of books devoted to Music or Arts might be hiding some further titles about the Beatles, their music, films, careers, and/or picture books on them. Usually, the paperback editions are what people sell or give away to used book shops. The hard covers are much more difficult to locate.

It can't hurt to inquire with the shop owner about Beatles books and where they might be located. Many of them are so eager for your business, that they take requests, often having a card file of books wanted, and will call you if your book should turn up. Their prices are usually fixed on used books, so they are not likely to raise the price just because you show an interest.

The exception is the specialty book store. Science fiction book stores, for instance, are more aware of the collectibility of books in general, and since they may come across some Beatles titles in their search for SF, you might do well to check them out, too. Because of my continued interest, one such place made an even greater effort to get such books for me. They ended up raising their normal prices several dollars a book, but I realized they were also probably paying more to get me what I wanted.

Some used book shops run a search service for a commission, and will locate even the most difficult of rare books for you. I know collectors who have given them titles like *The Lennon Factor* and *Body Count* and have gotten satisfaction, even though it may take months, if not years, for such rare books to be finally unearthed.

There are around 1500 bookstores in the U.S. which deal exclusively or primarily in used books, so there may be one or more very near you. If you want to find one without calling every book dealer listed in your area yellow pages under "Book Dealers — Retail," you can go to your local library and ask to see a reference book called *American Book Trade Directory* (Bowker). It is an address list arranged alphabetically by state, then by city within state, and provides a marginal notation which identifies the types of books handled by each book store. The designation you should watch for is "Antiquarian," which usually means the store has or will search for used or out-of-print books.

Old Beatles books can be found anywhere books in quantity might end up. Library sales, for instance, occur frequently in every city. Even though a library book is not valued as highly as a Near Mint original copy of the book, they still are a bargain at the sale price of 25–50 cents. Library books tend to have markings indicating ownership, and are therefore considered "defaced" or less than Mint by collectors. Prices are figured at the Very Good condition rate or less.

Any place books are sold is a potential source . . . I attend local science fiction conventions, and in their "huckster room," as they call it, I often find Beatles books, and even magazines. These experts are tuned in to the whole genre of pop culture and whatever is popular or faddish. In other words, collectibles are usually well represented. Because prices on SF books, even rare fifties editions, are so much less than sixties Beatles books, these dealers are likely to set very decent prices on even the rarest of Beatles books. I found *In His Own Write* in Mint condition for $4.50,

HELP!
THE BEATLES

Released by United Artists

A Random House Book

One of the nicer hard-cover picture books from 1965. Hard to find, in Near Mint condition it would be worth $35. *Price Guide No.: 451*

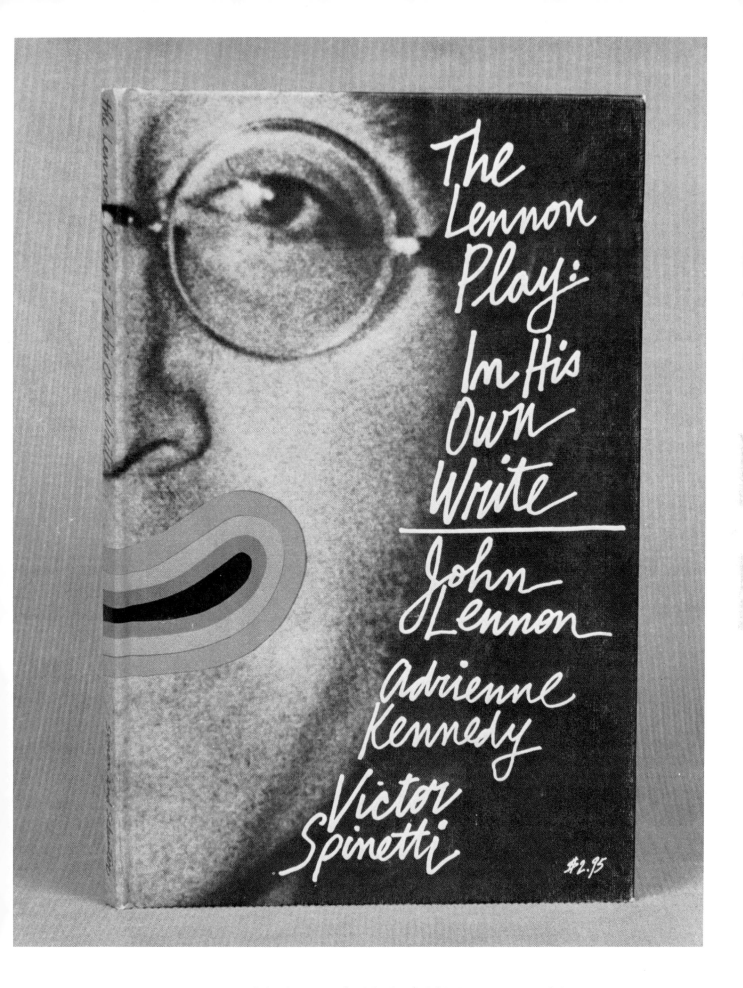

A rarely seen 1968 U.S. hard-cover book. Valued at $20-25. *Price Guide No.: 458*

and an uncirculated copy of one of the very first Beatles magazines, *Around The Beatles*, for just a few dollars.

If you want to widen your search for books and magazines outside your local area, you can do so by mail. You *could* copy out all the addresses of "Antiquarian" book dealers by paging through *American Book Trade Directory*, but there is an easier way. Try to locate a copy of a book called *Buy Books Where — Sell Books Where: A Directory of Out of Print Book Dealers & Their Specialties*, by Ruth Robinson and Daryush Farudi (third edition, 1981, Robinson Books), which does all the hard work for you. For magazines, a listing of back-date periodical issue dealers appears in a reference book called *Magazine Industry Market Place* (Bowker), which is also probably at your local library. The address list will indicate whether a search service is available from the dealer, or whether they will only search their own stock.

You may be able to submit quite a lengthy list of titles you want to have located by such mail-order book and magazine search services, and the good part is that it usually costs you nothing if they can't find what you are after (make sure there is no charge *just for searching*). If they do find something for you, they will usually let you know, describe the condition of the item, and quote you a price (which you should expect to be inflated because of their having searched, profit margin, etc.). You should also inquire beforehand about conditions whereby you would be able to return the item and get your money back if you are dissatisfied with it once it arrives.

As an alternative to writing and paying postage for a stack of individual letters to book dealers, there is a specialist book trade publication called *AB Bookman's Weekly* which reaches some 8,000 subscribers who buy and sell rare, used, and out-of-print books, and in which you can place a paid advertisement. Many "ads" are similar to classified ads in newspapers — a few lines, nothing fancy. For information and rates, write to: Antiquarian Bookman, Box AB, Clifton, NJ 07015.

SEARCHING FOR RECORDS

Searching for records is only slightly different from searching for books, mainly because there are fewer stores which specialize just in "oldies-but-goodies." Plenty of stores *do* feature at least a used record *section*, however. Once you learn to by-pass the more conventional chain stores and get into the little, privately owned and more out-of-the-way shops, you'll start finding more unique and collectible items.

Check the yellow pages for a beginning and call around to see if they have a used record section. These same places may offer a selection of imports, and possibly even under-the-counter bootlegs, and may also be good sources for promo material, record collector magazines, and so on. Once again, to widen your search beyond your immediate locale, you might try and get a hold of a copy of *The Record Collector's International Directory*, by Gary S. Felton (Crown, 1980), which lists names, addresses, store hours and services of rare record dealers in around seventy different record categories. The same rules of cautious inquiry and guarantees apply to buying records mail-order as they do to books, of course.

Record store owners are usually quick to spot a really valuable piece of wax, and they (and their friends) get first pick of anything really decent. So, your chances of discovering an unclaimed Butcher cover or **Two Virgins** still sitting in the racks of used records are pretty slim. But it has happened, and the quest for such finds is part of what makes this hobby intriguing.

So far, I've never been lucky enough to find anything both cheap *and* rare in the used records bins, but I do find lots of old Apple albums by Badfinger, Mary Hopkin, James Taylor, records like **Magic Christian**, along with Denny Laine, solo Beatles, and Yoko Ono albums. If the condition is *good* or better, and the price is only $2.00--3.00, then you've still made a nice addition to your collection.

In England, street stalls, particularly in such areas of London as Soho, are a common sight. They often feature rows of used singles for cheap prices (under $1.00), and I have found a wealth of Beatles-related and novelty songs here. It's a great place to check for Lennon/McCartney compositions which other artists recorded, especially the early '63--64 material they gave to friends, whose singles are now worth $5.00 and up. I've also discovered a lot of Mike McGear/Scaffold 45s, and Beatles Parlophone releases, which differed from U.S. versions.

A few U.S. shops even stock used singles now, and not just the common repressed hits on the oldies labels. They may also have import oldies with rare picture sleeves, some of which are valued in the double digits and are just as hard to locate as the rarer U.S. sleeves. An odd store here and there may even be run by a fellow collector, who may specialize in finding really rare collectibles: Butcher covers, German *My Bonnie*s, Frank Ifield records, etc. But, in most cases, their prices will be comparable to or even more than what you'd expect to pay at any of the Beatles conventions around the country. But at least such a store may be able to help you when you've struck out everywhere else and you just *have* to have a certain item for your collection.

On the completely opposite side of the fence is the *junk shop*, which is much more geared to the budget of most of us. However, what you lack in dollars, you had better be prepared to expend in time. If you want to make a habit of buying Beatles goods at these places, your finds will probably be few, far between, and filled with lots of frustrating moments.

In this category lies the *Salvation Army*, the *Goodwill*, and all kinds of thrift shops. Among all the used clothing (you may even find a Beatles sweatshirt . . . I found a Monkees one once!), are lots of discarded rubbish, and hopefully a valuable Beatles record or book. I found a Very Good condition copy of **Life With The Lions** at a Goodwill once for only 99 cents. Inspired by this easy find, I went back a month or so later only to discover someone had priced a poor condition 45 of *I Want To Hold Your Hand* (sans sleeve) for $3.00, and a cut-out copy of **Let It Be** (the common U.S. one) for $10.00 — neither of which are worth anything at all to a collector.

An incredible amount of patience and perseverance is required to slog through junk shop after junk shop in search of something worthwhile. This type of shop usually houses the *rejects* from garage sales, so anything really exciting probably never makes it this far. But, it is the rare exception from which legends are made!

A less wasteful expenditure of time might be the *antique shops* in town, instead. At least here you are dealing with professionals who recognize the value of things both old *and* collectible, and worth preserving as part of pop culture. Many antique dealers, however, are not interested in anything as current as sixties memorabilia, so you still have to do a lot of scouting around. If you are lucky enough to find a shop that does specialize in "fads," "youth culture," etc. — such as Shirley Temple, Mickey Mouse, Coca-Cola, Elvis, and hopefully the Beatles — then you'll have hit the jackpot. You can get a pretty good idea of what is available by calling around, and asking a few pertinent questions. You'll want to check to see whether they have any Beatles items in stock now, and also if they ever carry such items. This will at least alert them to your interest, and they may try to get items for you in the future. They all want to make a sale, so if they are aware of your interests, they are more likely to come up with something.

Since these dealers are buying from original sources themselves (garage sales, estate sales, or from customers selling items to them), you have to be prepared to pay the extra for their commission or profit. Still, considering the high sums real Beatles rarities go for at conventions and through mail order, you can still come out ahead. You may be able to make an offer, or negotiate a price, that is 50 to 75 percent less than you'd have to pay a professional Beatles dealer. I once bought a set of Mint "Yellow Submarine" clothes hangers for $40.00, easily a hundred dollar item at a "Beatlefest."

There are also street sales and mall shows of antiques going on all year round in most large cities,

and these are worth at least a cursory browse through. They are just like flea markets, and you can learn to glance across tables quite quickly, keeping a sharp eye out for something of potential. Antique dealers might even have movie memorabilia, which could produce posters, lobby cards, or stills from one of the Beatles' films.

You need a lot of *optimism* to be successful in these pursuits. You need an attitude of faith that just around the corner something marvelous will turn up. If you can hold on to a belief that, in the very next shop or at the next table, you'll find that elusive promo copy, or a Beatles pillow for $5.00, or an original Beatles Christmas disc for 98 cents, then this sort of venture was made for you. But if you don't believe in that kind of fantasy, or your patience starts to wear thin, and your time gets too valuable (as does your gas) . . . then you have to start thinking of contacting the professionals.

RECORD COLLECTING MAGAZINES

I start with the one place left where you still might get a bargain now and then: the record collector magazines. *Goldmine* in the U.S., *Trouser Press*, or *Record Collector* (U.K.), for instance, all have page after page of collectibles, either at low set sales prices or in their auction lists.

Set sale on one-of-a-kind items means that it is first come, first served, so it's vital to have a first class (or air-mail) subscription to these magazines, and to take care of your orders promptly. Most of the really rare Beatles items, however, are usually up for bid in auctions. Learning how to read the small print and how to bid effectively is an art form all in itself.

Most dealers in these magazines begin by giving you some information on how they grade their records and merchandise. It helps if they tell you what *they* mean by "Mint," "Very Good," and "Good" condition. When they don't give you any tips at all, you are bidding blind; often their concept of *Mint* can be far removed from yours. In that case, it is essential that they give guarantees, and refunds if not satisfied. If they don't mention refunds in the beginning of their ad, then you can't take it for granted that they offer them. You'll be best protected by dealing with established dealers, especially ones that run ads frequently; obviously, they have satisfied customers who keep coming back or they wouldn't be able to afford the repeat ads. Also, try to ascertain if the items they are listing are *originals* or might possibly be counterfeits. This is not always so easy to determine from a description only, but an honest dealer will tell you when something is a reproduction, a second pressing, or a bootleg. Some dealers even state at the beginning of their ads that all items are guaranteed original. In some cases, though, a dealer might not even be aware that their sale item is a fake, because current duplicating jobs can be so precise.

So, it still pays to bid conservatively. If they have a phone number, you might even want to call and ask a few extra questions that might help you tell whether they are offering originals or copies. Some clues contained in the ad may help you out: do they have several copies of the item in question; are several items in the same ad of questionable status (items that are known to be counterfeited, or common re-issues); do they claim everything is Mint and still sealed no matter how rare, and so on? These tips can alert you to at least be suspicious enough to want to be sure about your bid. You don't want to bid a fortune on a **Two Virgins LP** that ends up a counterfeit.

If you keep a file of your own bids, you will gradually start to see a pattern emerge in terms of the prices which items are going for in these kinds of collectors magazines. They will not necessarily be the same prices being paid at conventions and through mail order from specifically Beatles-oriented dealers. By keeping track, you learn which bids made it and which bids could have succeeded if an additional dollar or two had been offered. I tend to keep my bids at 50 to 75 percent of the value for which an item might be resold at top of the market prices. But if you really want something badly for your own collection, then you might consider bidding full value.

Be careful, though, not to overpay if you even intend to resell the item. Some dealers have a pretty unique idea of what "Near Mint" means. I have seen some incredibly shoddy merchandise passed off at Mint-minus, when I would hardly rate it a Good-plus. I come out very badly when I pay Mint-minus prices for Good-plus items, especially when a true collector will not even look twice at anything lower in quality than Very Good-plus.

Since the majority of people bidding in a non-Beatles record collecting magazine are going to be unaware of the "real" value of Beatles items, they are just as likely to wildly overbid as underbid. As a result, I have better luck in getting magazines, gum cards, and books in these magazines than I do getting any particularly sought-after Beatles records, because of too much competition from these other record collectors (who are not necessarily Beatles fans, and who needlessly pay outrageous, ill-informed prices for things). Non-Beatles fans are starting to become aware of Beatles records as investments, and are paying high prices now with visions of big profits years later — or so they imagine. So, we are not only competing with our own peers in Beatle fandom, but also with the average record collector, who may be mainly into surf, or heavy metal, but who wants to make a killing someday on a Beatles collection.

When I've made a lot of bids with one dealer, I may enclose a stamped, self-addressed envelope for them to notify me of the winning bids on the items I'm interested in, whether or not I personally won. This helps me to keep track of what the items are going for, so I can make wiser bids in the future. If I'm only off a few cents or a few dollars, I'd probably be willing to raise my bid next time and try again.

Most of my earliest mistakes centered around not reading the fine print thoroughly. Sometimes, an item is listed for its sleeve only, or maybe record only, no jacket. I once bid a good price on **Life With The Lions**, but received only the jacket — worthless without the record! When I looked at the ad again, I saw in small type "jacket only." I learned an expensive lesson then about double checking on my bids to verify that I'm really bidding on something I want, and that my bid is sensible in relation to condition and variation, etc.

It is important to keep your skepticism, along with your sharp eye for the finer details. A record dealer whose specialty is *not* the Beatles may just assume *everything* with their name on it is *rare*. They sometimes mistake common bootlegs, currently being sold by Beatles dealers for $7.00–8.00, as rare imports, believing the markings bootleggers inscribe on the wax or jackets — mostly as a joke — to be sincere. So, they end up pricing it ridiculously high. Giving them the benefit of the doubt on these things, often they cannot tell a counterfeit or reproduction from the real thing. Many rare promos and other expensive Beatles records have been duplicated, so you have to be careful when buying any item you cannot examine in person.

When bidding by mail, some dealers even encourage you to call beforehand to learn the current top bid, which makes it a lot less of a shot in the dark. Also, you can save a lot of time in letter writing if you can learn by phone about those bids you don't want to top.

Once you've read a few of these magazines, you'll become familiar with the jargon of the trade. At first it may all seem like hieroglyphics, but after a few practice bids, you'll be able to spout the lingo with the best of them.

RECORD GUIDES & GATHERINGS

You can pick up extra tips from reading existing price guides such as the "Bible" of the business: Osborne and Hamilton's *Record Album Price Guide* (third edition, O'Sullivan, Woodside & Co., 1980), for sale in most major book stores, and their *Popular & Rock Price Guide for 45's* (O'Sullivan, Woodside & Co., 1981). Their Beatles section, though, is not as complete as a serious Beatles collector needs. It does not list all variations on every item, and it can still leave you confused about which edition you actually have. Also, since prices have been escalating on Beatles items so rapidly these past few years, even the latest edition of the book cannot tell you the current price an item is *really* selling for (at top market value, anyway). However, many serious record collectors religiously set all their prices by this book, and you can make some good deals because of that fact.

I bought a Beatles EP, **4 X 4**, from an experienced dealer (but one who specialized in Elvis), and he wanted book price for it, which was then $25.00 for a Mint copy. It was really only Very Good-plus, but worth $50.00 a couple of years ago at "Beatlefest," and is probably worth $75.00 at least by now.

Another book that might supplement your knowledge and be very useful to you when buying and bidding is Charles Reinhart's *You Can't Do That* (Pierian Press, 1981), a guide to Beatles bootlegs, counterfeits, novelty, and related records. A lot of valuable information is imparted here about telling originals from the fakes, as well as a descriptive listing of all known bootlegs. To keep up to date on new bootleg releases, you might consider subscribing to the *Hot Wacks Quarterly* ($9.00/yr; P.O. Box 2666, Station 'B', Kitchener, Ontario, Canada N2H 6N2).

Attending rock-and-roll shows, collectors swap meets, and record conventions is very similar to dealing with the sellers in the record collecting magazines; often, it is the very same people bringing their wares to customers in person. The magazines, in fact, announce and run ads for the various shows which go on all over the country all year. And "Rockages" puts on rock-and-roll conventions in New York City a couple of times a year that rival "Beatlefest," with thousands of collectors/fans attending and more major dealers than anywhere else. But every city holds them on at least a small scale; even Minneapolis (where I live) has "record buyers open markets" every couple of months. Just browsing through an issue of *Goldmine* can give you an extensive listing of dates of upcoming shows. *Record Collector*, in Britain, advertises dozens of shows going on all over that country.

Obviously, the advantage here is being able to check out the merchandise in person. Some dealers even bring a record player, albeit a cheap one that doesn't really give a perfect audio grading! At least you can quickly cull out the poor quality merchandise from those truly in Near Mint condition, instead of having to accept on faith a dealer's advertised standards. Prices are usually reasonable on most old records here, as dealers want to move their goods in quantity. However, because of the publicity about the value of Beatles items in recent years, and especially lately, these dealers are beginning to imagine instant riches like everyone else, and consequently have put amusingly ludicrous prices on some rarities. At one recent show, a copy of **The Family Way** was priced at $200.00! On the other hand, such dealers sometimes let real gems slip right past them. I discovered a *promo* copy for *Please Please Me* in a pile of singles for only $15.00; resale value would be at least $60.00–75.00.

You might also want to turn these shows to your own advantage by becoming a dealer yourself, if you have any extra records around. Prices for tables are low at most smaller shows, and you can make enough selling your own duplicates and old castoffs to be able to afford some Beatles collectibles instead. In your garage sale and flea market shopping, you may have come across non-Beatles records and memorabilia that other record collectors are interested in. A record price guide book can help you determine what is, and what is not worth picking up on these buying expeditions. And a record show is a good place to unload them. If you keep your prices low, you can sell most anything! Another advantage of having your own table is that it allows you to get in early when the dealers set up and thereby have the first look at everything that is available.

The record collector magazines might also be used to sell off your own excess, and make some cash for new purchases. You can not only run your own ads to sell items but, if you haven't found particular items yet, you can run a *want* ad as well. Since these magazines are being read by hard core record fanatics, this is the most likely place to go for help. It can't hurt to advertise.

The Beatles pillow, also licensed by NEMS, comes with either blue or red backside. It has doubled in value in

8.

Eventually, you may want to work up to the real hub of buying and trading activity and deal with the professionals in the business. These people make the Beatles their full- or part-time work (or at least their *full-time* hobby), and their specialization in this area makes them the most useful outlet for merchandise, information, and guidance.

Your best bet is to go where you'll find more of them under one roof than any place else: a Beatles convention. Every serious Beatles fan/collector owes it to themselves to experience at least one such show. Every year there are at least a half a dozen in the U.S. alone, and two or three in Europe. It's well worth the price of admission and any distance you might have to travel to attend, just for the contacts you can make. You'll be able to deal with people *at least* as knowledgeable as you and, in some areas, even more well versed in the intricacies of collecting. After all, *you* may only get to one convention a year if you are lucky, while many of the dealers there will travel from show to show, selling at as many as eight in that same time period. Firsthand, they see what sells, they hear what is in demand, and what isn't, and they come across rarities of every description and variation, and are witness to obscurities rarely seen any place else.

Conventions attract thousands of fans (average attendance is probably 3,000--5,000 over a weekend), and nearly a hundred or more dealers who come in from all over the country and even abroad. The largest conventions take place annually in Chicago, Los Angeles, and New York, and have recently become a regular feature in Houston, Boston, and Connecticut. Conventions on a smaller scale (attendance of 1,000 or less, and around 25--50 dealers) are likely to take place in any city, and have already occurred in Minneapolis (1978 and '79), Cleveland, Atlanta, Philadelphia, San Francisco, Seattle, and so on. Wherever there is someone willing to promote and finance such an endeavor, the possibility exists for a future show.

DEALING WITH DEALERS

It's always wise advice to know the person you are dealing with. This is your chance to meet these people in person and check them out. Many of them also deal through their mail-order business and, if you're not already, you can get on their mailing lists here. So, in many regards, a convention is the perfect place to begin your collecting career. But, if it is already your last resort and all the original sources and second-hand shops are used up and played-out, then

you may have to put aside your old notions and store those dreams of bargains in your back pocket, for at a convention you'll be facing top of the market prices. What an item sells for here is, in my opinion, the number one determinant of its value. Based on prices at a convention, you can tell if an item is a bargain or a ripoff if found for sale from other sources. The reason is primarily that the competition, all being in the same room together, tend to balance one another out, and it becomes possible to calculate the best "going rate" price for an item.

Dealers have to be keenly aware of the value of everything that passes before them. They have to compete. Since they are all pushing the same product — the Beatles — each dealer struggles to make the best deal, while making the most money. Someone who doesn't know their product as well as the next person may be underselling to their own disadvantage, and may also pass up opportunities to buy items that might have brought a quick and profitable turnover.

Many fans view the Dealers Room with disgust. They are geared to finding bargains in basements, attics, and garages, in used record bins, and so on. They think back to their own teenage years, when they first bought gum cards five for a nickel, when Beatles dolls sold for under $3.00, and picture sleeves were still only 89 cents. No wonder they wince when they see price tags that are ten, twenty, even 100 times more than they originally paid. Automatically, and without complete justification, they think "ripoff," and blame the dealers for wanting to get rich quick from what is, to them, just a hobby.

But dealers wouldn't be asking outrageous prices if there weren't so many fans ready and willing to pay them. The demand for original rarities and true collectibles far outweighs the at-hand supply.

When you examine the situation closely, you can see that the pluses of a convention's dealers room balance out the minuses. After all, the prices may be high, but they are more likely to be the correct value, not just an arbitrary figure placed on an item by someone completely without knowledge of the field. This is very important if you ever want to resell your collection, if you want to insure your collection, or if you just want to be satisfied that you got the proper price on an item. If you drastically overpay on some item (say, $200.00 for **The Family Way** album at a record swap meet), you'll never see it appreciate in value enough to make a profit with it.

Also, as I mentioned, the competition between so many dealers gathered in one place acts as regulator over the situation of pricing, and stabilizes them into some degree of uniformity. If one dealer is selling a Beatles pillow for $50.00 or a book, such as *In His Own Write*, for $35.00, others are encouraged to price along similar lines. Other variables have to be considered, of course: condition, scarcity, variations, packaging, edition, etc., but if all is equal, then the pressure is there for dealers to compensate and conform to the prices of their neighbors. Some dealers stick to outrageously high prices despite the examples of their fellows, perhaps hoping the cheaper items will sell fast and theirs will be the only choices left, or perhaps they paid high prices to begin with and cannot afford to lower the prices now. At least you have the final option at such gatherings, and you have more of a chance for *comparison* shopping than any place else.

TIPS ON "CONVENTIONEERING"

The opportunity to *select* is, in my opinion, the biggest plus factor of all for the convention. Nowhere else will every dealer be prepared to supply specifically what you are after. Although some dealers have buttons, t-shirts, or photos of other rock stars, approximately 80 percent of the items displayed will be Beatles items. So, you can avoid the time-consuming chore of digging through crates of unrelated (to the Beatles) records, the expended energy, and the letdown of high hopes when nothing worthwhile is found. At a Beatles convention, you'll find *plenty*; taking the best advantage of all this bounty should be your major concern.

When dealing with the "experts" at a Beatles convention (self-styled or otherwise) you should expect the same high standards you'd demand from any specialty dealership or business. You expect them to know their product, to be able to explain the reasons for its value, and to back up their wares with guarantees. They have expectations from *you*, too. They expect you to know a collectible when you see one, to know what you want and what you don't want, and to have some understanding of prices based on condition, variation, and so on. It works out best for *both* parties when expectations are met on both sides.

You can increase your odds immensely by getting a head start at the tables: *get in early*. Too many people erroneously think that the best shopping time is after the initial crowds thin out. It may be more pleasant, sure, to be able to actually examine all the merchandise at your leisure, without the hassles of being pushed, shoved, and crowded against the tables. But if you are serious about finding anything worth collecting at these conventions, especially if you are after the really unique and valuable items, then you owe it to yourself to be one of the first in the door. It hurts to keep having to tell people on the second day, that yes, we did have that book, or

that record, but it sold long ago — in the opening hour, in fact.

A fact to get used to is that the best merchandise disappears even *before* the doors open. As the dealers are setting up (1–3 hours before the show begins), the other dealers (and their friends and workers) have the first crack at everything. Some hard-core collectors make a point of working for a dealer at these shows, for the express purpose of getting in ahead of the crowds and getting the chance to see everything, even as it is being unpacked!

Some of the dealers have few scruples about buying from each other specifically to mark the price of something higher at their own table. They feel that anyone who has items underpriced (in their eyes) is fair game. So, should a first-time dealer set up at such a show and want to sell their Beatles items cheaply (or even reasonably), they'll inevitably be bought out quickly, and very probably by their fellow dealers.

By the time the first fans walk in the door, most truly one-of-a-kind things offered relatively inexpensively will have already been sold, at least once. It may be for sale again, but the price has undergone instant inflation! So, if you can't get in when the dealers do, then at least be sure and be at the head of the line when the door opens.

After the first hour or two, nothing much remains in the rarities department. Memorabilia is the first to be scooped up, at least any with an affordable price tag on it. Vastly overpriced items may sit around all weekend, but if the deal is fair then the item doesn't last long at all. U.S. fans are especially hungry for the original paraphernalia that went along with Beatlemania in 1964–66. Those collectors who know the field are quick to spot the real gems from the common goods, and grab those exceptional finds without hesitation. Some items are so rare they may never appear at another convention again.

The records which disappear the quickest, besides any that are underpriced, are the Beatles' Christmas discs, promo copies of any early Beatles singles, and the rarest of the picture sleeves (the ones least often seen). First edition hardcovers of John Lennon's two books are quickly purchased, as are promo pieces of particular uniqueness. Any Apple promo items are so rarely seen that they will probably not make it past the first few minutes either. By the end of the first day, dealers are left largely with the items they had in quantity to begin with. Usually, this consists of: common bookstore books, bootlegs, handmade items (artwork, crafts, t-shirts, belt buckles, etc.), and lots of photographs and buttons. I'm not saying there is nothing to buy the second day — there's still plenty there, but the nicest *collectibles* are usually long gone.

You need to heed the same advice at a Beatles convention that you would automatically remember at flea markets, junk shops, collectors' shows, etc.: *inspect everything closely*. Counterfeits and bootlegs, reproductions, etc., are more likely to turn up here as anywhere else. If you know your dealer and trust him/her to give you an honest deal and an honest answer to your questions, then you'll be one step ahead in the game. If you suspect an item is not an original, and it is always prudent to be skeptical these days (no one can keep up with how many things are duplicated, new items are remade every month, and in many cases the job is very professional), then your best advice is to bring the questionable items to a dealer you trust. Or, if the item can't be moved, then ask a friendly dealer to come and examine it for you. If they have an original to compare to, even better.

It's very possible that if you've been collecting long enough you already know many of the current crop of dealers, and should be able to protect yourself from any ruses they might try and employ. A certain percentage of dealers today are not fans at all (as opposed to those that attended the first conventions in 1974, who were almost *all* fans). This new breed has come into the field as a business venture only. Some of them couldn't tell a legitimate item if it hit them in the face. Knowledge is your protection. Dealers expect *you* to know what it is you want; otherwise, how you spend your money is your affair.

You can spare yourself grief just by shopping around a bit and doing a little comparing and questioning. If you see an item for $40.00, and then a similar one for $9.00, one of them is almost certainly a fake. Better to have some doubts than to naively assume one dealer is giving you that much of a savings. As noted, anything severely underpriced that might be a hot seller is not going to survive the dealers (and friends) own pre-show perusals of the room. Even if a dealer is not planning on reselling at the same show, they may need it for their mail-order list, or their own store back home.

You cannot take for granted *anything* at these conventions. Large quantities and low prices together usually indicate a counterfeit. But quantity alone does not *have* to mean it isn't the real thing. Some items *do* turn up years later in warehouses. Sometimes a manufacturer, who has stored it all this time, will approach a dealer and offer them the product. The Beatles tray, for instance, worth $35.00–50.00 now, has become a common memorabilia item ever since dozens of them were wholesaled to a few dealers. Beatles wigs have just started to turn up in quantity because the manufacturer in England decided to sell his back stock of them, seventeen years after the fact. A few years ago, it was tennis shoes and, for a while, they were a common item selling at $25.00–30.00; now they've become a rarity again and the price has soared to $50.00–100.00 a pair! Sometimes, books or magazines sit in publishers' overstocked inventories and then suddenly

appear in mint condition. *Beatles On Broadway* was one such case, and the copies you see for sale are originals even though the price is kept low. A few once very rare records have surfaced recently and have managed to retain their value; **I Apologise**, with all its original inserts from the Beatles' 1966 Chicago press conference, sold for $30.00, and the Beatles' EP **Souvenir Of Their First Visit To America** is going for $18.00–25.00 despite the stacks of them available.

Such inconsistencies make it extremely critical that you exercise caution when buying, and also that you retain the ability to recognize the real thing when you do see it! It can definitely be difficult at times and, in some cases, nearly impossible, so unless you can swear by the reputation of the dealer, it is best to weigh all the factors involved, ask around and then trust your best judgment.

Remember, anything easy to duplicate has either already been duplicated or is a potential target for it. Anything that can be bought plain, and then overprinted with the Beatles' pictures on it is an easy item to "recreate": pouches, scarves, t-shirts, beach towels, pens, pins, buttons, posters, and so on. Some things that will probably never be recreated, like the "Flip Your Wig Game," the "Yellow Submarine" Corgi Co. toy, etc., just have too many parts and complexities that make them too expensive to reproduce in limited quantities. Anything else you can consider fair game.

A convention doesn't *have to* be filled only with suspicion and negativism. If you shop wisely and deal with reputable persons (and they *are* out there), you can do better here than anywhere else. Where else can you find in one room: Butcher covers (peeled and unpeeled), bootlegs, imports, promos, rare first edition books and magazines, posters, t-shirts, picture sleeves, rare albums, buttons, jewelry, gum cards, Beatles toys, stationery, photographs, autographs, fan clubs to join and newsletters to read . . . the whole gamut in one big room?!

TRADING & AUCTIONING AT CONVENTIONS

It's quite common for fans to bring their own extra items to conventions, some to make extra money to buy new items, and others with the intention of "trading up." They hope to make a few deals for cash or merchandise and end up with an item in even better condition than the one they came in with. Dealers are usually more than willing to at least discuss your offers. They are always looking for additional merchandise, especially rare collectibles which move quickly; or, you may have something they know someone else is specifically looking for. However, most dealers will only offer you 60 to 75 percent of the value they will later put on the item, especially if they are paying you cash. If

This Beatles tray, manufactured in the U.K., is a common memorabilia item but still sells easily at $25-30 each.
Price Guide No.: 736

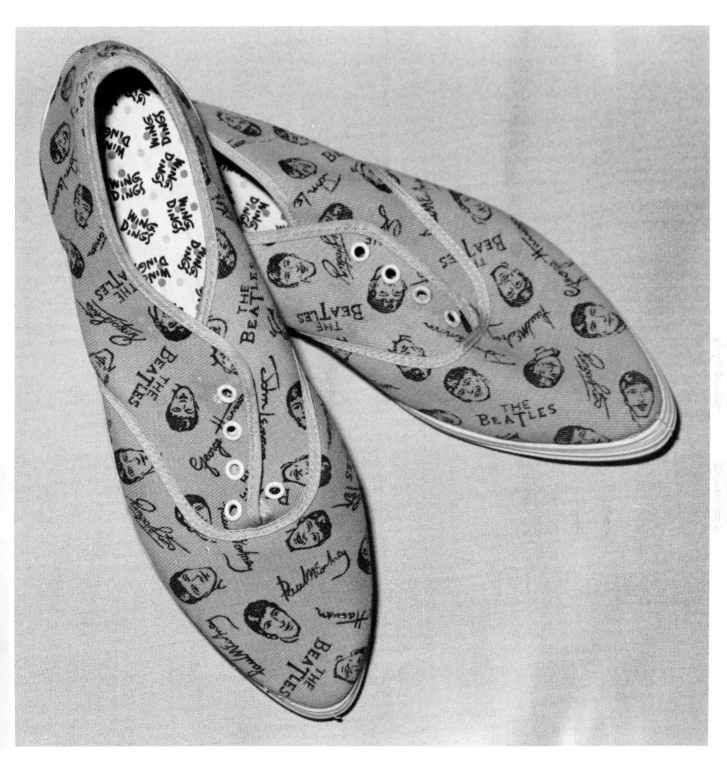

Beatles tennis shoes come in an assortment of colors and styles: light blue and pink, low back and also (more rare) high back models. Those above, in Mint condition, are worth about $50-75, perhaps more if still in the manufacturer's original box. *Price Guide No.: 728*

they are trading merchandise, they may make it a more even trade. Remember, *you* leave with the money or the goods, *they* still have to find another buyer for the item you left them. Dealers are obviously most willing to trade evenly (value for value) for items they have in quantity, in return for a one-of-a-kind rare record, book, or piece of memorabilia.

Dealers aside, you may also make useful sales and trades with some of the thousands of fans you'll meet while waiting in lines, or taking a break in the halls or lounges. Fans may be able to offer a better deal, in fact; they may want what you have more than a dealer might, for one thing and, in addition, they have less overhead to worry about (cost of tables, employees, advertising, displays, and capital for new merchandise for the next show!).

Fans bring in their extras in paper bags, suitcases, briefcases, and record boxes. An interesting idea for future shows (and one already in practice at record conventions) is to set aside a room or an area of the dealers room for the average fan to set up and sell their own small quantity of items. Instead of having to pay full price for a table for the entire weekend, a percentage could be charged for a one-day rate, or a half-table rate. It might add a lot of variety to what is currently being offered by the "professionals."

There is one other means for fans to both buy and sell at a Beatles show and that is *the auction*. Most conventions hold at least one during the weekend event. Most of the items end up coming from the dealers, because they are the most prepared for it, and they (ideally) put up their rarest and most valuable items. Sometimes, they sneak in common goods, hoping that the final going price in the heat of the bidding will be better than the one they placed on it at their table. So, before you start getting too carried away, be sure you have thoroughly checked out the prices in the dealers room. I have seen ordinary photographs (available for $5.00 in the dealers room) go for $20.00 in the bidding; books that were on sale for $12.00 take in $25.00, and so on. There's no reason to lose money, when you can easily note what's available for what price beforehand.

Some items that you can't buy at a table are put up in an auction: one-of-a-kind items that are hard to price and are better off finding their value in competitive bidding; for example: autographs, paintings, gold records, rare memorabilia, promo displays, and other unique items.

Not only the dealers, though, may put up items, so if you've brought something valuable along, make sure that it gets to the auctioneer early in the day. If you have something special, worth more than the average collectible, or something so unusual it is hard to price, this would be a good place to see what you can get for it. You can also indicate a *minimum* bid on your item so you don't lose it for a few dollars.

You can sometimes come out in super shape by picking up rare items that no one else bids for. Bidding can be fierce on some items, while surprisingly subdued on others. I have seen really marvelous pieces of memorabilia go unbid on, or sold for *less* than the asking rates in the dealers room. In other cases, I have seen items, not all that remarkable, sell for incredibly high sums. A Blue Meanie puppet of *recent* manufacture went for over $100.00 once and, although cute, I saw it later in a store for $25.00! Auctions are always lively and interesting and worth your while to sit through. You never know what to expect at them. Once, someone brought in *Ringo's tie* (and a photo of him wearing it!), and another time it was *Paul's bowler hat* from "A Hard Day's Night"! (The tie went for $81.00, the hat for $400.00.)

To find out about conventions (if you are not in a city where one regularly occurs), you need only be on the regular mailing list of a Beatles-oriented publication or sales list. Dealers always inform their readers/customers about upcoming shows; after all, they want to see as many prospective buyers turn up as possible.

MAIL-ORDER SPECIALISTS

Dealers who specialize in mail-order sales will run periodic, if not constant ads in such music or collector publications as *Rolling Stone, Goldmine, Record Collector*, maybe even *Circus, Creem, Trouser Press*, etc. Once you get on their mailing lists and start receiving their sales catalogs, brochures, flyers, or ads, you'll get an even deeper education in the art of Beatles collecting.

Since every dealer is different, offers a different product, sets different standards, and so forth, generalizations are hard to make. There are some who will sell only *original* collectibles and who won't touch anything else. They give guarantees on their wares, and are good people to work with when you want to be certain of what you are getting. They are usually fans themselves and will discuss trades, answer your questions, and generally try to help you with all your collecting needs. They offer a wide selection of rarities, and their price typically reflects the quality of the merchandise they carry: top of the line. Bargains are few, but you'll at least get what you pay for without fear of any fakes sneaking in.

The other type of dealer is the one who sells mostly, if not only, remakes, bootlegs, counterfeits, and such newly made merchandise as t-shirts, buttons, posters, and so on. They usually have extensive catalogs, often with pictures of the goods, and can serve as an excellent source for all the new items that come out each year but are never found in your local stores. Because of the quantity involved, these dealers can offer low, or at least affordable prices on their items and, as long as they clearly indicate that their goods are new or second pressings, reissues, etc., they can be as much of a help to you as the dealers of collectibles. Some dealers offer a little of each (collectibles *and* new merchandise) and try for a personal touch in working with you. These people try to fill *your* want lists whenever they can, and act as kind of a central clearing house for all your collecting needs: buying, selling, trading, advertising, etc.

Another variety of dealer specializes in legitimate imports which also rarely make it to the majority of U.S. stores: records and books on the Beatles manufactured in Europe, Japan, South America, such items are more easily bought through these specialty Beatles dealers than through local stores, which must special-order them. Beatles dealers order these items in quantity so their prices will probably be lower than what your neighborhood record/book store could manage, even if they *would* try to get it.

The risks in mail-order buying are the same as in record collecting through the magazine auction/set sale ads. You have to be prudent. If you're not already dealing with people you know and trust, then make your first orders small ones. See what kind of service you get — not only how fast, but how reliable. What is the quality of the merchandise, etc. If the dealer offers a "return option" on his goods should they not meet *your* standards, then you can feel safer about proceeding. Mail ordering from most Beatles dealers will be smooth and satisfactory. After all, they want to do a good job, they want you to keep coming back for more and bring your friends, too. They can't afford to burn their bridges behind them by ripping off their customers. In addition, the Beatles fandom/dealers community is a close-knit one — everyone knows everyone else. After eight years or so of conventions and other areas of communication, none of them are operating in a dark and secret void. So, those who don't conform, play by some set of decent rules and, in effect, try to ruin the reputation of the business as a whole, are going to find the word is out about them, and will find it as hard to get new merchandise as it is to get new customers.

One unavoidable risk exists, though, with small businesses like this (often operating just this side — or perhaps *that* side — of the law) is that they may suddenly fold up, be closed down, or go bankrupt overnight. If this happens, you're probably out of luck, even if they still owe you $100.00 worth of merchandise. We're not talking about something as secure as Sears, which is going to be around forever, but, instead, mere one-person (maybe two or three at the most) basement sales operations in most cases. Most of them mean well, but they have a lot of problems with factors beyond their control: shipping in merchandise from overseas, ordering on credit, crack-

downs on bootlegs, customs regulations, unreliable suppliers, and so on. An understanding of these problems and a patience with these kind of dealers will usually work to your advantage in the long run. Those dealers still in business after a half dozen years or so must be doing *something* right!

Obviously, mail order has plenty of advantages for you as well and is still the number one way most fans buy their Beatles merchandise. You can be receiving sales lists from dozens of dealers at the same time, all of which you can look over and select from at your own leisure. You don't have to compete with crowds and lines, and you can save up to buy what you can afford, and buy when you can afford it. You may have to wait three to six weeks for an item, but if you have that kind of patience, you'll have the fun of receiving lots of surprises in the mail.

Most of the dealers who frequent the conventions put out mail-order lists of some kind or other during the year to tide them over between shows, and to sell their excess and quantity items. You can sign up for most of them right there at the convention. In addition, getting to know these dealers better through the mail will benefit you later on at the next convention. As a preferred customer, one whose name is familiar to them, dealers will try extra hard to get you a good bargain, maybe even pulling out that extra special item from under the table. Some dealers routinely put aside their *very* best and rarest merchandise especially for favored customers, so if you know a dealer it doesn't hurt to ask after such goodies. A friendly face in the crowd at a convention can be a big plus in making a wise purchase in such an atmosphere of avarice.

FAN CLUB NEWSLETTERS & FANZINES

There is also a worldwide network of fan clubs with their own monthly, bi-monthly, or quarterly fanzine publications which wise collectors and fans can subscribe to. Although the majority of them do not sell anything, and those that do, sell only a few items (usually), they can be a tremendous help in keeping you informed, updated, and aware of the whole convention and fandom scene. Even more than any sales catalog or bulletin, the fanzines are *geared* to helping fans with whatever questions they have concerning the Beatles, collecting, prices, and new items available.

Fanzines do regular reviews of all new Beatles items that come onto the market, be they legitimate, imports, or remakes. It's a great help to the collector to know what is out there in the first place! No better source presents itself than these magazines for keeping abreast of the scene, as they serve no other function than to spread the news about the Beatles, and help fans communicate with each other.

My own publication, *The Write Thing*, runs a

regular "Collectors Column" in each issue, addressing itself to different aspects of the collecting problem, as well as answering readers' questions about values, how to tell counterfeits, what's rare and what isn't, and so on. With over 2,000 members worldwide, if I can't help them, someone else out there in this group of dedicated and hard-core fans and collectors will.

Most fanzines also run ads for their members who buy and sell collectibles, and this can be another alternative to turn to when you are ready to get into the mail-order scene. After all, you are reaching the most hard-core audience possible, and fan clubs rarely charge as much as commercial publications for ads. Members' ads are a *service* of the club and you can take advantage of them by buying *from* your fellow fans, or selling *to* them. This is also a good place to run your *wanted* ads. You'll be reaching hundreds, even thousands in some cases, and these are the very people most likely to have duplicates of the item you most need in *your* collection.

The few fanzines that do sell items usually can give fair prices on their product because they have them in quantity, because they are specializing in only the Beatles, and because they are running the sales as another service to their members, not just as a cold business proposition. They need to keep and preserve the good will of their members. People get to know their fan club editors/presidents, and even fellow members (through penpal lists, letters, articles, etc.) and feel almost like family. This spirit of kinship is one that helps make collecting extra rewarding and enjoyable.

The sources discussed in the last three chapters are all ones which I have used to one degree or another in locating Beatles items over the past decade or so. I have had varying amounts of success with different avenues, but each is worth checking into until you find the method most right for you and your own collecting needs. Time, money, energy, patience — all should be taken into consideration when you start. Also, depending on how much you are looking for, or *what* you are looking for, some of these means may be extremely useful, while others might prove worthless. But, for those open to all possibilities, and who want to get involved in the *fun* of collecting as a hobby and who can greet new discoveries with curiosity and enthusiasm, then I hope I've opened a few new doors, shed some new light on a confusing area, and helped you to expand your collection.

9.

What Do You Do With It Now?

Now that you've invested all your spendable income and all your free time to build a respectable collection of Beatles valuables, you probably are beginning to worry about its safekeeping, its preservation, and its future.

First of all, you want to protect the items that can yellow and/or deteriorate with age. What's the point of lovingly cutting out a clipping you really want to hang on to, if it will crumble and turn brittle with age before you can show it to your children, let alone your grandchildren?

All paper items — magazines, photos, clippings, picture sleeves, etc. — need special handling and care. Ads abound (in *Goldmine*, for instance) for the storage bags you should be using to keep all your magazines and paper sleeves in; you can also usually find them in collector-oriented record and magazine shops. Plastic (clear polythene) bags are perfect for temporary safekeeping, or for packaging if you are selling the item. Costing only three to seven cents apiece, they let you price and/or describe each item with peel-off stickers (available at office supply stores) that never have to touch the article itself. But, for your *long term protection*, you'll want something that doesn't allow any deterioration. The following advice comes from Paula Sigman, the assistant archivist at the Walt Disney Archives in Burbank, California:

" . . . studies now recommend the use of mylar where plastic storage is desired, since mylar is inert and should prevent additional damage to the already acidic pages of magazines and clippings, and books. E. Gerber Products supplies mylar record storage bags and acid free boxes as well as magazine size bags. Write for a catalog: E. Gerber Products; Box E; Center Lovell, ME 04016.

[The bags then can be stored in] acid free archival document boxes, which are available from the archival supply companies. These companies also produce all kinds of acid-free folders, which are recommended for filing clippings. You can write: Hollinger Corp; P.O. Box 6185; 3810 Four Mile Run Dr.; Arlington, VA 22206 for a sample catalog."*

If you have just one or two favorite clippings, you might check into a service offered at your area

Historical Society. The Minnesota Historical Society, for instance, will take a clipping and have it encapsulated in plastic for $5.00, or dipped in a solution for longer preservation for a total of $7.00. You can give a call to the museums, colleges, or the like in your area that might offer a similar service. It would certainly be worth looking into if you have paper items in your collection with either monetary or sentimental value which you'd like to keep just as nice as possible. And if you ever wanted to sell them for the kind of prices collectible antiques may bring in twenty-five to fifty years time, then you owe it to your future profits to take some time and trouble now.

As for photographs, if you have some special ones in your collection, then treat them right. See that they get professionally mounted. If you are unfamiliar with the proper procedures yourself, then visit the specialists: the frame shops. At least with that solid mounting board for backing, your photos will keep their shape and not wrinkle or curl, bend or rip.

Pictures do fade with the years and can lose their color. So, use good judgment in where you store your collection, keep it away from humidity and direct sunlight. The best you can do for a valuable photograph is have it mounted with acid-free mounting materials, and then framed in glass. Non-glare looks nicer if you have any plans to exhibit or display the photo, but either kind will add to the longevity of the item.

Some items can be kept in top condition *and* made easier to exhibit and personally enjoy at the same time. Your gum card collection for example, will fit into the display albums they sell for baseball cards. These are advertised in mail-order catalogs, or sold by sports cards collectors (addresses are given in sports cards collecting books available in libraries or bookstores). Many picture sleeve collectors display their sleeves in photo albums with 8 x 10-inch clear plastic pages. These are the most practical ways for either exhibiting or selling your paper items.

Picture sleeve collectors always take the 45 rpm record out of the sleeve and then preserve the sleeve separately. Keeping the record in its sleeve is what brings on the telltale ring wear which devalues a sleeve instantly from Near Mint to Very Good at best. It can also speed up seam splits. So, if you've got a new sleeve or one you've paid a good price for, and you want it to retain (and/or increase) in value, then be sure to guarantee that by keeping its condition as new looking as possible. Signs of age mean wasted dollars for you.

---

*Reprinted from *The Write Thing*, issue 33, May/June, 1981.

After you've protected your collection, you might consider protecting *yourself* — against theft, loss, or disaster. The things we grow attached to, even though inanimate, are endowed with special meaning to us, and their loss can be devastating. No matter how safe you feel where you live — apartment or home, city or suburbs — things do happen; not just robberies, but fire, flood, and so on. Pure peace of mind alone is worth the time and fees involved in having your collection insured.

Contact your *present* insurance agent. Whether you have a homeowners or renters policy, your collection can be insured under a "personal articles floater" (in the category "fine arts") and attached to your present policy. It can even be your parents' policy, if you are living at home and your collection is there. Most agents won't write a separate policy if you are not already a client, so it is easier and cheaper to talk to the agent currently handling the rest of your household or auto insurance requirements.

Without a separate policy, or specific policy attachment identifying exactly what you have, you would have a hard, if not impossible time winning a settlement should there be any reason to file a claim for loss or damage to your collection. But, when you take out a special policy just on your collection, then the company is *accepting the values* you assign your goods when they bill you for the coverage. And it will be there in writing for future claims.

You must list ("itemize") your most valuable pieces individually: Butcher cover, the higher priced rare records, sleeves, books, magazines, memorabilia, autographs, etc. But you can also group items of equal value. Examples might be: 200 photos @ $1.00 = $200.00; twenty magazines @ $10.00 = $200.00; 100 records @ $8.00 = $800.00, etc.

You'll be amazed at how fast your collection's value will mount up once you start listing it all. Don't forget photo albums, scrapbooks, posters, promo items — even clippings. When you have a quantity of such smaller items, even those little things would cost a fortune in replacement costs.

List the values at the *current* market prices. If you paid $3.00 for a Beatles doll in 1966, and it would cost you $30.00 to buy it at a Beatles convention today, then list it as $30.00. Price guides such as *Collecting The Beatles* or mail-order lists you receive can be used to verify prices if you ever need to do so for any claims.

Insurance is a highly regulated industry, and the rates which state governments permit carriers to charge do differ, but the average is about 20 cents per $100.00 worth of goods. Your $300.00 Butcher cover should therefore cost about 60 cents a year for you to protect. After all, if the neighbor's dog chews it up, where would you get another $300.00 to buy a new one? So, insurance is relatively inexpensive when you consider how much you stand to lose should un-

expected disaster strike. Just remember to *keep your coverage current* as your collection grows in size. Every year or so, you should send in an updated inventory of your collection to reflect both the new purchases acquired, and the new prices of all the rest of the items in your collection which increased in value due to inflation. This way, if anything happens, you'd be reimbursed for exactly what it is worth, not for what it was worth last year, and perhaps hundreds of dollars ago.

Now that you've had this $10–20,000 collection nicely bagged, mounted, and protected, what do you do with it? Do you let it sit on a shelf and collect dust, with only your own eyes to gaze upon it? Well, most of us don't do more than personally enjoy it in our own homes. Perhaps we have it neatly stored away for the day it can be a nest egg to retire on, although even when poverty calls we can hardly bear to sell any part of it.

A few more enterprising souls have taken the initiative to exhibit their collections for others to appreciate and enjoy. At recent "Beatlefest"s, Rick and Terry Thomas of Ohio have set up a Beatles museum, with an amazing display of collectibles, ranging from "Yellow Submarine" memorabilia, unique Beatles toys, and paraphernalia from the early sixties as well as rare records, books, magazines, gum cards, and so on. Fans and collectors can view in person these items they've only heard or read about otherwise. They can compare the original collectibles like the Thomas's have with some of the replicas being passed off in the dealers' room nearby. When you see for yourself that the real, original Beatles scarf has fringe, you'll recall this when you see the new ones now being sold.

Not everyone can set up at a convention, but other places in your own area may lend themselves to a nice one-time exhibit, though. If your collection is large enough and you are interested in letting others see it, you might want to contact local museums, banks, schools, libraries, malls, or whatever appeals to you. All of these are possibilities. Other fans can learn from seeing what really exists out there, and you'll be aiding the hobby of collecting. You'll probably make some interesting contacts with other people who share your interests along the way, too.

There are also collectors' magazines, antique guides, and local newspapers that might be interested in doing a feature on your collection. You may want to write about or photograph the rarities in your collection for publication in one of these. It depends on how much you'd care for the notoriety and the attention to your collection this will all bring. But if you've already made provisions for your collections' safekeeping, then it could be worth the trouble. It can be fun to show off what you've had to work so hard to put together.

One last piece of well-meant advice is: what about a *will*? Have you ever thought what would happen to your collection, so painstakingly sought out, purchased, preserved, and insured, after you're gone? Will your relatives pack it off to the Goodwill? Or, will your sister take it to the next convention and sell it, or your husband distribute it among your friends? This may be fine if it is what you *want*. But if it isn't, then you should set down in writing (and have it legally attended to) just exactly what you *do* want done with it all.

Perhaps special items *should* go to special friends, and the rest sold. If so, you should indicate which goes to whom. Or, maybe you want the best of it to go someplace special where it can be enjoyed and appreciated by future Beatles fans in the next generation. If your collection harbors items of particular interest and uniqueness — rare photos, memorabilia, letters from the Beatles, autographs, etc. — you might consider leaving it to a Beatles museum.

Currently, Cavern Mecca (18 Mathew St., Merseyside, Liverpool, England) is the principal place to have begun such a project. They have established a museum for all fans the world over to enjoy and learn from, and especially to instruct the future fans who come to this "mecca" for the beginnings of Beatlemania. It has the support of Paul McCartney, his family, and friends (Victor Spinnetti, for one).

In London, there are plans to open a branch of the Victoria and Albert Museum which, like our Smithsonian, preserves the best of the historical past. They will exhibit and describe "artifacts" such as their stage outfits, instruments, contracts and letters, photographs and records, in addition to the memorabilia. Both places will help to insure that these wonderfully special times, and all their memories, stay vivid in the minds of future generations. If you believe that is a pretty "noble" cause, then you might like to see that the most prized of your possessions ends in places like these. I know I would like mine to.

The original Beatles scarf comes in red, blue, and yellow on a white background, and has fringes around the edges.
Price Guide No.: 720

10

How to Use the Price Guide

Beatles items are distributed into twelve different major categories to make them easier to locate. Within each category, they are alphabetized by title (records, books, and magazine sections), artist (Beatles-related records section), or generic designations (e.g., pen, doll, jewelry, tickets, t-shirts, etc., as in the memorabilia, promo, movie, and special items sections). A few miscellaneous subcategories involving arbitrarily assigned designations did not lend themselves to organization, and so are not alphabetized at all.

The prices listed are those for materials in Near Mint condition, as this is the most common top grading used by dealers, and the condition most hard-core fans are seeking. (See the Glossary in this book for more detailed definitions of grading terms relating to condition.) Some Very Good prices are supplied when the price spread on a given item is interesting and relevant. *Condition* (next to authenticity) is the most important consideration when buying or selling collectibles. Most collectors want only Near Mint to Mint items for their collection, but many times start with Very Good items and "trade up." However, if you want the item for the sake of the music, or utility, then a counterfeit or a replica at a fraction of the cost might be just the right thing for you.

I have tried to list all the known variations of each item, and note how much it is worth in each of these different states. In many cases, a price cannot be attached to an item unless you know *exactly* which variation is being offered. In other cases, packaging and contents play a vital part, so these factors are all discussed and individually priced when possible.

Mentioned earlier in this book, but worth repeating, is that fact that prices have been gathered from a wide range of sources, with the most *common* prices actually paid being the ones listed. In this way, a price outrageously off the mark, either on the high or low side, was eliminated. So, instead of taking an "average," I noted every price I saw, and then determined a mid-range (and most usually seen) figure. The range given is small, but should at least indicate that most items cannot have just *one* set price, but rather a variable price which changes from dealer to dealer.

The prices reflected in this book come from dealers all over the world: from those at Beatles conventions, rock-and-roll shows and swap meets, to those who sell over the counter in specialized shops, and those who put out Beatles oriented mail-order lists. I have been recording such prices now for four years

(personally attending over twenty-five Beatles conventions in the last eight years), and have tried hard to get a price on every Beatles item I saw or heard about. For most items, I was able to gather over half-a-dozen price notations from a variety of different, knowledgeable dealers in different parts of the United States. A few of the really unique items that I have come in contact with or heard about, but never actually seen sold or priced, are included, but with the letters NPA (no price available) in the price column.

NOTES ON PRICE GUIDE SECTIONS OR COLLECTING CATEGORIES

RECORDS (LPs, EPs, 45s)

The principal album section of the Price Guide first offers things like anthology, fan club, foreign, interview, pre-Beatles, solo, and other original albums, followed by a separate listing of the original group albums. Succeeding categories cover group singles, solo singles, and then extended play (EP) and compact records.

Most records listed are U.S. releases. To list all foreign pressings would have been a lifetime compilation job. A few of the more desired and sought after foreign discs *are* included, though, especially those with different titles or covers that make them particularly collectable in the U.S. No attempt has been made to list the prices these records might sell for in countries outside the U.S., as this was not possible. Suffice to say that the situation may be completely different in each country, item by item, depending on individual supply and demand.

Many records have been counterfeited, both wax and picture sleeve in many cases. Instances of counterfeiting that are known are detailed, with price given for the counterfeit as well as for the original. This practice is mainly designed to help distinguish one from the other, and to simply alert you to the existence of the counterfeit, not because I think counterfeits should necessarily count as true collectibles. (More detailed information on the subject of counterfeits and how to tell them from originals is included in the chapter called "The Counterfeit Controversy." Also, the book *You Can't Do That* by Charles Reinhart (Pierian Press, 1981) has some useful notes on this area of collecting.) The list in this book is nowhere near being complete, mainly because new items are counterfeited every month, and it is impossible to keep up with the outpouring. I have noted, then, just those that I am currently aware of; any item *may* be copied, though, so caution and judgment are essential when buying high-priced records.

A few records are listed in both U.S. and U.K. versions, when both are in equal demand or particularly collectable by U.S. fans (e.g., **The Christmas Album**, which goes by a different title and jacket in the U.K.). Some records, such as the **Scouse The Mouse** LP or *Zoo Gang* as a 45 rpm B-side, are *only* available commercially in the U.K., but are desirable to U.S. fans, so they are listed as well.

The list of records includes only those that are considered collectibles, so even though this book was completed in mid-1982, you won't find current releases listed because they are still sold in stores at retail prices. Many of the older solo albums and singles fall into this category as well; some LPs are already to be found in the cut-out bins at *less* than the original retail price!

BOOTLEGS

There are literally hundreds and hundreds of bootlegs of Beatles recordings around, in 12-inch, 10-inch, and 7-inch forms. To list them all with prices would be superfluous, as most of them fall within a similar price range anyway. The common price for a discontinued, out-of-print bootleg record LP is $6.00--$12.00, with $10.00 being the most usual cost. An old 45 might cost $3.00--$6.00, hardly much different than what the new ones cost. Exceptions and variations are listed in this guide, along with samples of the more common varieties. (A detailed discography of bootlegs can be found in the book *You Can't Do That*.) Still, new boots are pressed regularly, and old bootlegs are even remade, so the price situation can fluctuate. Although most redone boots have some difference or variation that sets them apart, the hard-core collector will usually want the first pressing, just as they do with other records.

PROMOS

Promotional versions probably exist for every commercially made record released. The ones listed in this book are the most unusual, or those most sought after, as collectibles. Some promos are particularly rare because they contain alternate versions or song variations that were never on the succeeding commercial release. Such differences, and their current values, are all given in the Price Guide section. Collecting promo records is becoming an increasingly expensive hobby, as "instant" collectibles are created when a record company suddenly decides to change a release at the last minute (after the press copies are out, but before the commercial version is in the store). Thus, the new promo version of *The Beatles Movie Medley* was immediately valued at $50.00. A

hard area to predict or keep up with!

The most desirable promo records are listed first in this guide, followed by the rare and high-priced white label U.K. promos. The more common Beatles promo 45s are all listed separately. All the recent solo-Beatles singles, LPs, etc., have promo versions as well, but only a selection of each are included in this guide because the price range for all of them are similar (exceptions are noted). Most promos without variational differences that set them apart are selling for $8.00--$10.00 in Near Mint condition (and even Mint condition). Since promos are not sold commercially in stores, but sent to radio stations, the press, and record stores, the usual condition they are seen in is Near Mint or even uncirculated Mint.

Lastly, a short listing of some additional promo LPs, acetates, and test pressings is included, to give you an idea of the scope of the field and provide a starting point if you are interested in pursuing a collection of these more esoteric recordings.

PICTURE SLEEVES

Picture sleeves are a breed apart, as their value may exist independently from the record they were originally sold with. They may also be counterfeited even when the record they came with is not.

Many fans question why the price is often the same for the picture sleeve whether the record is included or not, and why the sleeve is worth *more* than the record in most cases. The reasons are that the records were pressed in much greater quantities than the original picture sleeves and, secondly, many people kept their records, cleaned them and preserved them from damage, but they either didn't keep the sleeve at all or, when they did, the condition deteriorated over the years and the sleeve is often in poor shape by now (due to anything from ring wear, water damage, writing or other defacement, seam splits, etc.). Collectors today want to find the *best* examples possible, so the picture sleeve market continues to be an active and important one for fans and dealers.

Those records which do have a separate value independent of the packaging are indicated, but in the rest of the cases, I have listed the records and picture sleeves together, with the value actually being in the sleeve.

To locate picture sleeve values, turn to the two "singles" sections of the Price Guide, where The Beatles' group singles are given first in alphabetical order, with the solo-Beatles singles alphabetized separately afterwards.

BEATLES-RELATED RECORDS & NOVELTIES

The Beatles-related records are all listed by *artist or group* in the Price Guide, even though in some cases the material is better known by title. The novelty record section then reverts back to the most familiar type of arrangement for that class of recordings, song title. The records listed are those most frequently encountered, or those most in demand or most interesting to collectors. Thousands of cover versions of Beatles songs exist on singles and on albums, but the majority of these are not of interest to collectors and the value (to Beatle fans anyway) is minimal.

A sampling of Beatles novelties are included in this work, just to give a general idea of the field. But, like bootlegs, a common price range for most such records is $1.00--$4.00 without a picture sleeve, and perhaps a bit more if the sleeve exists and features anything "Beatleish." All the most interesting items and any exceptions have been noted in this guide. (For a complete discography, see *You Can't Do That*.)

A Beatles-related record must meet one of the following conditions:

    a. The artist is (literally) related or has family ties.

    b. The artist was once a member of The Beatles, or worked with one or more of The Beatles in some recording capacity.

    c. The material on the recording was written/produced by one or more of The Beatles.

    d. One of The Beatles plays on the recording.

    e. The record is on The Beatles own Apple label.

    f. Record is a cover version of Beatles material, may picture Beatles caricature, wigs, or some take-off of name on cover or sleeve.

A Beatles novelty record is one which:

    a. Has a Beatles theme to it.

    b. Is a take-off on The Beatles' style, name, or newsworthiness.

    c. May be humorous, have a serious message, or contain a tribute.

Value is in the recorded material itself, in most cases. Those records with picture sleeves are indicated. For LPs, the jacket and recording must both be intact for the album to have value.

BOOKS AND MAGAZINES

The majority listed are U.S. publications, but exceptions when interesting and relevant are noted. All are listed by *title*. If there were reprintings, different editions, etc., these variations have all been noted. Price differences are noted for hardcover and paperback editions as well. Again, only *collectible* books and magazines are listed; even though there are dozens more available in book stores, the fact that these are still for sale commercially eliminates them as

collectibles at the present time. As they go out-of-print and become hard to find, we may see their value increase and thus become sought-after items. Magazines have a shorter shelf life than most books and may become collectors' items within weeks of their disappearance from the shelves. Since so many new books and magazines are published these days, the emphasis in the guide is on the older, more "established" collectibles.

SPECIAL ITEMS

Promotional items are included in this category, as well as highly prized collectibles like autographs, gold records, sheet music, and so on, which are hard to classify in the other sections. All are listed by generic name and alphabetized accordingly. Even though this section could have been indefinitely expanded, only a relatively small sampling has been included. New promotional items are flooding the market constantly, and counterfeiting is a problem here, too. It is impossible to keep up with it all, so one can only advise caution.

MEMORABILIA

Again, all items are listed generically in three sections: Apple promo items; sixties memorabilia; and "Yellow Submarine" memorabilia. Descriptive information is given, including manufacturer, types, variations, etc., whenever known. The Beatles pictures, names, and autographs were pasted, printed, and embossed on almost every conceivable type of product, so only those items actually seen for sale, seen on display, or described in print are included in this guide. In a few cases, the items are so rare that I have never seen a price tag on them, but similar items might give a basis of comparison or a standard to go by in determining value if you are buying, selling, or just appraising your own collection. Counterfeits, when known about, are indicated.

In conclusion, and to repeat myself again, these prices should not be taken as "The Bible," but more as a *guide* to serve as a beginning and a reference point in estimating the value of your present collection, in helping you to determine a price you might want to charge if you are selling Beatles items, or the price you might expect to pay if you are buying them.

Many people will argue that the prices are too low in one instance, or too high in another. Keep in mind, however, that these are prices actually charged and/or paid as recently as early 1982. They are not figures I just plucked out of the air. As they change, *and change they will*, this book can still serve as a basis of comparison. The price differences *between* items is to me just as important an attribute of this book as the prices themselves. You can see at a quick glance just which items are the most valuable, and also which are much more common.

I hope this proves useful to you, that you have a lot of fun with it, and that you find everything you're looking for! Good luck!!

Collecting The Beatles

PRICE GUIDE

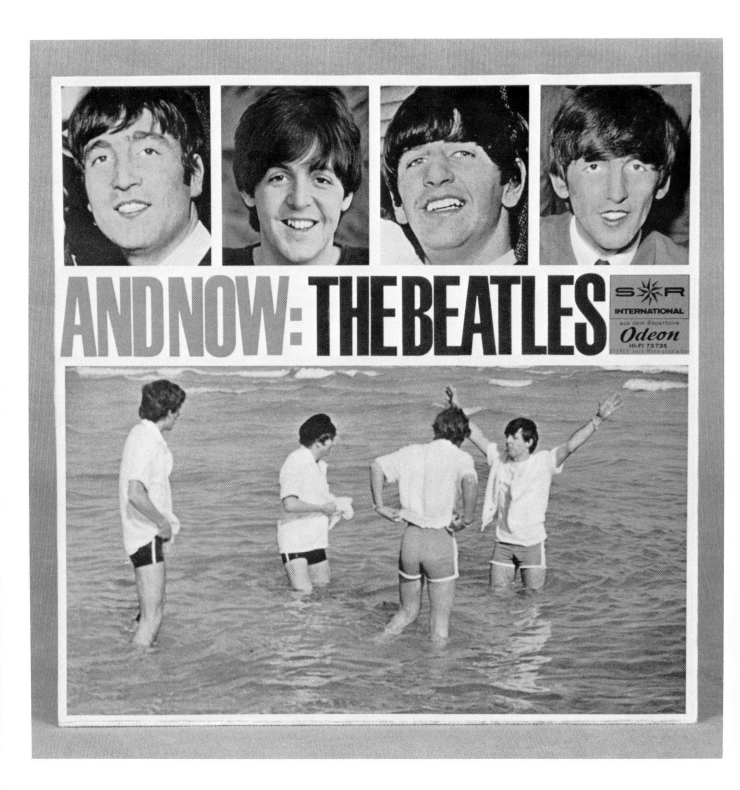

Original copy of a rare German release, valued at $50. *Price Guide No.: 5*

Label and Record Number	Title	Description	Condition Near Mint	Very Good	Good
1. Atco 33--169	**AIN'T SHE SWEET**	Stereophonic	$55–100	$75	
		Monophonic	$40		
		White label promo	$100--135		
2. Parlophone	**AIUTO** (Italian **HELP**)	Different fold out cover	$30		
3. Clairon 601	**AMAZING BEATLES**	Stereophonic	$30–50	$25--40	
		Monophonic	$20–25		
		Mini-cover on back of sleeve	$60--100		
4. Radio Pulse-beat News	**THE AMERICAN TOUR WITH ED RUDY** (News Documentary No. 2)	With 34 page booklet	$55--100		
		Without booklet	$35--40		
	THE AMERICAN TOUR WITH ED RUDY (News Documentary No. 3)		$40–50		
	Counterfeit		$8		
	Bootleg	White cover	$5		
	Reissue no.2	No booklet	$8–10		
5. Odeon 73735	**AND NOW: THE BEATLES** (Very rare German record club release)				
6. BV66	**BEATLE VIEWS** 1966 U.S. tour	Original	$15–25		
		Counterfeit (Limited quantity)	$6--10		
7.	**LES BEATLES** with Tony Sheridan	France 10 inch	$250		
8. Polydor 236–201	**THE BEATLES FIRST** (U.K. August 1967 reissued)		$30		
9. Parlophone 383083	**BEATLES GOLDEN GREATEST HITS** (Sweden)	Club edition 1965	$7		
10. Parlophone PMCS 306	**BEATLES GREATEST HITS** (Sweden)		$25		
11. Parlophone 7534--33	**BEATLES GREATEST HITS VOL. 1 & 2** (Australian)		$25		
12. Parlophone 1506	**BEATLES IN ITALY** (Rare Italian release — champagne cover)	Original open-out cover	$60--125		
		Second pressing — doesn't open out	$15		
		Counterfeit — doesn't open	$10		
		Picture disc	$15--25		
13. EMI/Parlophone 1A-062-04632	**BEATLES IN ITALY**	Reissue — Holland (Different cover)	$12–15		

B
E
A
T
L
E
S

A
L
B
U
M
S

Label and Record Number	Title	Description	Condition		
			Near Mint	Very Good	Good
14. PBR International 7005/6	THE BEATLES TAPES (Two record set of David Wigg interview and 8 page booklet)	Blue vinyl Regular issue	$20 $10		
15. Capitol 2125	BEATLES VS BEACH BOYS		$200		
16. Polydor 2484073	BEATLES VS BEE GEES (Rare Argentinian)		$350		
17. VJ DX30	BEATLES VS FOUR SEASONS	Original stereophonic with poster	$200–300	$150–200	
		Without poster	$100	$50–60	
		Monophonic with poster	$110	$50–80	$30–40
18. MGM SE 4215	THE BEATLES WITH TONY SHERIDAN	Stereophonic	$100	$60	
19. Polydor 46432	THE BEATLES WITH TONY SHERIDAN (U.K. April 1964)	Red label	$100	$85	
20. Capitol St 2094	CHARTBUSTER VOL. 4 (Two Beatles songs)		$40	$30	
21. Apple SBC–100	(BEATLES) CHRISTMAS ALBUM (U.S.)	Original Counterfeit U.S.	$50–75 $12–15	$40–50	$25–35
22. Clarion 609	DISCOTHEQUE IN ASTROSOUND (Original discotheque hits)	Stereophonic Monophonic	$50 $25–50		
23. Foundation 1001	DO IT NOW: 20 GIANT HITS (One Beatles cut: *Nowhere Man*)	Stereophonic	$15	$8	
24. Zapple ST 3358	ELECTRONIC SOUND	Still sealed Original not sealed	$20–22 $10–14	$5–10	
25. Apple TV SS8	THE ESSENTIAL BEATLES (Australian import)		$30		
26. London MS 82007	THE FAMILY WAY (Soundtrack by Paul McCartney)	Original	$50–75	$50	$35–40
		Monophonic promo	$80–100	$75	
		With promo 45 — rare	$125–150	$95	
		Counterfeit	$8–12		
		Australian import different cover	$10–15		

Label and Record Number	Title	Description	Condition		
			Near Mint	Very Good	Good
27. Apple LYN 2154	FROM THEN TO US (U.K. Beatles Christmas LP, different cover)	Original Counterfeit U.K.	$60–80 $8–10	$40–50	$25–35
28. VJ Pro 202	HEAR THE BEATLES TELL ALL	Mono. original 70's reissue (stereo) Counterfeit w/no spine writing	$45–75 $5–9 $6–8	$35–45	$30–35
29. 109	HERE'S TO VETERANS (McCartney is DJ)		$25–30	$15	
30. Sterling Prod. 9995–6481	I APOLOGISE by John Lennon (Promo from *Chicago Tribune* 1966)	With original picture insert Bootleg in white sleeve	$30 $6–8		
31. Polydor 24–4504	IN THE BEGINNING THE BEATLES – CIRCA 1960 (Released in 1970)		$10–12		
32. VJ 1085	JOLLY WHAT! THE BEATLES & FRANK IFIELD ON STAGE	Ifield cover – stereophonic Monophonic Rare Beatles drawing on cover – monophonic Rare stereophonic with oval VJ label (Ifield cover) Counterfeit	$35–50 $15–25 $400–700 $70 $10	$25–35	
33. Zapple ST 3357	LIFE WITH THE LIONS (UNFINISHED MUSIC NO. 2)		$50–75	$35–50	$20–25
34. Apple SW 3362	LIVE PEACE IN TORONTO Plastic Ono Band	With original rare calendar Without calendar Reissue	$50–60 $15 $8–9	$35–40 $12	$25–35 $10
35. Polydor J 74557	MEET THE BEAT by Tony Sheridan and the Beat Brothers German club issue	10 inch stereo-	$200–350		
36. MGM E 4215	MY BONNIE	Stereophonic Monophonic	$60–70 $35		
37. EMI Starline SRS-5013	NO ONE'S GONNA CHANGE OUR WORLD		$50–75	$50	$30–35
38. ESP 63019	PASS ON THIS SIDE	TV offer	$10	$8	

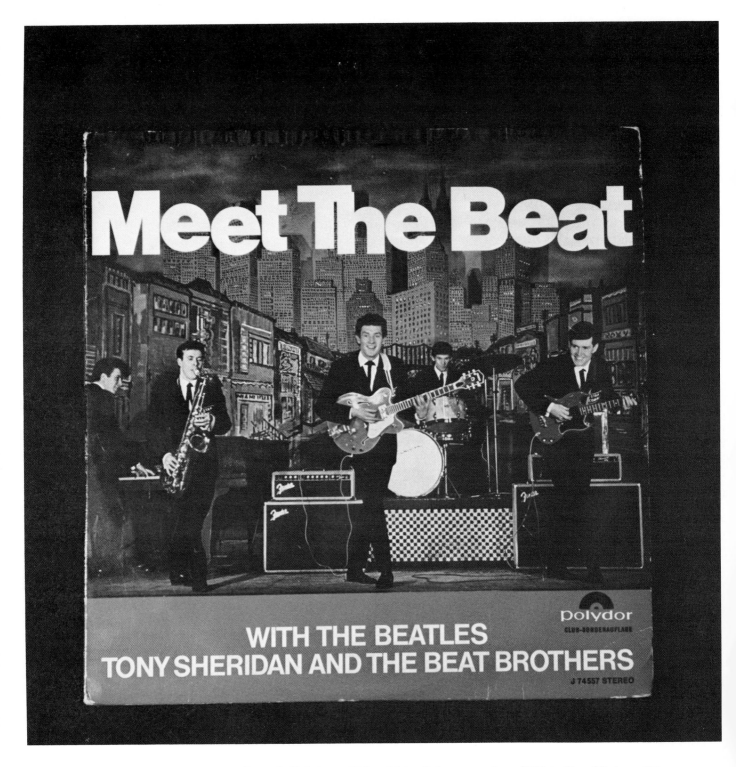

A very rare **10-inch** German Record Club issue. This might sell for as much as $300 in Near Mint condition.
Price Guide No.: 35

The World Wildlife Fund charity album, which includes John Lennon's original version of *Across The Universe*. Valued at $75-100 in Near Mint condition. *Price Guide No.: 37*

Label and Record Number	Title	Description	Condition		
			Near Mint	Very Good	Good
39. ODEON J060--84973	POR SIEMPRE BEATLES (Released in Spain — different cover)	Monophonic	$10–15		
40. Capitol SN--12009	RARITIES U.S.	Green label series (scheduled for 1979 release but pulled) with white cover	$50–100	$50	
	Second issue	Blue cover (as in boxed set)	$45–50	$35–45	
	First issue – different songs	Open out cover	$7--10		
	Second issue	"Prod by George Martin" added and butcher cover	$7–10		
41. Adam VIII	ROOTS	Original inner sleeve had ads	$50–75	$40--50	$30--35
		Counterfeit	$8--17		
42. Savage BM69	SAVAGE YOUNG BEATLES	First press – 1964	$20	$15	
		1966	$18		
		Counterfeit	$8		
43.	SCOUSE THE MOUSE (U.K. only. Very rare.)		$100–150		
		Counterfeit – purple	$15		
44. VJ 1092	SONGS PICTURES & STORIES (Original is fold-out cover) (Counterfeit "Songs & Pictures" no fold out)	Bracket label stereo	$250	$150--200	
		Bracket label mono	$60	$35--45	$25
		Oval label – Monophonic (Earlier press)	$75	$65–70	
		Oval stereophonic	$300	$200--250	
		Counterfeit	$8		
45. Metro MS 563	THIS IS WHERE IT STARTED by Tony Sheridan & The Beatles	Stereophonic	$50–70	$30–45	
		Monophonic	$30		
46. Apple T–5001	TWO VIRGINS (UNFINISHED MUSIC. NO. 1)	First press – in brown wrapper – hole for heads cut out sealed with sticker	$100–125		
		No seal but in original brown wrapper	$50–75		
		U.K. version – rare	$60–75		
		Original but no wrapper	$45–60	$40–45	$30–35
		Counterfeit brown wrapper has no open hole cut	$8--10		

Label and Record Number	Title	Description	Condition		
			Near Mint	Very Good	Good
47. Apple 3361 Sapcor Odeon EAS	WEDDING ALBUM (boxed set)	With all contents Original U.S. U.K. version Japanese import	$50--85 $65--85 $20--35	$50--60	$40--45
48. Parlophone 3045	WITH THE BEATLES (Australian import)	First pressing — original jacket Current issue minor differences	$30 $10		
49. Apcor—1	WONDERWALL	With original insert Stereophonic — no insert Monophonic — no insert	$18 $7--15 $7--9	$7--9	
50. Electrola— EMI 27--408--4	THE WORLD'S BEST (German import)	Original Counterfeit Dutch import	$35--50 $7--10 $16		

Original Group Albums

Label and Record Number	Title	Description	Near Mint	Very Good	Good
51.	ABBEY ROAD	Picture disc	$30		
52. United Artists UAS6366	A HARD DAY'S NIGHT (3 variations)	Monophonic original label	$20	$15	
53. Capitol ST 2080	THE BEATLES 2ND ALBUM	Monophonic Stereophonic	$15 $10	$10	
54. Capitol ST 2358	BEATLES VI	Monophonic — original label ("see label for correct order") Monophonic — corrected order	$20 $15	$5--15	
55. Capitol T 2228	BEATLES 65	Monophonic	$15	$12	$10
56. Capitol TB 02222	THE BEATLES STORY	Original mono- phonic Original stereo- phonic Stereophonic — Apple	$25 $20--25 $15	$20	$10--15
57. Capitol 2386	HELP!	Original label	$15	$12--15	

B
E
A
T
L
E
S

A
L
B
U
M
S

Label and Record Number	Title	Description	Near Mint	Very Good	Good
58. VJ 1062	**INTRODUCING THE BEATLES** (13 variations) *most common edition Version 1 from 1963 has *Love Me Do* and *P.S. I Love You* Version 2 from 1964 has *Please, Please Me* and *Ask Me Why* Counterfeits list version 1 but play version 2	Promo — blank back version 1 — rare	$250--300		
		Stereophonic VJ in brackets, version 2	$100	$85--100	$60--70
		Stereophonic VJ in oval, version 2	$150	$60--100	
		Stereophonic VJ in oval, version 1	$300		
		Stereophonic in brackets, version 1	$150--200		
		Monophonic, oval label, version 1	$75		
		Monophonic — brackets label, version 1	$60		
		Monophonic — oval label, version 2	$100		
		*Monophonic — brackets version 2	$25	$15	$10
		Original with ads on back cover — rare, version 1	$250--300		
		Counterfeit	$5--10		
		Reissue by VJ in 1970s	$5--8		
		Cut-out	$3--4		
59. Apple PXS 1 or Apple PCS 7096 Apple AR 34001	**LET IT BE**	U.K. boxed set with book	$125--175	$85--100	
		Canada boxed set	$175		
		Book with box — no LP	$100	$90	
		U.S. never issued with book, opens out	$8		
		Cut-out	$2--5		
60. Capitol SMAL 2835	**MAGICAL MYSTERY TOUR** (Last monophonic LP issued)	Stereophonic with booklet	$15	$10--12	
		Monophonic with booklet	$20		
61. Capitol 2047	**MEET THE BEATLES**	Original Rainbow label, stereophonic	$20	$15	
		Monophonic	$15		
62. Capitol T2576	**REVOLVER**	Original stereophonic label	$15		
		Monophonic	$15		
63. Capitol T2442	**RUBBER SOUL**	Original label Stereophonic	$15	$10	
		Monophonic	$15	$10	

Label and Record Number	Title	Description	Condition		
			Near Mint	Very Good	Good
64. Capitol SMAS 2653	**SGT. PEPPER'S LONELY HEARTS CLUB BAND**	All inserts	$15--20	$7--9	
Capitol SEAX 11840		Picture disc	$20--25		
		Marble from Canada	$10--12		
65. Capitol T2108	**SOMETHING NEW**	Original label	$15		
66. Apple SWBO 101	**"WHITE ALBUM" – (THE BEATLES)**	With all inserts, stereophonic, original label	$20	$12--15	
	*Some collectors value lower numbers more.	*Low number stamped on front, original label and inserts	$20--25		
Apple PCS 7067/8	U.K. version French version	Monophonic rare with inserts	$75		
		White vinyl	$20--30		
		Reissued U.K. monophonic 1981	$25		
67. Capitol T 2553	**YESTERDAY AND TODAY** Trunk cover	Record club issue, green label, true stereophonic	$45	$25	
		Monophonic – original label	$20	$15	$8
		Stereophonic – original label	$20	$8--20	$8
	Butcher cover	*First state stereophonic	$300–400		
		First state monophonic	$300		
		First state S.S.	$300+		
		S.S. unpeeled (truck cover over)	$250	$200	
	*First state – never covered by trunk cover. Very few known stereophonic first states in existence.	Unpeeled – stereophonic more than monophonic	$200–300	$150--200	$75--125
		Peeled – stereophonic more than monophonic	$200+	$125--200	$75–100

Other

68.	Japanese Beatles albums	Early LP's deleted now	$35–50		
69.	U.K. colored vinyl	Magical Mystery Tour – Yellow	$12		
		Abbey Road – Green	$12		
		Let It Be – White	$12		

Six (out of seven) of the Beatles' annual Christmas discs, which were sent to fan club members only and never

Label and Record Number	Title	Description	Condition Near Mint	Very Good	Good
70. Capitol 5222	*A HARD DAY'S NIGHT/ I SHOULD HAVE KNOWN BETTER*	*With picture sleeve	$14–20	$7–14	
71. Atco 6308	*AIN'T SHE SWEET*	Promo With picture sleeve Record only	$80–100 $75 $8–10	 $50–70 $6–7	 $50
72. Polydor NH52–317	*AIN'T SHE SWEET/IF YOU REALLY LOVE ME*	Record only	$30		
73. Capitol 72144	*ALL MY LOVING/THIS BOY*	Canada	$15		
74. Capitol 5964	*ALL YOU NEED IS LOVE*	With picture sleeve	$6–9		
75. Capitol 5235	*AND I LOVE HER/IF I FELL*	With picture sleeve	$15–25	$12–15	
76. Apple 2531	*BALLAD OF JOHN & YOKO/OLD BROWN SHOE*	With picture sleeve	$17–25	$13–17	
77. Capitol 5150	*CAN'T BUY ME LOVE/ YOU CAN'T DO THAT*	With picture sleeve	$150–175	$125	$80–100
78. Beatles Ltd. (Fan club)	Christmas singles	1963 – U.K. 1964 – U.S. on cardboard square 1965 – with picture sleeve 1966 – with picture sleeve (Pantomime, Everywhere it's Christmas) U.K. 1966 – U.S. on postcard 1967 – (Christmas Time Is Here Again) U.S. – postcard U.K. – with sleeve 1968 – (Happy Xmas) with picture sleeve 1969 – (Happy Xmas) with picture sleeve	$80–150 $75–125 $75–100 $55–65 $70–75 $60–65 $35–45 $35–45 $20–35	$75 $65–75 $50 $50 	 $60 $40 $35

_____

*In most cases the value is in the sleeve. Records alone are listed only if of collectible value.
(All items original, first release — unless otherwise stated.)

B
E
A
T
L
E
S

S
I
N
G
L
E
S

The U.S. edition of the 1964 Beatles' Christmas disc, mounted on cardboard. This Very Good++ copy would be worth approximately $100. *Price Guide No.: 78*

The 1966 Beatles' Christmas flexi-disc. This Very Good+ copy would go for at least $50. *Price Guide No.: 78*

The 1967 Beatles' Christmas flexi-disc from the U.K. This Near Mint copy is valued at $35-40. *Price Guide*

A 1968 Beatles' Christmas flexi-disc worth about $35-40. Price Guide No.: 78

A Beatles Christmas flexi-disc from 1969. Not as valuable as Christmas records from earlier years. *Price Guide*

Label and Record Number	Title	Description	Condition		
			Near Mint	Very Good	Good
79. MGM 13227	*CRY FOR A SHADOW/WHY*	Promo	$60--75	$50--60	
		Record only	$15		
		With picture sleeve	$50--80	$40	$35
Polydor 52--275	U.K.	U.K. release	$26	$20	
80. VJ 587	*DO YOU WANT TO KNOW A SECRET/THANK YOU GIRL*	Record only	$6		
		With picture sleeve	$25–30	$17–20	
		Promo	$65		
81. Capitol Starline 6064	*DO YOU WANT TO KNOW A SECRET/THANK YOU GIRL*	No picture sleeve issued	$20--25	$17	
82. Capitol 5371	*EIGHT DAYS A WEEK/I DON'T WANT TO SPOIL THE PARTY*	With picture sleeve	$6--15		
83. VJ 522	*FROM ME TO YOU/THANK YOU GIRL* (1963 release)	Promo	$75--100	$65--75	$45–50
		Oval label – no sleeve issued	$50--55		
84. Capitol 2056	*HELLO GOODBYE/I AM THE WALRUS*	With picture sleeve	$15--20	$13--15	
		With original fan club insert and sleeve	$25–30		
85. Capitol 5467	*HELP/I'M DOWN*	With picture sleeve	$14–20	$9--14	
86. Capitol 5327	*I FEEL FINE/SHE'S A WOMAN*	With picture sleeve	$10–16	$6–9	
87. Parlophone DP562	*IF I FELL/TELL ME WHY*		$40		
88. Capitol 5234	*I'LL CRY INSTEAD/I'M HAPPY JUST TO DANCE WITH YOU*	With picture sleeve	$25–35	$16--25	$15
89. Capitol 5112	*I WANT TO HOLD YOUR HAND/I SAW HER STANDING THERE*	With picture sleeve	$15--22	$12–18	$10
90. Parlophone R 5084	*I WANT TO HOLD YOUR HAND/THIS BOY*	U.K. 1963 – record only	NPA		
91. Capitol 6066	*KANSAS CITY/BOYS*	Green Starline Series, no sleeve	$15		
92. Odeon 22671	*KOMM, GIB MIR DEINE HAND/SIE LIEBT DICH*	Original German release	$50–60		
		Counterfeit	$5		

One of the rarest Beatles singles of all: Decca 31382 from 1962. With a pink label, it can sell for $500+; with a regular black label, it may bring $200+. *Price Guide No.: 104*

Label and Record Number	Title	Description	Condition Near Mint	Very Good	Good
93. Capitol 2138	*LADY MADONNA/THE INNER LIGHT*	With picture sleeve With fan club insert and picture sleeve	$10–17 $20–30	$7–15 $15–18	$5–10
94. Apple 2764	*LET IT BE/YOU KNOW MY NAME (LOOK UP MY NUMBER)*	With picture sleeve	$10–15	$6–10	
95. Apple 2832	*LONG & WINDING ROAD/ FOR YOU BLUE*	With picture sleeve	$12–15	$8–10	
96. Tollie 9008	*LOVE ME DO/P.S. I LOVE YOU*	With picture sleeve Record alone Promo	$25–30 $4 $60	$20–25	$15
97. Capitol 72076	*LOVE ME DO/P.S. I LOVE YOU*	Canada – orange swirl	$30		
98. Capitol 6062	*LOVE ME DO/P.S. I LOVE YOU*	Green Starline Series – no sleeve	$30		
99. Parlophone R 4949	*LOVE ME DO/P.S. I LOVE YOU*	Original U.K. release with red label	$50–85	$35–50	
100. Parlophone SD 5937	*LOVE ME DO/PLEASE PLEASE ME*	With picture sleeve special release Sweden only	$12		
101. MGM 13213	*MY BONNIE/THE SAINTS*	With picture sleeve Record alone Promo	$25–40 $8 $60	$18–25 $4	$15
102. Polydor 24673	*MY BONNIE/THE SAINTS* (two versions) With German intro With English intro	Original 1961 release – rare Fan club reissue 1978 (500 pressed)	$150–250+ $15–18	$125	
103. Polydor NH 66-833	*MY BONNIE/THE SAINTS* Issued 5/63 and 2/64	U.K.	$150+		
104. Decca 31382	*MY BONNIE/THE SAINTS* U.S. 1962	Pink label – rare Black label	$250+ $200+		
105. Capitol 5587	*NOWHERE MAN/WHAT GOES ON*	With picture sleeve	$12–15	$8–12	
106. Capitol 5651	*PAPERBACK WRITER/ RAIN*	With picture sleeve	$12–15	$7–12	
107. Capitol 5810	*PENNY LANE/STRAW- BERRY FIELDS FOREVER*	With picture sleeve	$20–25	$12–18	

B
E
A
T
L
E
S
S
I
N
G
L
E
S

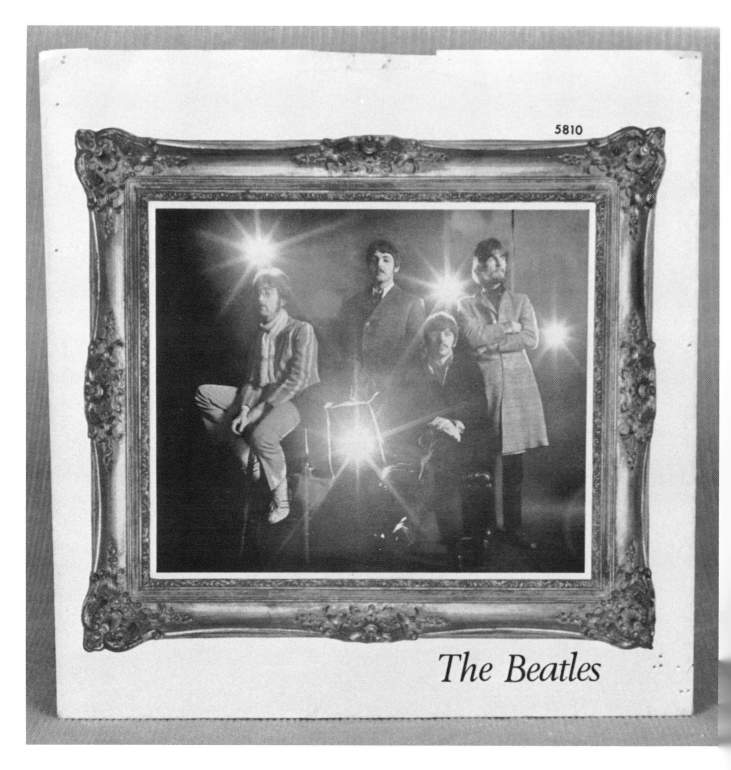

Front side of the picture sleeve for the U.S. version of *Penny Lane/Strawberry Fields Forever* **(45)**. This copy has pin holes which reduce its value to around $15, but a Near Mint copy would fetch $25. *Price Guide No.: 107*

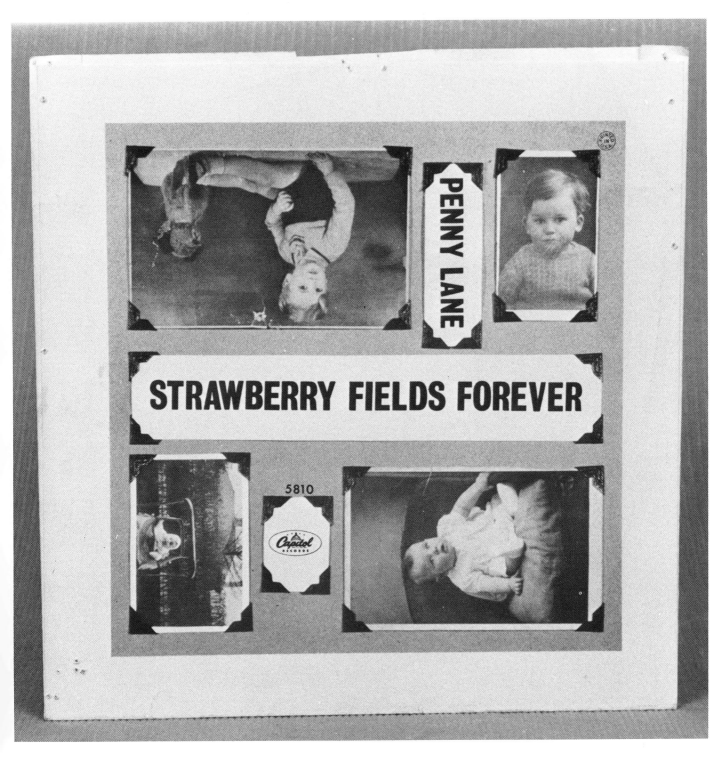

Flip side of the U.S. picture sleeve for *Penny Lane/Strawberry Fields Forever* **(45). Such a sleeve in Near Mint condition would bring $25.** *Price Guide No.: 107*

Label and Record Number	Title	Description	Near Mint	Very Good	Good
108. VJ 498	*PLEASE PLEASE ME/ASK ME WHY* (Beatles unknown in U.S. — February 1963 — sold poorly)	Misspelled on label with two "ts" in name	$115–150		
		Misspelled promo	$300		
109. VJ 581	*PLEASE PLEASE ME/ FROM ME TO YOU*	With picture sleeve	$80–100	$60–65	$50–60
		Record only — oval or brackets label	$6		
110. Capitol 6063	*PLEASE PLEASE ME/ FROM ME TO YOU*	Green Starline	$25		
111. Parlophone R 4983	*PLEASE PLEASE ME/ THANK YOU GIRL*	Rare red label	$100	$75	
112. Capitol 6064	*ROLL OVER BEETHOVEN/ MISERY*	Green Starline	$20–30		
113. Capitol 72133	*ROLL OVER BEETHOVEN/ PLEASE MR. POSTMAN*	Canada release	$15		
114. Swan 4152	*SHE LOVES YOU/I'LL GET YOU*	With picture sleeve	$18–25	$15–18	$10
		Record only	$5		
		Promo	$150		
		Rare blue label	$150		
		Rare white label with red print	$100		
		Counterfeit (white label)	$3		
115. Swan 4182	*SIE LIEBT DICH/I'LL GET YOU*	Red print	$40–50		
		Counterfeit (print is purplish, not red)	$3		
116. Capitol 5255	*SLOW DOWN/MATCHBOX*	With picture sleeve	$25–35	$17–25	$15
117. Atco 6302	*SWEET GEORGIA BROWN*	Promo	$100		
		Record only	$15–25		
118. Polydor NH 52-906	*SWEET GEORGIA BROWN/ NOBODY'S CHILD*	German release	$300+		
119. Polydor 52-324-B	*SWEET GEORGIA BROWN/ SKINNY MINNIE*	With picture sleeve	$200		
		Record only	$50	$20	
120. Capitol 5407	*TICKET TO RIDE/YES IT IS*	With picture sleeve	$25–40	$18–25	$15

The *Sweet Georgia Brown/Skinny Minnie* (Polydor NH 52 324 B) is quite a valuable item, the record alone selling for $50+. With picture sleeve, it is worth perhaps $200 in Near Mint condition. *Price Guide No: 119*

Vee-Jay Records issued this sleeve in 1964 to package their 45s at Christmastime. The value of the sleeve alone is at least $35 in Near Mint condition. *Price Guide No.: 127*

Label and Record Number	Title	Description	Condition		
			Near Mint	Very Good	Good
121. Tollie 9001	*TWIST AND SHOUT/ THERE'S A PLACE*	Record alone: Black label Yellow label	$6 $8	$3 $4	
122. Capitol 6061	*TWIST AND SHOUT/ THERE'S A PLACE*	Green Starline	$20--25		
123. Capitol 5555	*WE CAN WORK IT OUT/ DAY TRIPPER*	With picture sleeve	$15–20	$8–12	
124. Target Starline	*WE CAN WORK IT OUT/ DAY TRIPPER*	Rare — sold poorly	$125		
125. Capitol 5715	*YELLOW SUBMARINE/ ELEANOR RIGBY*	With picture sleeve	$12--17	$10–12	$6–10
126. Capitol 5498	*YESTERDAY/ACT NATURALLY*	With picture sleeve	$13--15	$8--12	$5--8

Other

Label and Record Number	Title	Description	Near Mint	Very Good	Good
127. VJ Christmas sleeve	BEATLES "Wish You a Merry Xmas" limited release with *DO YOU WANT TO KNOW A SECRET* and *PLEASE PLEASE ME*	Record and sleeve (same value sleeve alone)	$30–50	$20--30	
128. Target Labels	Oldies series	Record only — no sleeves issued	$5--10	$4–5	
129. Capitol	Original Orange Swirl Label	Without sleeve, common numbers Hard to find numbers, 5150, 5234, 5235, 5255, 5407	$5 $5--8	$3--5	$1

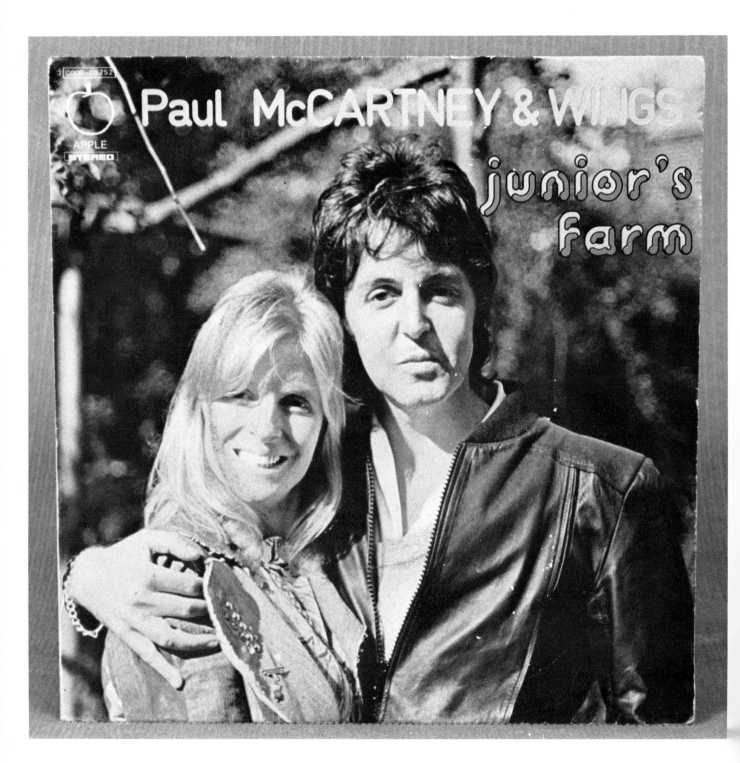

An example of a foreign picture sleeve, in color. The value of sleeves for solo Beatles material is often based on picture quality. This one is worth $5-10 in Near Mint condition. *Price Guide No.: 168*

Label and Record Number	Title	Description	Near Mint	Very Good	Good
130. Apple 1849	*BACK OFF BOOGALOO/ BLINDMAN*	With picture sleeve With blue Apple	$4--8 $10	$3--6	
131. Apple 1836	*BANGLADESH/DEEP BLUE*	With picture sleeve	$5--10	$5	
132. Apple 2969	*BEAUCOUPS OF BLUE/ COOCHY–COOCHY*	With picture sleeve	$20–30	$15–20	$8–10
133. Dark Horse K 17327	*BLOW AWAY/SOFT TOUCH*	With picture sleeve, U.K. With picture sleeve, U.S. (hard to find in some parts of U.S.)	$5 $2--5		
134. Apple 1813	*COLD TURKEY/DON'T WORRY KYOKO*	With picture sleeve Counterfeit (original has black background white skull — boot is reversed)	$80–150 $3	$50--70	$35--50
135. Apple 1877	*DARK HORSE/I DON'T CARE ANYMORE*	With picture sleeve	$25–35		
136. Apple 1879	*DING DONG/HARI'S ON TOUR EXPRESS*	With picture sleeve	$5--7	$3--5	
137.	*FASTER*	Picture disc only, U.K.	$18–30		
138. Columbia 3-11020	*GETTING CLOSER*	With picture sleeve, hot pink title issued with first pressing only	$25–35		
Columbia R-6027	*GETTING CLOSER/ BABY'S REQUEST*	With hard picture sleeve, U.K.	$5		
139. Apple 1847	*GIVE IRELAND BACK TO THE IRISH*/version one and two	With yellow picture sleeve, title and lyrics	$10–15	$6–8	
140. Apple 1809	*GIVE PEACE A CHANCE/ REMEMBER LOVE*	With picture sleeve	$17–25	$13–18	$8
141. Apple 1882	*GOOD NIGHT VIENNA/ OO--WEE*	With picture sleeve	$3--5		
142. Capitol 4274	*GOT TO GET YOU INTO MY LIFE/HELTER SKELTER*	With picture sleeve	$2		

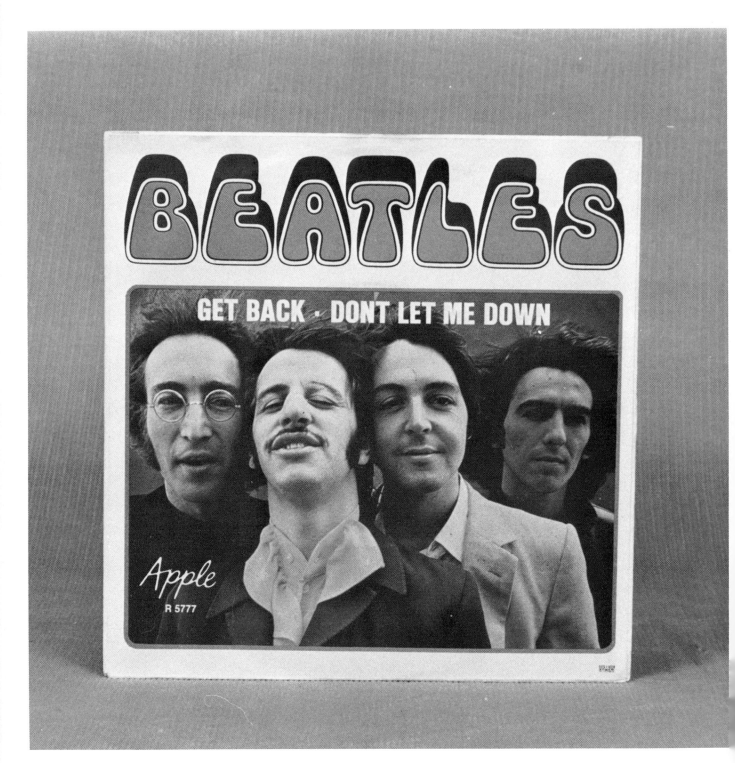

A foreign picture sleeve from the later period of the Beatles' career. This one, in Very Good condition, is valued at **$7-10.** *Price Guide No.: 168*

Label and Record Number	Title	Description	Near Mint	Condition Very Good	Good
143. Apple 1842	*HAPPY XMAS (WAR IS OVER)/LISTEN THE SNOW IS FALLING*	With sleeve on green vinyl	$5–10		
		Reissue Holland EMI	$5		
		Black label with faces, U.K.	$4–7		
144. Apple 1818	*INSTANT KARMA/WHO HAS SEEN THE WIND*	With picture sleeve	$20–25	$10–18	$10
145. Apple 1831	*IT DON'T COME EASY/ EARLY 1970*	With picture sleeve	$10–12	$4–8	$5
146. Capitol 4091	*LISTEN TO WHAT THE MAN SAID/LOVE IN SONG*	With picture sleeve	$3–5		
147. Dark Horse 8844	*LOVE COMES TO EVERY-ONE*	Only 1,000 pressed with picture sleeve	$50–100	$50	
148. Apple 1851	*MARY HAD A LITTLE LAMB/LITTLE WOMAN LOVE*	With picture sleeve, both titles printed	$10–25	$10–18	$10
		With only first title printed — common	$5–8	$5	
149. Apple 1868	*MIND GAMES/MEAT CITY*	With picture sleeve	$3–5		
150. Apple 1827	*MOTHER/WHY?*	With rare picture sleeve	$35–45	$30–35	
151. Capitol 4504 Capitol R6018	*MULL OF KINTYRE/GIRLS SCHOOL*	With picture sleeve	$3–8		
		U.K., with hard picture sleeve	$5		
152. Apple 2995	*MY SWEET LORD/ISN'T IT A PITY*	With picture sleeve	$8–15	$7–12	
153. Capitol 4347	*OB-LA-DI OB-LA-DA/ JULIA*	With picture sleeve	$2		
154. Apple 1876	*ONLY YOU/CALL ME*	With picture sleeve	$3–5		
155. Apple 1865	*PHOTOGRAPH/DOWN AND OUT*	With picture sleeve	$3–5		
156. Apple 1830	*POWER TO THE PEOPLE/ TOUCH ME*	With picture sleeve	$12–17	$10	$5
157. Apple 1881	*STAND BY ME/MOVE OVER MS. L*	No sleeve	$5		

A foreign Beatles picture sleeve, in color, from the later period and valued at approximately $10-18. Earlier and more rare picture sleeves from overseas may go as high as $35-40. *Price Guide No.: 168*

Label and Record Number	Title	Description	Near Mint	Condition Very Good	Good
158. Parlophone R6039	*TEMPORARY SECRETARY/ SECRET FRIEND*	With color jacket, 12 inches	$15--20		
		Black jacket, 12 inches	$8		
159. Dark Horse 8294	*THIS SONG/LEARNING HOW TO LOVE YOU*	With picture sleeve	$6--10		
		Promo sleeve different	$25--35		
160. Capitol 1/335 Parlophone R6037	*WATERFALLS/CHECK MY MACHINE*	With picture sleeve	$5--10	$6	$3
		U.K. hard cover	$5--10	$6	$3
161. Apple 1828	*WHAT IS LIFE?/APPLE SCRUFFS*	With picture sleeve	$7--10	$5--7	$5
162. Apple 1848	*WOMAN IS THE NIGGER OF THE WORLD/ SISTERS O SISTERS*	With picture sleeve	$6--10	$3--6	
163. Capitol Parlophone R 6029	*WONDERFUL CHRISTMAS TIME/RUDOLPH THE RED-NOSED RAGGAE*	With picture sleeve U.K.	$4--5 $4--5		
164. Apple 1884	*YOU/WORLD OF STONE*	With picture sleeve	$7--10	$4--5	
165. Apple 1870	*YOU'RE SIXTEEN/DEVIL WOMAN*	With picture sleeve	$5--8	$3--4	
166. Apple R 5997	*ZOO GANG/BAND ON THE RUN*	U.K. release only, no picture sleeve	$4--5		

Other

167. Apple 45s	Various titles	Record alone — no picture sleeve	$1--3		
		With Apple black sleeve — green print	$3--4		
168. Foreign 45s	Beatles and solo — various titles	With picture sleeve (the older or more colorful, unique the picture on the sleeve, the higher the value. Beatles more valuable than solos.)	$8--30		

A promo disc for THE BEATLES' SECOND ALBUM. This Capitol Compact disc with picture sleeve is more rare than the one for MEET THE BEATLES (which is worth $100+), and is probably valued at over $200. Front and

Label and Record Number	Title	Description	Condition		
			Near Mint	Very Good	Good
169. Capitol EP R 5365	4 x 4	With picture cover Record only	$65--80 $18--20	$40--50	$35--40
170. Capitol EAP 1-2121	**FOUR BY THE BEATLES**	With picture cover Record only Bootleg – Different cover and songs	$75–90 $18–20 $5–8	$50–65	$40--50
171. Parlophone SMMT 1/2	**MAGICAL MYSTERY TOUR**	U.K. — Monophonic with booklet	$16		
172. Capitol SXL 2047	**MEET THE BEATLES**	Jukebox compact with picture cover and title stripes With picture cover Picture cover only Record only	$100--150 $100--125 $50--60 $50--60		
173. Polydor H 21-610	**MY BONNIE**	U.K. (1963)	$50–90		
174. Capitol SXA-2080	**SECOND ALBUM**	Jukebox compact with picture cover and title strips Picture cover (sleeve only) Record only	$95–125 $40--60 $40	$70–75 $30	
175. Capitol SXA 2108	**SOMETHING NEW**	Jukebox compact rarest of all With picture cover and title cards With picture cover Record only	 $225 $175 $60	 $50	
176. VJ 1-903	**SOUVENIR OF THEIR VISIT TO AMERICA**	With original jacket: Oval label Bracket label With "Ask Me Why" in larger letters Record only	 $25--30 $30–35 $40--45 $8		

Other

177. Russian EPs	Various titles and songs	No covers — rare	$28+		

E
P
S

&

C
O
M
P
A
C
T

R
E
C
O
R
D
S

THE BEATLES'
SECOND OPEN-END INTERVIEW

SIDE ONE   PRO 2598   TOTAL TIME 4.45

DJ: Something brand new coming up for you now ...THE BEATLES SECOND ALBUM...AND ...The Beatles THEMSELVES! — John, Paul, George and Ringo.... Welcome back to the (—station—)

DJ: Well JOHN... what's the big SECRET behind the Beatles' PHENOMENAL SUCCESS, anyway?

DJ: (Laugh) George. I understand your latest single "Can't Buy Me Love" is not only a hit HERE, but in OTHER countries as well!

DJ: Gee that's great!

DJ: Well, they're buying up your records in THIS country, THAT'S for sure!

DJ: Say, RINGO... about your Beatle OUTFITS ... How did your Beatle decide on getting THOSE, do you remember?

DJ: I guess a lot of young BRITONS are WEAR-ING this get-up now, aren't they?

DJ: (Laugh) Say, is there a REASON why so many of your songs have "ME" or "YOU" in the title like "Please Please Me"...uh....

DJ: Yeah, well is this sort of a GIMMICK with you, then?

DJ: (Laugh)... or even "BEETHOVEN," like this NEXT one here!
(MUSIC SNEAKS IN B.G.)

DJ: Well, John, Paul, George and Ringo...Thanks very much for being on the show here with me.

DJ: Now, here's the LATEST ...from the brand new BEATLES' SECOND album...the rompin', swingin' "ROLL OVER BEETHOVEN"...The fantastic sound of THE BEATLES!

MUSIC: ROLL OVER BEETHOVEN
(BMI) —
Up to end — T 2080

Capitol

Produced by Jack Wagner

CAPITOL 33 COMPACT
THE BEATLES' SECOND Open-End
33⅓ SIDE 1 PRO 2598 Total Time: 4:45
INTERVIEW
"ROLL OVER BEETHOVEN" (BMI)
From the album "THE BEATLES' SECOND ALBUM" T-2080
Especially prepared for Radio-T.V. programming
Produced by Jack Wagner
MFD. BY CAPITOL RECORDS, INC. U.S.A.
Capitol Records

Label and Record Number	Title	Description	Condition Near Mint	Very Good	Good
178. Apple P-1883	*AIN'T THAT A SHAME*	Monophonic/sterophonic	$70	$50	
179. Warner Bros.	*ALL THOSE YEARS AGO*	Twelve inch	$25--30		
180. Apple KAL004	*APPLE FILMS PRESENTS*	Promo	NPA		
181. Capitol P-B5100	*BEATLES MOVIE MEDLEY*	With interview on B-side	$50+		
182. Capitol	*BAND ON THE RUN* Open end interview	Disc jockey copy with script	$25--50		
		Counterfeit	$12--15		
183. Capitol	*BEATLES OPEN END INTERVIEW* "Meet the Beatles" promo	1964 DJ 7-inch with jacket	$100	$75	
		Counterfeit	$4--5		
184.	*BEWARE MY LOVE/LET 'EM IN*	Twelve inch French disco mix	$20		
185.	*BRUNG TO EWE BY*	Promo for **RAM** with media kit, letter, open end interview	$40--60		
		Counterfeit	$8--10		
186. Columbia	*COMING UP*	Twelve inch white label, rare limited edition	$60--70		
187. Dark Horse PRO-649	*DARK HORSE 33 1/3* Interview LP	Dj promo	$30--50		
188. ABKCO 1970	*DIALOGUE FROM* **LET IT BE**	One sided test pressing — May 1970	$15--25		
		Bootleg	$4		
189. Atlantic DSKO 93	*DROWNING IN THE SEA OF LOVE*	Twelve inch disco single	$15--20		
190. Napra	*GET OFF*	Ringo and others, anti-drug messages	$25+		

Label and Record Number	Title	Description	Condition		
			Near Mint	Very Good	Good
191. Capitol P-4506	*GIRL*	Monophonic/stereophonic disc jockey copy for single that was never released with picture sleeve	$65--85		
		Picture sleeve only, common	$5--10		
192. Columbia 23-10940	*GOODNIGHT TONIGHT/ DAYTIME NIGHTTIME SUFFERING*	Twelve inch short and long versions with full picture cover	$10--12		
		First version with white cover	$2--6		
		Promo kit with 45, photos, postcard, special cover	$25--50		
193. Capitol	*GREATEST MUSIC EVER SOLD*	Three Beatles songs, one John, one Ringo	$12--25		
194. Capitol P-2720	*HELTER SKELTER*	Monophonic/stereophonic dj copy — was originally slated as A side	$15--20		
195.	*IBBB INTERVIEW* by Tom Clay	1964--65 45s	$50		
196. Cotillion 105 Atlantic PR 104	*JOHN LENNON ON RONNIE HAWKINS*	Promo	$25--30		
		Test pressing	$40		
		Long and short raps	$25		$12
197. Capitol	*KFWB INTERVIEW*	Promo	$60	$40--50	
		Counterfeit	$4		
198.	*KNUZ RADIO INTERVIEW*	1964 seven inch souvenir record	$60	$40--50	
199. Apple	*KYA PEACE TALK*	1969 interview with John Lennon	$85	$35--50	
		Counterfeit copy	$3--4		
200. Warner Bros.	*LIFE OF BRIAN* Promo	George and others interviewed	$20+		
201. Capitol	*MAYBE I'M AMAZED*	Twelve inch	$30--50		

Label and Record Number	Title	Description	Condition Near Mint	Very Good	Good
202. Columbia	*McCARTNEY INTERVIEW*	Dialogue promo originally to dj's with 2 LPs	$50--65		
		Reissue with 1 LP	$5--10		
		Counterfeit with 2 LPs	$10--15		
203. Fairway Records	*MURRAY THE K AS IT HAPPENED*	1965 seven-inch with picture sleeve	$50--100		
		Original single without picture sleeve	$25--30		
		Legitimate reissue with new sleeve, 1979	$5		
		Bootleg 45	$2		
204. Decca	*MY BONNIE*	Rare pink promo	$250+		
205. Capitol P-5810	*PENNY LANE*	With horn ending which only dj copies had	$60--100	$40--50	
206. Apple SWAL 3413	*RINGO*	With long version of *Six O'Clock*	$45--50		
207. Epic 8-50403	*SEASIDE WOMAN*	Twelve-inch red vinyl	$20--25		
208. Epic	*SEASIDE WOMAN* Boxed set U.K.	Seven-inch yellow vinyl boxed with frisbee, postcards, badge	$25--40		
209. A&M SP 7548	*SEASIDE WOMAN*	Twelve-inch regular vinyl — U.K. — color picture sleeve	$8		
210. Apple P-1883	*SLIPPIN & SLIDIN*	Monophonic/stereophonic promo never commercially released	$60--70	$50	
211. Disc & Music Echo	*SOUND OF THE STARS* Interview with the Beatles	Flexi-disc	$75+		
212. Geffen PRO A 919	*(JUST LIKE) STARTING OVER*	Twelve-inch	$35--50	$50	
213. Geffen 49-604	*(JUST LIKE) STARTING OVER*	Seven-inch promo with picture sleeve	$10--15		

A promo album from United Artists to promote the film "Help!" Rarely seen, it is valued at $200+. *Price Guide No.: 218*

The Wall's Ice Cream promo EP from Apple Records, featuring the Beatles' "first four" on their new record label (1968). Valued at $200. *Price Guide No.: 222*

Label and Record Number	Title	Description	Near Mint	Very Good	Good
214. Parlophone R6039	*TEMPORARY SECRETARY*	One-sided promo	$40–50		
215.	*THIS SONG – THE STORY BEHIND*	Promo with picture sleeve with details on how song came to be – for dj's	$25–35	$20–25	
216. Apple	*UNA SENSAZIONALE INTERVISTA DIE BEATLES* (Italy) With Kenny Evertt	With picture sleeve With Apple four record set Also known as Kenny Evertt interview – counterfeit copy	$30–50 $200+ $3–4		
217. United Artists	*UNITED ARTISTS PRESENTS A HARD DAY'S NIGHT*	Red label plain sleeve – interview and songs	$250		
218. United Artists	*UNITED ARTISTS PRESENTS HELP*	Red label plain sleeve – interview and songs	$250		
219.	*VANCOUVER BEATLES PRESS CONFERENCE*	Rare interview, seven-inch (1964)	$100		
220. Geffen	*WALKING ON THIN ICE*	Twelve-inch with long version – rare U.S.	$25–30		
221. Geffen 49683	*WALKING ON THIN ICE*	Seven-inch with lyrics	$10–12		
222. Apple CT-1	*WALLS ICE CREAM* Promo, various artists	EP July 1969 special promo re-lease for Walls Ice Cream Co. in U.K. only (boxed set)	$200+		
223. MA 1137	*WHAT'S IT ALL ABOUT* Beatles part 1		$35		
224. Tiger Radio 560	*WQAM – MIAMI*	1964 seven-inch radio interview Counterfeit	$70 $3–4		

White Label Singles

Label and Record Number	Title	Description	Near Mint	Very Good	Good
225. Parlophone R 5160	*A HARD DAY'S NIGHT/ THINGS WE SAID TODAY*	White label promo	$175+		
226. Atco 33-169	*AIN'T SHE SWEET*		$100+		

Label and Record Number	Title	Description	Condition Near Mint	Very Good	Good
227. VJ 587	DO YOU WANT TO KNOW A SECRET/THANK YOU GIRL	Blue and white label with brackets	$50+		
228. Parlophone R 5084	I WANT TO HOLD YOUR HAND	White label promo	$200+		
229. Tollie 9008	LOVE ME DO/P.S. I LOVE YOU	White label promo	$50--70		
230. VJ 903	MISERY/TASTE OF HONEY	With blue script, dj	$60		
231. VJ 498	PLEASE PLEASE ME	White label promo with blue script	$75--100		
232. VJ 522	THANK YOU GIRL	White label promo	$70		
233. Parlophone R 5015	THANK YOU GIRL/ FROM ME TO YOU	White label promo	$275+		
234. Parlophone	Other Beatles singles with white label promos		$175--185+		

Beatle Promo 45s

Label and Record Number	Title	Description	Condition Near Mint	Very Good	Good
235. Capitol P 5964	ALL YOU NEED IS LOVE/ BABY YOU'RE A RICH MAN	Promo copy with rare trumpet ending	$45--70		
236. Capitol P 5150	CAN'T BUY ME LOVE	One-sided stereophonic	$75		
237. Capitol P 2056	HELLO GOODBYE	Promo		$40	
238. Swan	I'LL GET YOU	One-sided promo with white label	$90--150		
239. Capitol P 2138	LADY MADONNA	Promo	$40--50		
240. Swan 4182	SIE LIEBT DICH/I'LL GET YOU	First pressing white label with "Don't Drop Out"	$40--50		
		Without "Don't Drop Out"	$100		
241. MGM 13227	WHY/CRY FOR A SHADOW	Promo copy — rare	$75--100	$50--65	$35--45
242. Various	Other titles	Promos	$50--75	$40--50	

Solo Promo 45s

243. Apple 1829	*ANOTHER DAY*	Promo	$25	
244. Apple 1849	*BACK OFF BOOGALOO*	Blue Apple with picture sleeve	$15	
		Promo – U.K.	$8	
245. Apple/20th Cent./Fox	*BANGLADESH*	One-sided	$100	
Apple 1836		Monophonic/ stereophonic	$35	
246. Dark Horse 8763	*BLOW AWAY*	Monophonic/ stereophonic promo	$8--10	
247. Apple P-1877	*DARK HORSE*	Monophonic/ stereophonic promo	$12–15	
248. Apple 1879	*DING DONG*	Monophonic/ stereophonic promo	$10–15	
249. Apple 1862	*GIVE ME LOVE*	Monophonic/ stereophonic promo	$10	
250. Apple 1882	*GOODNIGHT VIENNA*	Monophonic/ stereophonic promo	$10--15	
251. Capitol P 4274	*GOT TO GET YOU INTO MY LIFE/HELTER SKELTER*	Promo copy	$15	
252. Apple 1842	*HAPPY XMAS*	Promo copy	$30	
253. Apple 1869	*HELEN WHEELS*	Monophonic/ stereophonic	$15	
254. Apple 1818	*INSTANT KARMA*	One-sided promo	$30	
		Monophonic/ stereophonic with picture sleeve	$12–15	
255.	*I'VE HAD ENOUGH*	Monophonic/ stereophonic	$12	
256. Capitol P4293	*LET 'EM IN*	Monophonic/ stereophonic	$10	

120

PROMO RECORDS

Label and Record Number	Title	Description	Condition Near Mint	Very Good	Good
257. Capitol 4625	*LONDON TOWN*	Monophonic/ stereophonic	$8		
258. Dark Horse 8844	*LOVE COMES TO EVERYONE*	Monophonic/ stereophonic	$8		
259. Apple 1851	*MARY HAD A LITTLE LAMB*	Promo	$25		
260. Apple 1868	*MIND GAMES*	Monophonic/ stereophonic	$12–20		
261. Capitol SPRO 8747	*MULL OF KINTYRE*	Promo	$8		
262. Apple 1861	*MY LOVE*	Monophonic/ stereophonic	$25		
263. Apple 2995	*MY SWEET LORD*	Monophonic/ stereophonic	$10		
264. Apple 1880	*NO NO SONG*	Monophonic/ stereophonic	$10		
265. Apple 1853	*NOW OR NEVER* John Lennon produced for Yoko	With picture sleeve	$15	$13	
266. Apple 1876	*ONLY YOU*	Monophonic/ stereophonic	$10		
267. Apple P1882	*OO-WEE*	Monophonic/ stereophonic	$10		
268. Capitol P4256	*SILLY LOVE SONGS*	Monophonic/ stereophonic	$10	$8	
269. Apple 1885	*THIS GUITAR (CAN'T KEEP FROM CRYING)*	Monophonic/ stereophonic	$15		
270. Dark Horse Apple 1877	*THIS SONG*	Promo with promo sleeve	$25–30		
271. Apple 1837	*UNCLE ALBERT/ ADMIRAL HALSEY*	Monophonic/ stereophonic	$25		
272. Geffen 49644	*WOMAN/BEAUTIFUL BOYS*	Promo copy	$10		
273. Apple 1884	*YOU*	Monophonic/ stereophonic	$10		
274. Apple 1870	*YOU'RE SIXTEEN*	Monophonic/ stereophonic	$10		

P R O M O   R E C O R D S

Label and Record Number	Title	Description	Condition		
			Near Mint	Very Good	Good
275. Atlantic	Ringo's singles: *HEY BABY, DROWNING IN A SEA OF LOVE, A DOSE OF RnR, LIPSTICK TRACES*, etc.	Promo copies	$5--7 ea.		

Other Promo LPs, Acetates & Test Pressings

276.	*ELECTRONIC SOUND*	Promo	$150		
277. London MS 82007	*FAMILY WAY*	U.S. monophonic promo	$80--100		
278. Capitol 11642	*THRILLINGTON*	Very rare promo	$100+		
279. Various	Test pressings: One sided demo pressings	Seven-inch Beatles and early 1970s (usual price) Mid and late 1970s	$20–30 $15--20		
280.	Test pressings	Twelve-inch LPs (usual price) Later 1970s	$25–40 $20		
	WINGS OVER AMERICA	Test pressing	$100		
	HOLLYWOOD BOWL	Test pressing	$75		
	WHATEVER GETS YOU THROUGH THE NIGHT	Test pressing	$25--50		
281. Various	Acetates – Metal				
	AT THE SPEED OF SOUND	Test acetate	$150		
	SHE LOVES YOU	Test acetate	$80		
	COMING UP	Test acetate	$150		
282.	Pocket Discs: *HEY JUDE*	Rare three minute, three-inch disc made by Capitol--U.S. on a black Apple with white print	$75–100		
283.	*GET BACK*	Rare three minute, three-inch disc made by Capitol--U.S. on a black Apple with white print	$75–100		

PROMO RECORDS

Label and Record Number	Title	Description	Condition		
			Near Mint	Very Good	Good

Group Bootlegs

284. Walrus **ALIVE AT LAST IN** $7--14
     TVC 1001 **ATLANTA**
     CBM 1001 **LIVE AT THE ATLANTA** On blue wax $30
     or TMQ **WHISKEY FLAT**
     OPD 67-2/ Really Hollywood Bowl or
     70418F Philadelphia 1964 show
     etc.

285. RUT 546 **ALL YOU NEED IS CASH** Rutles TV sound- $50
     track, first pressing

286. Audio **ALPHA OMEGA VOL. 1 & 2** Sold on TV $25--30 ea.
     Tape **Boxed sets of four LPs each**
     ATRBH
     3583 and
     ATRB 4

287. Napoleon **AND THE BEATLES WERE** Sometimes listed $16
     11044 **BORN** as Italian import
     (From Hollywood Bowl)

288. CBM **AS SWEET AS YOU ARE** $12--15
     3316 (Also known as **DON'T PASS**
     ME BY YELLOW MATTER
     CUSTARD)

289. TMOQ **AT THE HOLLYWOOD** Regular issue $10--12
     S-208 **BOWL** Various vinyl $25
     (Also called **BACK IN '64** colors
     AT THE HOLLYWOOD
     BOWL, etc.)

290. Zakatecas **BEATLEMANIA 1963--69** European import $40
     ST 57 **TWENTY NEVER PUB-** color cover
     633 XU **LISHED SONGS**

291. Joker-Saar **BEATLES AND ROLLING** Two record set $12--18
     SM 3591 **STONES**
     (Beatles/Stones live)

292. Idle Mind **BEATLES AT SHEA** $15--20
     1180 **STADIUM (SHEA AT LAST)**
     CBM **SHEA, GOOD OLD DAYS** Color cover $20--30

293. Tobe Milo **BEATLES GET TOGETHER** Ten-inch EP
     401--2 500 on yellow $15--25
     500 on black $15

294. PRO **BEATLES BY ROYAL** With picture sleeve $6--8
     1108 **COMMAND** EP on color vinyl

Label and Record Number	Title	Description	Condition		
			Near Mint	Very Good	Good
295. Capitol SPRO 9462	BEATLES COLLECTORS ITEMS	Looks like regular Capitol release, first pressing	$25--35		
Capitol SPRO 9463		Second pressing (color faded, *Paperback Writer* replaces *I'm Down)*	$15--25		
296. Tobe Milo 4Q 11/12	BEATLES STUDIO OUT-TAKES	Ten-inch EP	$15--20		
297. Original Rock 1003	BEATLES VS CARL PERKENS		$40		
298. Tobe Milo 10Q 1/2	BEST OF TOBE MILO	Ten-inch EP	$20		
299. "Capitol" SEAX 11950	CASUALTIES	Picture disc w/butcher cover	$30		
300. CBM 3906	CAVERN CLUB		$30		
301. CBM 211	CINELOGUE: LET IT BE	From soundtrack	$25		
Wizardo	CINELOGUE: A HARD DAY'S NIGHT	From soundtrack	$25		
King Kong 634	CINELOGUE: MAGICAL MYSTERY TOUR	Two LPs	$15		
302. Berkeley 102	DECCA AUDITION TAPES	From BBC radio show November 1962	$12		
303. Circuit LK 4438	DECCA TAPES	Picture disc	$25--40		
304. Circuit	DECCA TAPES	With picture jacket	$8--10		
305. Deccagone PRO 110 A/B--1107	Eight different titles	45s with picture sleeve, color vinyl	$4--6 ea.		
306. TAKRL 1374	EMI OUTTAKES		$8		
307. TMOQ 2	FAB RAVER SHOW		$8--12		
308. De Wintraub 426	FIVE NIGHTS IN A JUDO ARENA	With color jacket	$12--15		
309. Ruthless Rhymes LMW-281F	FROM US TO YOU, A PARLOPHONE REHEARSAL SESSION	Ten-inch, various color vinyls	$15		
		Reissue, regular vinyl	$7--8		

Label and Record Number	Title	Description	Condition		
			Near Mint	Very Good	Good
310. TMOQ BGB 111 TMOQ 71024, etc.	GET BACK SESSIONS	From **Let It Be** outtakes On green vinyl	$12 $25		
311. BC Records V36766 or CBM 209	GET BACK TO TORONTO		$12		
312. Phoenix 44784	HAHST AZ SON	Two LPs, color cover	$15--20		
313. CBM WEC 3624	HAVE YOU HEARD THE WORD	With picture jacket	$25		
314. Beat 1 or Idle Mind 1162	INDIAN ROPE TRICK		$10--12		
315. CBM 15 or KB 10	KUM BACK	Very early bootleg plain white sleeve	$15+		
316. Image Disc 2043/526	LIVE AT JUDO ARENA	In picture disc — limited	$25--35		
317. Instant Analysis 1034	LIVE IN MELBOURNE, AUSTRALIA 7/16/64		$16		
318. CBM 3794	LIVE IN WASHINGTON D.C.		$14		
319. CBM 1005	L.S. BUMBLEBEE		$20		
320. CBM 3585	NEVER RELEASED MARY JANE		$20		
321. NW 8 AR8-69	NO. 3 ABBEY ROAD	With color jacket	$8--15		
322. GRC 1000	ORIGINAL GREATEST HITS	One of earliest bootlegs with laminated cover — 1967 — TV offer	$50--65+		
323. Berkeley 2009	PEACE OF MIND		$8--10		
324. Various	RENAISSANCE MINSTRELS VOL. I--IV		$15--25		
325. SOK Prod.	*REVOLUTION/HOW DO YOU DO IT*	45 with sleeve, color vinyl	$4--5		

Label and Record Number	Title	Description	Condition Near Mint	Very Good	Good
326. VeeJay EP1-903	*SOUVENIR OF THEIR VISIT TO AMERICA*	Picture disc, seven-inch	$15+		
327. New Sound NR 909-1	**SWEET APPLE TRAX**	Two LPs with black-and-white picture sleeve	$12–15		
328. Wizardo 343	**SWEET APPLE TRAX**	Two LPs with black-and-white picture, two volume set, 1969 picture	$15–25 ea.		
329. Image Disc 909 1A/B	**SWEET APPLE TRAX**	Limited pressing, picture disc	$25–45		
330. TWK 0169A 1YHO-10	**SWEET APPLE TRAX** (Re-released as **BLACK ALBUM**)	1981 with poster, two LPs	$20–30		
331. Idle Mind 1176 Ruthless Rhymes	**20 x 4**		$15–20		
332. Melvin Records MM02	**21 (BEATLES)**		$8		
333. Pro 909	**TWICKINHAM JAM**	EP w/picture sleeve on green vinyl	$10–16		
334. Audifon L-7	**WATCHING RAINBOWS**	Color cover Monochrome cover, EP on color vinyl	$15–25 $7–10		
335. CBM 2 C1/101 TMOQ 513	**YELLOW MATTER CUSTARD** (Same **AS SWEET AS YOU ARE**)		$10–12		
336. Audifon BVP 005	**YOUNGBLOOD**		$12–16		
337. Tollie ep 18901	**TOLLIE EP:** *Love Me Do, Twist & Shout, There's a Place, P.S. I Love You*	Only 15 pressed, rare boot	$15–150*		
338. VJ 103-4	**VJ EP**	Limited pressing	$15–150*		

---

*No legitimate Tollie or VJ EPs were ever made — these bootlegs were a joke and only a few were made.

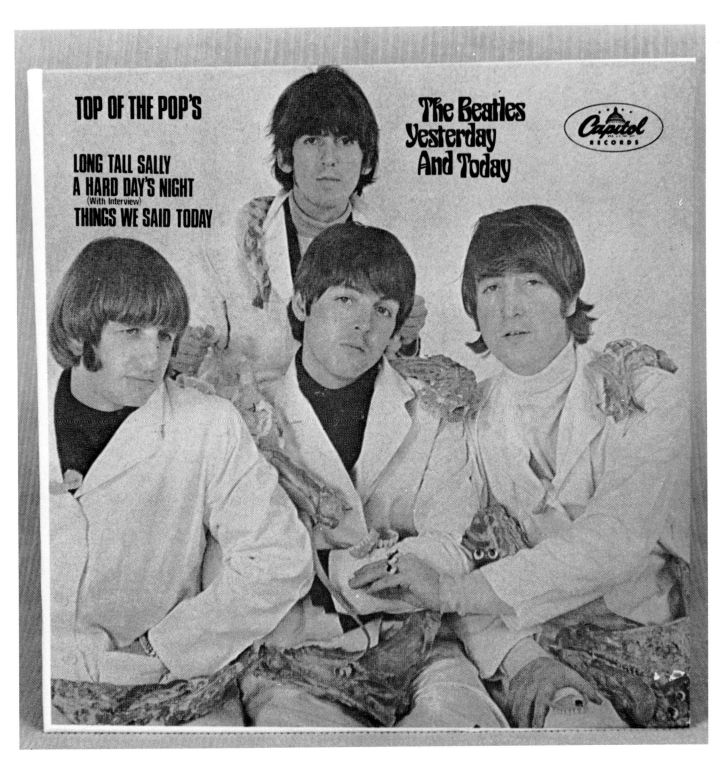

This bootleg EP features an outtake photo from the Butcher Cover session. Currently out-of-print, it is valued at about $15. *Price Guide No.: 339*

339. Various	Various titles	Bootlegs, plain white covers or inserts	$6--10		
		Color covers — out of print	$12--15		

Solo Bootlegs

340. Audifon R 6015	**A GUITAR'S ALRIGHT JOHN . . . .**	Ten-inch color vinyl LPs (picture jacket).	$15--20		
		Reissue on regular vinyl.	$7--8		
341. BB J 1 A/B	**BRITISH BLUES JAM** John Lennon and Rolling Stones		$20		
342. Berkeley 46 Wunderland W 49000	**(WINGS) FLY SOUTH** (Australia, 1975)	Two LPs, laminated cover	$12--16		
343. Wizardo 380	**FLY SOUTH**	Blue and multi-color with insert — rare	$40		
344. TMOQ	**GREAT DANE** (Wings European tour)	Two LPs	$10--12		
345. TK BWM 1803	**JOSHUA TREE TAPES** (John Lennon)	Rare	$15--20		
346. Tobe Milo 4Q13/14	**LIFE WITH LENNONS**	Ten-inch EP — numbered copies	$20--30		
347. PRO 1234 A/B	**NASHVILLE DIARY**	EP with picture sleeve	$6--10		
348. HAR 169	**ORIENTAL NIGHTFISH**	Two LPs on marble vinyl	$16		
349. Unknown	**VANCOUVER '74** (George Harrison live)		$16		
350. Idle Mind Prod. 1117- 1119	**WINGS FROM THE WINGS** (LA Forum 1976)	Boxed set of 3 LPs on color vinyl, red, white, blue	$30--35		
351. WOW 1616	**WINGS OVER THE WORLD**	Two LPs from TV	$25--50		
352. Wizardo 505	**WINGS (76 TOUR)** Various cities	With insert, 3 LPs	$30		

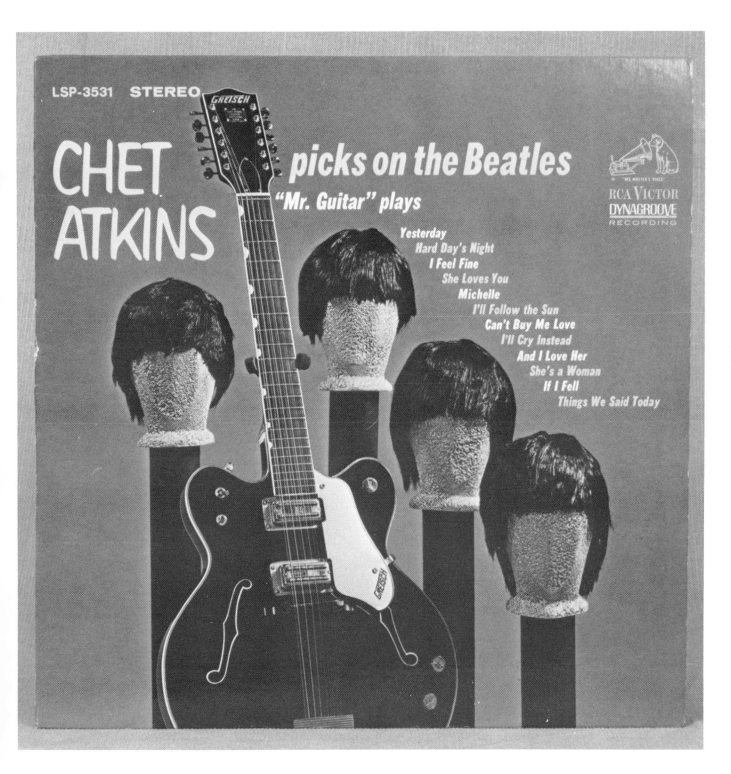

This Beatles-related LP — hundreds of artists have done "cover versions" of Beatles material — rates special interest because of the novel jacket design and Atkins' friendship with the Beatles. The LP is worth about $8, the more rare jukebox EP with jacket about $10. *Price Guide No.: 354*

Another interesting example of a Beatles novelty record. The LP version is worth approximately $15-18 in Mint condition. The jukebox EP with jacket would bring $8-10. *Price Guide No.: 361*

Label and Record Number	Title	Description	Condition		
			Near Mint	Very Good	Good
353. Decca F11916	APPLE JACKS *Like Dreamers Do*	45 — U.K. Lennon/ McCartney compo- sition	$5		
354. RCA LSP 3531	ATKINS, CHET **Picks on The Beatles**	LP 1966 EP — 6 songs for jukebox with title card	$6--8 $6--8		
355. Marma- lade 598-005	BARBER, CHRIS *Catcall*	Written by Paul McCartney	$30		
356. Savage 71	BEST, PETE **Best of The Beatles**	LP	$6--12		
357. Cameo 391	BEST, PETE *Kansas City/Boys*	Single	$8		
358. BW 726	BLACK, CILLA *Step Inside Love*	45 — written by Paul McCartney — U.K.	$3--5		
359. Apple 1800	BLACK DYKE MILLS BAND *Thingumybob*	45 — Produced by McCartney	$20–30		
360. Recar 2012	CALDWELL, LOUISE HARRISON **All about The Beatles**		$30–40		
361. Liberty 3388	CHIPMUNKS **Chipmunks Sing The Beatles**	EP for jukebox with picture jacket	$8--10		
362. Liberty 55134	CHIPMUNKS *All My Loving/Do You Want To Know A Secret*		$5--8		
363. Capitol 3928	CHRISTIE, JOHN *4th of July*	With picture sleeve written by Paul McCartney	$8--10		
364. EMI 3977	COUNTRY HAMS *Walking In The Park With Eloise/Bridge On The River Suite* (really McCartney and friends) *Price before reissued in Holland in 1981 — current price may be less because of quantity of current issue.	Written by James McCartney, original release with picture sleeve EMI Holland reissue Seven-inch picture disc	$50–75 $5 $7–15		

Beatles' producer George Martin put out four albums of instrumental Beatles hits. This one, in Mint condition, might be worth $10-15. Similar to the LP listed under *Price Guide No.: 375c (Appendix III)*

Label and Record Number	Title	Description	Condition Near Mint	Very Good	Good

365. Parlophone FOURMOST   45s written by
     R5078   *I'm In Love*   Lennon $5
     R5056   *Hello Little Girl*   and McCartney $5

366. Ringo   HENTSCHEL, DAVID   Ringo instrumental $13--20
     Records **Startling Music**
     11372

367. Capitol HOLLYRIDGE STRINGS   Five instrumental $6--8 ea.
     2116   **The Beatles Songbook** LPs
     2202   **The Beatles Songbook Vol. 2**
     2429   **The New Beatles Songbook**
     2656   **The Beatles Songbook Vol. 4**
     2876   **The Hollyridge Strings Play**
              Magical Mystery Tour

368. Apple   HOPKIN, MARY   U.K. 45 with rare $15
     34   *Let My Name Be Sorrow* picture sleeve

369. Apple   IVEYS   Rare Italian version $150
     90150   *Maybe Tomorrow*   with picture sleeve
                                   Holland version $25

370. Scratch LAINE, DENNY   U.K. 45 w/picture $2--4
     HS401   *Japanese Tears*   sleeve
     Scratch   U.K. LP $12--15
     SCRL   **Japanese Tears**
     5001

371. Atlantic LEE, PEGGY   45 written by Paul $3--4
     3215   *Let's Love*   McCartney

372. Jerden   LENNON, FREDDIE   45 by John $25--50
     792   *That's My Life*   Lennon's father

373. Apple 23 LOMAX, JACKIE
              How The Web Was Woven U.K. single $15
     Apple 1819 **How The Web Was Woven** U.S. w/picture $8
                                   sleeve

374. Apple   LOMAX, JACKIE   U.S. with picture $8
     1802   *Sour Milk Sea*   sleeve

375. United   MARTIN, GEORGE   45 – U.K. $20--30
     Artists (Orchestra)
     UP 1165 *Love In The Open Air/*
     UA 50148 *Theme From Family Way* 45 – U.S. $20--30
     Dunhill By the BRASS RING $5
     Decca   By TUDOR MINSTRELS   U.K. $10--15
     F12536

376. Warner   McGEAR, MIKE   Special numbered $60--100+
     Bros. BS **McGear (LP)**   pressing (500, signed)
     2825 (U.S.)   Rare U.K. version – NPA
     K56051   opens
     (U.K.)   Regular U.S. version $5--7

From the movie "Son of Dracula," this Beatles-related Nilsson picture sleeve features Ringo Starr (seated). In Near Mint condition, its value is approximately $5-8. *Price Guide No.: 381*

Label and Record Number	Title	Description	Condition Near Mint	Very Good	Good
377. Carrere 144	McGEAR, MIKE *All The Whales In The Ocean*	Rare U.K. 45, very limited distribution	$20+		
378. Warner Bros.	McGEAR, MIKE *Leave It/Sweet Baby*	With picture sleeve, U.K. — flip written by Paul McCartney	$5--7		
379. Parlophone PCS 7047	McGOUGH–McGEAR	U.K. LP, rare 1968 produced by Paul McCartney	$100+		
380. Parlophone PM 144	MENDES, CARLOS *Penina*	Original from Portugal	$16		
		Reissue	$4		
381. RCA APBO 0246	NILSSON, HARRY *Daybreak*	With picture sleeve showing Ringo	$5--8		
382. Rapple AL1-0220	NILSSON, HARRY **Son Of Dracula**	LP with Ringo on cover	$12		
383. RCA 9298	NILSSON, HARRY *You Can't Do That*	Beatles song titles in lyrics	$7--10		
384. Apple SW3391	PEEL, DAVID **The Pope Smokes Dope**	Produced by John Lennon	$10–15		
385. Capitol 5175	PETER & GORDON *A World Without Love*	Written by Lennon/ McCartney	$5		
		With picture sleeve	$8		
386. Capitol 5579	PETER & GORDON *Woman*	Written by Paul McCartney under alias Bernard Webb and A. Smith	$5		
		With picture sleeve	$5–8		
387. Liberty 55806	PROBY, P.J. *That Means Alot*	Written by Lennon/ McCartney	$10--12		
388. Apple 15	RADHA KRISHNA TEMPLE *Hare Krishna Mantra*	With picture sleeve	$10		
389. Apple	RADHA KRISHNA TEMPLE **Hare Krishna Mantra**	LP	$30		
390. Electra 7306	RIFKIN, JOSHUA **Baroque Beatles Book**	1965	$8--12		
391. Warner Bros E723	RUTLES	Twelve-inch four-song promo on yellow vinyl	$10–15		
392. Capitol 5580	SELLERS, PETER *A Hard Day's Night/Help*	Comedy 45 Reissue 1981 U.K.	$8--12 $3		

Label and Record Number	Title	Description	Near Mint	Very Good	Good
393. Dark Horse 22002	SHANKAR FAMILY & FRIENDS With George Harrison	Promo	$10		
394. Polydor 52025	SHERIDAN, TONY *Ruby Baby/What I'd Say*	Original German release — rare	$250		
395. Fontana TF 603 (U.K.) 1525 (U.S.)	SILKIE, THE *You've Got To Hide Your Love Away*	Written and produced by Lennon/McCartney	$10–15		
396. Apple 3369	TAVENER, JOHN **The Whale**		$15		
397. Apple 3	TAYLOR, JAMES **James Taylor**	LP	$15		
398. Capitol ST 11642	THRILLINGTON, PERCY **Ram** instrumental	Promo, white label with different cover	$25		
399. EMI	THRILLINGTON, PERCY *Eat At Home/Uncle Albert*	U.K. 45	$25		
400. 20th Century Records TFM 3178	WELLS, MARY **Love Songs To The Beatles**		$15		
401. Apple 3412 3380 3373 3399	YOKO ONO **Feeling The Space** **Fly** **Plastic Ono Band** **Approximately Infinite Universe**	LPs	$6–10 $5–10 $5 $5–7		

Other

Label and Record Number	Title	Description	Near Mint	Very Good	Good
402. RSO 2394–141	ORIGINAL CAST **John, Paul, George, Ringo . . . and Bert**	1974 U.K. LP	$12–18		
403. Various	Lennon/McCartney compositions recorded by other artists, i.e., Billy J. Kramer, *Do You Want To Know A Secret*; Arthur Fiedler, *I Want To Hold Your Hand.*	45s	$3–6		
404. Various artists	**BEATLES TRIBUTE ALBUM**	Plain white cover	$12–15		
405. Audio Journal 1	BEATLES' BLAST IN STADIUM DESCRIBED BY ERUPTING FANS	Audio report 1965 — fan interview Remake — bootleg	$15–20 $10–12		

Label and Record Number	Title	Description	Condition		
			Near Mint	Very Good	Good

Novelties

Label and Record Number	Title	Description	Near Mint	Very Good	Good
406. Various	Beatles-related novelties and break-ins, nearly 400 different titles without picture sleeves. A few exceptions are listed below.	Most common price: LPs 45s	$5--7 $3--5		
407. MGM 14097	*BALLAD OF PAUL* by Mystery Tour	1969 (Death clues) promo Regular version	$25 $7		
408. Diamond 160	*BEATLE FLYING SAUCER* by Ed Solomon	Break-in	$12		
409. Beetle 1600	*BEATLEMANIA* by Prof. Bugg	Break-in	$9		
410. Cameo 302	*BOY WITH THE BEATLE HAIR* by The Swans		$12		
411. Tuff 378	*I UNDERSTAND THEM* by The Pattycakes		$12–15		
412. American Artists 20	*INTERVIEW WITH THE FAB FOUR* by Harv Moore	Break-in dj copy Regular version	$25 $10–15		
413. Novel 711	*INVASION* by Buchanan & Greenfield	Break-in	$12–20		
414. Warner Bros. 5475	*LETTER FROM ELAINA* by Casey Kasem		$5--7		
415. Smash 1885	*LITTLE BEATLE BOY* by The Angles	With picture sleeve	$10–12		
416. Capitol 5127	*MY BOYFRIEND GOT A BEATLE HAIRCUT* by Donna Lynn		$15		
417. Liberty 55680	*PEPPERMINT BEATLE* by The Standells		$15		
418. Annette 1000	*RINGO, I LOVE YOU* by Bonnie Jo Mason (Cher)		$12		
419. Capitol 2506	*SAINT PAUL* by Terry Knight (of Grand Funk Railroad)	1969	$5--7		

Label and Record Number	Title	Description	Condition		
			Near Mint	Very Good	Good
420. Foto-Fi 107	*STAND UP AND HOLLER* by FotoFi Four	Co-written by Nilsson, very rare to radio stations only	$25		
421. Challenge 59234	*WE LOVE THE BEATLES* by Vernon Girls	1964	$7		
422. London Int'l 10614	*WE LOVE YOU, BEATLES* by The Carefrees	With picture sleeve	$10–15		

Publisher	Year	Title	Description	Condition Near Mint	Very Good
423. Dell	1964	*A HARD DAY'S NIGHT* by John Burke	Paperback original edition	$10--15	$5--10
			Reissued by Melita Music, British cover	$5--6	
424. Chelsea House	1977	*A HARD DAY'S NIGHT* by Philip DiFranco (Frame by frame study)	Softbound	$5--10	
			Remainders table	$2	
425. Simon & Schuster	1965	*A SPANIARD IN THE WORKS*	First edition, original hardcover (earliest printing most valuable)	$30–35	$25--30
426. McFadden--Bartell	1964	*ALL ABOUT THE BEATLES* by Edward de Blasio	Paperback	$7–10	$5--7
427. Straight Arrow	1973	*AS TIME GOES BY* by Derek Taylor	U.S. hardcover	$10	
			U.K. hardcover (different)	$12--15	
			U.K. paperback	$8--10	
428. Mander	1978 1981	*BEATLE MADNESS* by Martin Grove	Paperback	$3	
			Reissue	Store price	
429. Signet	1968	*BEATLES, THE* by Anthony Scaduto	Paperback	$10--12	$8--10
430. Hutchinson & London	1964	*BEATLES, THE* by Norman Parkinson (photos) and Maureen Cleve (text)	Original softbound	$10	
			Large format with dust jacket, U.K.	$15	
			Reprinted by Melita Music U.K.	$5	
431. Christian Crusade	1969, 1971	*BEATLES, THE: A STUDY OF SEX, DRUGS & REVOLUTION* by Rev. David Noebel	Oversized paperback	NPA	
432. Cowles	1968	*BEATLES BOOK, THE* by E.E. Davis	Hardcover with dust jacket — velvet pictures of Beatles in psychelic — rare	$25--40	
433. Beatles Unlimited	1979	*THE BEATLES CONCERTED EFFORTS* by Jan Van de Bunt and friends (All live appearances listed)	Holland (in English)	$10	

**B
O
O
K
S**

	Publisher	Year	Title	Description	Condition Near Mint	Very Good
434.		1980/ 1981	*BEATLES CATALOGUE*	Thick volume of all Beatles items, posters, calendars, memorabilia, books, etc. Japan import.	$30	
435.	Warner Books	1975	*BEATLES COMPLETE QUIZ BOOK* by Edwin Goodgold	Softbound	$4--6	
436.	Delacorte	1969	*BEATLES ILLUS- TRATED LYRICS, VOL. I*	Original first edition hardcover with dust jacket	$20--25	
		1972 1981	by Alan Aldridge	Reissue, softbound	$15	
		1971	*BEATLES ILLUS- TRATED LYRICS,*	Hardcover with dust jacket	$25	
		1981	*VOL. II*	Reissue	Store price	
437.	Shinko Music	1976	*BEATLES PHOTO COLLECTION* (Glossy pictures of Beatles career and solos until 1975. Some color.)	Japan import	$25--30	
438.	Shinko Music	1973	*BEATLES PHOTOS* by Dezo Hoffman	Original issue in Japan	$25	
		1980		Reissue	$20	
439.	McGraw Hill	1968	*BEATLES, THE: THE AUTHORIZED BIOG- RAPHY*	Original first edition with dust jacket — hardcover	$25--30	$20--25
			by Hunter Davies	Book club edition	$20--23	$15--18
	Dell			Original printing paperback	$10	$7--9
	McGraw Hill	1978		Rev. ed. of hard- cover — different jacket	Listed store price	
440.	Putnam	1968	*BEATLES: THE REAL STORY*	Hardcover	$15--25	$10--12
	Berkeley		by Julius Fast	Paperback	$8--10	$7--8
441.	Lancer	1964	*BEATLES UP-TO- DATE* no author	Paperback	$7--8	$5--6
442.	Straight Arrow	1972	*BODY COUNT* by Francie Schwartz	Oversized paper- back	$25--30	
	Pyramid			Paperback	$20--25	$15--20
443.	Doubleday	1964	*CELLARFUL OF NOISE*	Hardcover with dust jacket	$25--35	$20--25
	Pyramid	1964	by Brian Epstein (Ghostwriter: Derek Taylor)	Original paperback Reissue (counter- feit)	$10--12 $4--5	$6--8

B O O K S

140

Publisher	Year	Title	Description	Condition Near Mint	Very Good
444. Grosset & Dunlap	1964	*DEAR BEATLES* by Bill Adler	Hardcover	$12--15	$8
			Paperback	$6--8	
Wonder Books			Hardcover	$10	
445. Simon & Schuster	1964	*EN FLAGRANTE DELIRE (IN HIS OWN WRITE)* by John Lennon	Different cover hardcover	$35--40	$25--35
446. Pendulum Illustrated Biography Series	1979	*ELVIS PRESLEY/THE BEATLES*	Softbound comic history	$5	
447. Apple Records	1968	*GET BACK* by Jonathon Cott	Softbound, issued with **Let It Be**, U.K. Book only without box set	$65--100	$50--75
448. A. Knopf	1970	*GIRL WHO SANG WITH THE BEATLES* by Robert Hemenway	Hardcover	NPA	
449. Simon & Schuster	1970	*GRAPEFRUIT* by Yoko Ono	Hardcover with dust jacket	$10--15	
			Softbound	$7--10	
450. Dell	1965	*HELP!* by Al Hine	Original edition	$10	$8
			Reprinted by Melita Music (out of print)	$8	
451. Random House	1965	*HELP! THE BEATLES* no author	Hardcover with pictures, rare	$25--35	$18--25
452. New England Library Ltd. Four Square Book	1964	*HERE ARE THE BEATLES* by Charles Hamblett	Paperback, U.K.	$11--15	
453. Bantam	1967	*HOW I WON THE WAR* by Patrick Ryan	Paperback with Lennon's picture on cover	$7--10	
454. Genesis Publ.	1980	*I ME MINE* by George Harrison with Derek Taylor	Hardbound, in box with signature. Limited edition of 2000 numbered copies. Box comes in black, brown or dark green.	$428*	
Simon & Schuster	1981		U.S. hardcover — no signature	$12.95	

*Note: Value may go up when all copies are sold. Lower numbered copies *may* be worth more eventually.

**B
O
O
K
S**

The Liverpool Souvenir Packet: the Beatles collection put out by the Liverpool City Council in 1974. It includes the booklet *Nothing To Get Hung About*, tour map, postcards, etc. Available only in the U.K. and now hard to find, it is currently valued at approxiamtely $12-18. *Price Guide No.: 461*

Publisher	Year	Title	Description	Near Mint	Very Good
455. Simon & Schuster	1964	*IN HIS OWN WRITE* by John Lennon	Hardcover first edition	$35--50	$25--35
Signet	1981	with *A SPANIARD IN THE WORKS*	Paperback	$2.95	
Penguin	1980	U.K. – original cover	Paperback	$5--6	
456. Futura	1976	*JOHN LENNON STORY* by George Tremlett	Paperback, U.K. only (out of print)	$8	
457. Stein & Day	1972	*THE LENNON FACTOR* by Paul Young	Poetry – inspired by Beatles era. Lennon on cover, rare hardcover	$35--50	$25--35
458. Simon & Schuster	1968	*THE LENNON PLAY* by John Lennon, Adrienne Kennedy and Victor Spinetti	Adapted from John Lennon's book hardcover	$25--35	$20–25
459. Straight Arrow	1971	*LENNON REMEMBERS* Jann Wenner Interviews John Lennon and Yoko Ono	Hardcover with dust jacket	$15	$10
Pyramid			Paperback – original edition	$8	$4--6
	1981		Reissue	Store price	
460. MPL	1975-- 1979	*LINDA'S DESK DIARIES* photos by Linda McCartney Originally sold through Wings Fun Club to members	*Nashville Diary 1975*	$25–35	
			Linda's Pix for '76	$20--25	
			Photos for '77	$10--15	
			Plates for '78	$10--15	
			Signs for 79	$10	
			Matey for '80	$10--12	
461. Liverpool City Council	1974	*LIVERPOOL SOUVENIR PACKET (THE BEATLES COL- LECTION FROM LIVERPOOL TO THE WORLD)* Included: *NOTHING TO GET HUNG ABOUT* by Mike Evans	Large format folder with thin softbound book sold by City Tourist Board to raise money for the city	$15–20	
462. Putnam	1964	*LOVE LETTERS TO THE BEATLES* edited by Bill Adler	Hardcover Softbound (was also reissued by Melita Music, U.K.)	$10–12 $4--6	$4–6
463. Penguin	1964	*LOVE ME DO* by Michael Braun	Paperback U.K. original edition Reissued by Melita Music (out of print)	$18–25 $8	$10–18
464. Bantam Books	1964	*MAGIC CHRISTIAN* by Terry Southern	Paperback with Ringo on cover	$3--4	

BOOKS

	Publisher	Year	Title	Description	Condition	
					Near Mint	Very Good
465.	Holt, Rinehart & Winston	1966	*MURRAY THE K: TELLS IT LIKE IT IS BABY*	Hardcover, Beatles chapter and pictures included. Introduction by George Harrison	$15--20	$12--15
466.	Futura	1975	*PAUL McCARTNEY STORY* George Tremlett	U.K. paperback also released in U.S. — common	$3	
467.	Creative Education		*ON STAGE WITH THE BEATLES* by D. Keenan	Hardcover	NPA	
468.	Dell	1964	*OUT OF THE MOUTHS OF BEATLES* by Adam Blessing	Beatles pictures with humorous captions, soft-bound	$10--12	$8
469.	Penguin	1966	*PENGUIN COLLECTION (IN HIS OWN WRITE & A SPANIARD IN THE WORKS)* by John Lennon	Original edition paperback (cover picture of Lennon wearing several glasses)	$8--10	
		1965		Color cover of Lennon as Superman	$12	
470.	Penguin	1980	*THE PENGUIN JOHN LENNON*	Australian soft-bound, picture of Lennon	$5	
471.	Bantam	1964	*TRUE STORY OF THE BEATLES* by Billy Shepherd	Paperback	$10--15	$7--8
472.	Star	1978	*TWIST OF LENNON* by Cynthia Lennon Twist	U.K. paperback original edition (out of print)	$8--10	
				Reissued by Melita Music	$4--5	
	Avon	1980		U.S. release — different cover — common	$2.50	
473.	Grosset & Dunlap	1968	*WORDS WITHOUT MUSIC* by Rick Friedman	Paperback	$5	$3
474.		1967	*THE WRITING BEATLE JOHN LENNON* (Compilation of two books)	Paperback	$10	$8

**B
O
O
K
S**

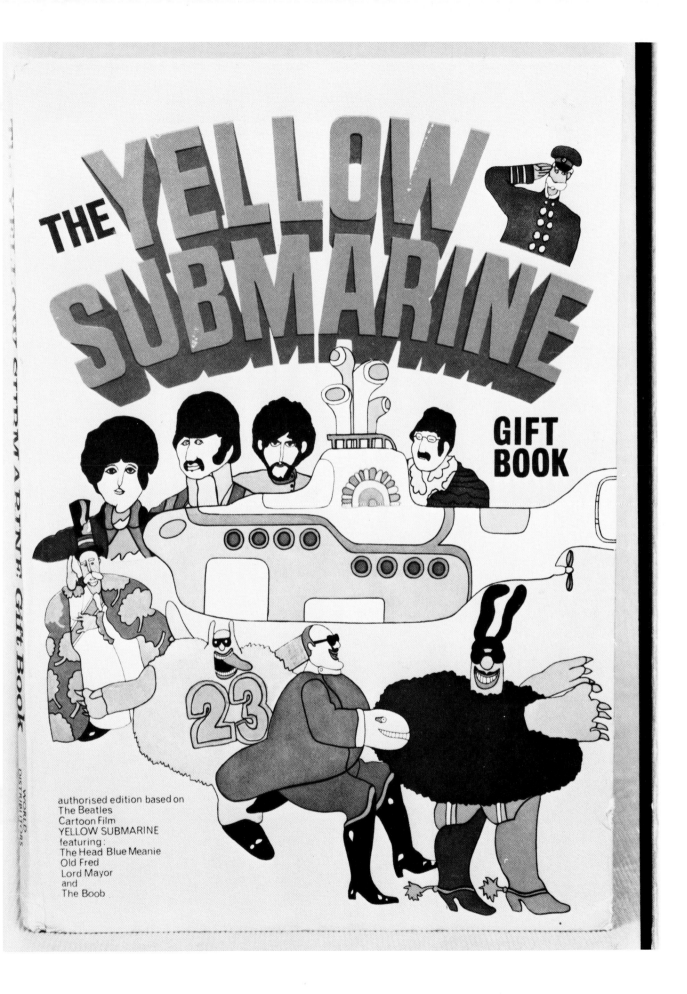

This rare hard-cover book sells for at least $35. *Price Guide No.: 477*

Publisher	Year	Title	Description	Condition Near Mint	Very Good
475. Simon & Schuster	1981	*WRITINGS OF JOHN LENNON* (Two books combined)	Grey cover, other-wise designed like *In His Own Write* (hardcover)	$8	
476. Signet	1968	*YELLOW SUBMARINE* by Max Wilk	Paperback with color drawings from film	$10	$7--9
North American Library	1968		Hardcover — rare	$15	
477. World Distributors	1968	*YELLOW SUBMARINE GIFT BOOK*	Hardcover	$25--30	

Other

478.		Songbooks:	Most common Beatles, range	$8--10	$5–6
		RAM	U.K., many pictures	$15	
		BACK TO THE EGG	U.K., many pictures	$12	

B O O K S

Title	Description	Condition	
		Near Mint	Very Good
479. *A HARD DAY'S NIGHT*	Published by Whiteman, common, color cover, quantity discovered in late 70s	$8--10	
480. *A HARD DAY'S NIGHT*	1964	$10	
481. *ALL ABOUT THE BEATLES*	Published by *Datebook* 1964	$10--12	$6--9
482. *ALL ABOUT US*	Thirty-two pages, black-and-white, 1965 – rare *16* magazine original sold by mail order only	$12--15	
483. *AVANT GARDE NO. 11*	Features John and Yoko's lithos, six pages of Bag One drawings	$15	
484. *BEATLDOM*	Teenage Kingdom of the Beatles, 66 pages, 1964	$15	
485. *BEATLEMANIA NO. 1*	Large format, 20 pages, 1964	$12--15	
486. *BEATLEMANIA*	Winter 1978, Charlton Publications, "The Beatles from Liverpool to Legend"	$3	
487. *BEATLES, THE*	By Beatles Publishing Corp., 1964	$15	$12
488. *BEATLES, THE*	Pyx Productions, 1964, mail order. Different radio station call letters.	$20	$18
489. *BEATLES, THE*	Color cover from Holland, 1964	$15	
490. *BEATLES, THE: A GIANT SCRAPBOOK*	By Rainbow, large format, color pictures, sold for 50p. originally	$7--10	
491. *BEATLES ARE BACK*	Published by MacFadden-Bartell, 1964	$10--12	$6–9
492. *BEATLES ARE BACK*	Published by Cousins Publication, 1976	$3--4	
493. *BEATLES ARE HERE*	MacFadden-Bartell, 1964	$10--12	$8–9
494. *BEATLES AT CARNEGIE HALL*	Panther Publications, 1964, U.K.	$15	$10
495. *BEATLES, BEATLES, BEATLES*	JLD Publishing, 68 pages, 1964	$12--15	$8–10
496. *BEATLES BY ROYAL COMMAND*	1963, U.K.	$10--20	$12--15
497. *BEATLES COLOR PINUP ALBUM*	Published by *Teen Screen*, color cover, 11 pages of color, 1964	$12--15	$9–10

═ Beatles Comics & Beatles Featured In Comics ═

Title	Description	Condition	
498. *BATMAN COMIC NO. 222*	"Dead . . . till proven alive" June 1970	$6	$3

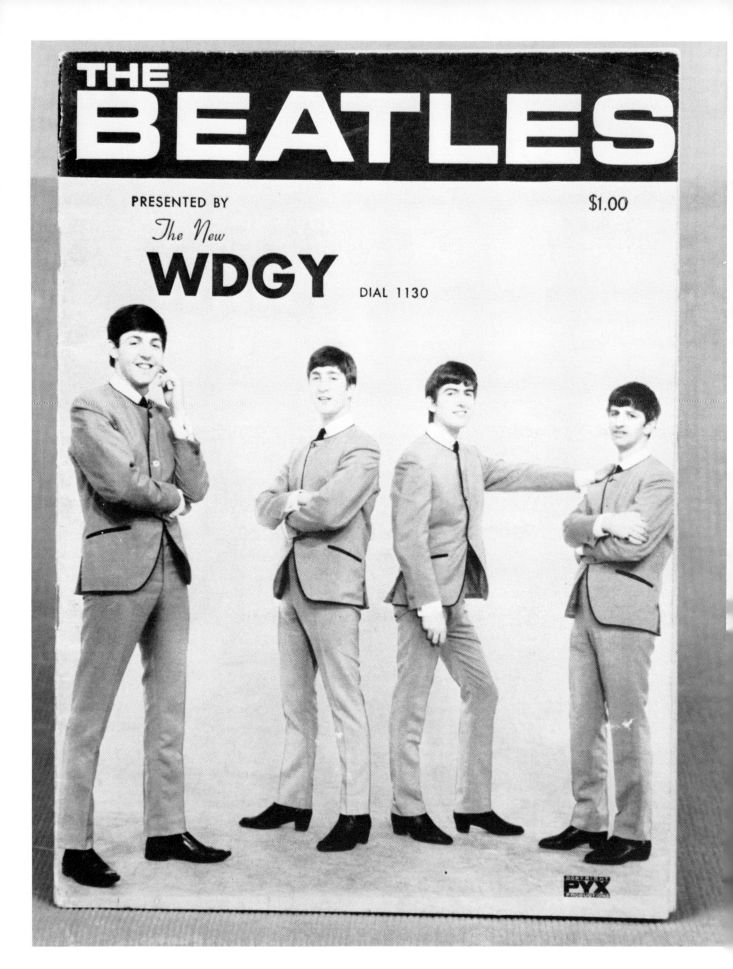

A mail-order magazine put out by Pyx. Many local radio stations sold them to area listeners in 1964, and they're now worth about $20 in Near Mint condition, $15 in Very Good. *Price Guide No.: 488*

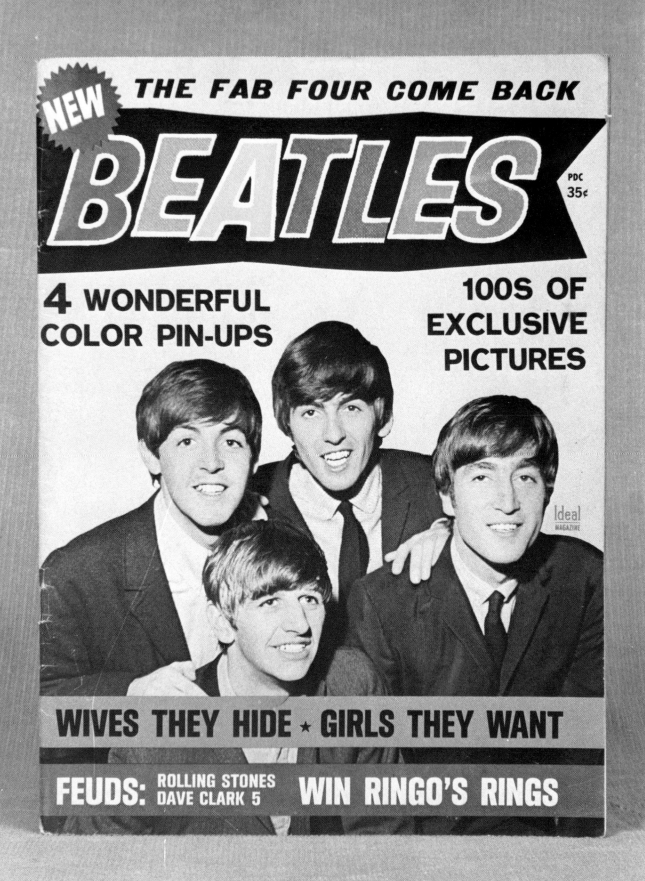

A 1964 U.S. Beatles magazine. With color cover and 68 pages, it is worth about $10-15 in Near Mint condition.
Price Guide No.: 506

Title	Description	Near Mint	Very Good
499. *BEATLES COMIC, THE*	Dell 1964, includes eight color pinups	$20--30	$18--20
500. *GIRLS ROMANCE NO. 109*	Beatles on cover	$6	
501. *HEART THROBS NO. 101*	Beatles on cover	$6	
502. *JIMMY OLSON COMIC NO. 79*	"Red-headed Beatle of 1000BC" September, 1964	$4	$2.50
503. *MY LITTLE MARGIE NO. 54*	Beatles on cover	$6	
504. *STRANGE TALES COMICS NO. 130*	"Human Torch & The Thing Meet The Beatles" Dell, March, 1964	$6--12	
505. *SUMMER LOVE, NOS. 46, 47, 48*	Beatles on cover	$8--10	

Title	Description	Near Mint	Very Good
506. *BEATLES: FAB FOUR COME BACK*	1964 Ideal Publications, color cover, 68 pages	$10--12	
507. *BEATLES FILM, THE*	Sun Printers, U.K., pop pics super special, color and black-and-white, 1964	$13--14	$10
508. *BEATLES FOREVER, THE*	1974	$5	
509. *BEATLES FROM THE BEGINNING*	Magnum Pub., 1970, 78 pages	$10	$7.50
510. *BEATLES HAIRDO'S & SETTING PATTERNS*	Dell Pub., 1,000 hints	$20	
511. *BEATLES IN AMERICA*	By Daily Mirror with black-and-white picture, 1964	$10--15	
512. *BEATLES IN PARIS*	Large format, pop pics special, U.K. newspaper	$10	
513. *BEATLES IN SWEDEN*	Large format, pop pics special, U.K. newspaper	$10	
514. *BEATLES MAKE A MOVIE (AHDN)*	1964 Magnum Publications, 66 pages	$12--15	$8--10
515. *BEATLES MEET DAVE CLARK 5*	1964 Kahm Pub., 66 pages	$10	$7.50
516. *BEATLES (MONTHLY) BOOK*	Originals no. 1--77 (issued in U.K., 1963--70), black-and-white covers except issues: 47, 53, 58, 68, which had color covers and centerfolds	$10--15	$5--8

M A G A Z I N E S, P A M P H L E T S & P R O G R A M M E S

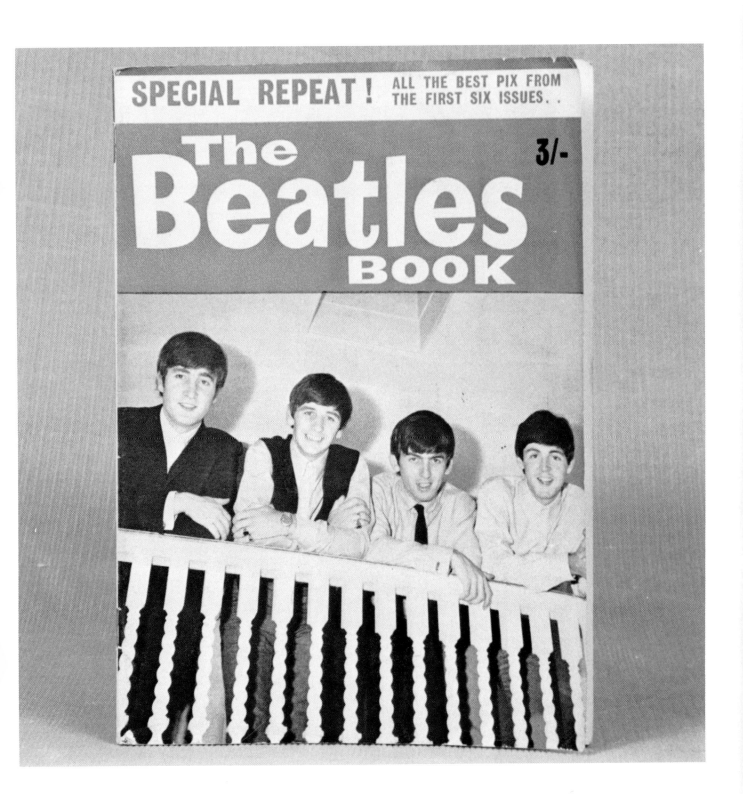

A special edition of the U.K. *Beatles Book* from 1964, so far not reissued. *Price Guide No.: 517*

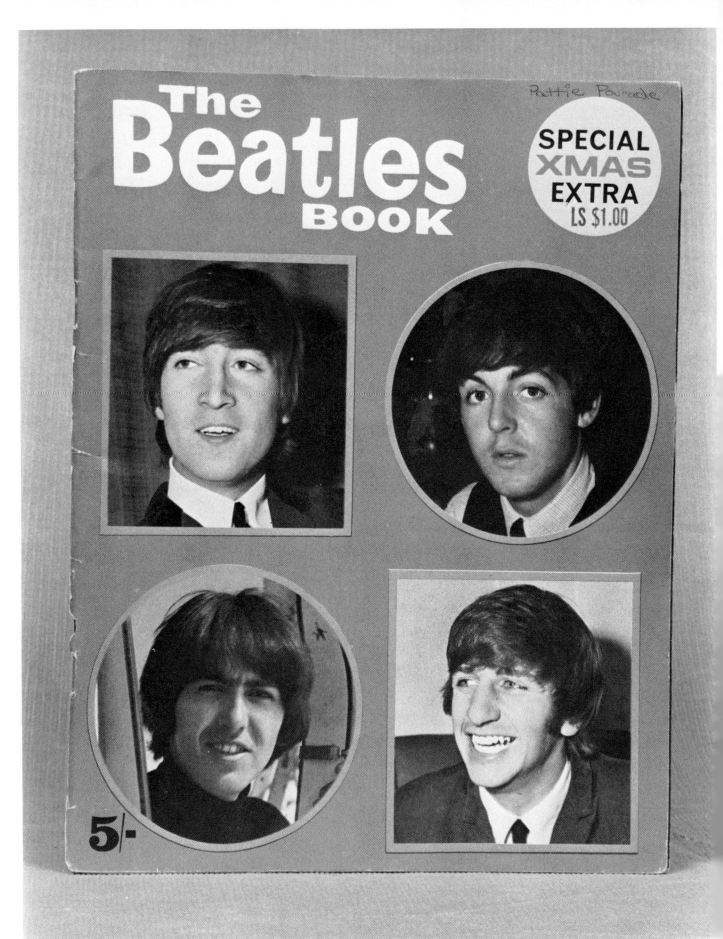

The hard to find special Christmas issue of *The Beatles Book* from 1965. Rare in the U.S., it is valued at $20. *Price Guide No.: 518*

Title	Description	Condition Near Mint	Very Good
	Reprinted by Beat Publications (same company) from same plates but with new cover and material added on in addition to original magazine reprinted in exact form*	$2.50–3 U.S. 70p U.K. current price	
	Original no. 1 most sought after	$16+	
517. *BEATLES (MONTHLY) BOOK, THE: SPECIAL REPEAT*	From *Beatles Monthly* reprints of best of issues 1–6, originals only	$15–20	
518. *BEATLES (MONTHLY) BOOK, THE: XMAS EXTRA*	Published by *Beatles Monthly*, U.K., both rare in U.S. 1965, 60 pages 1966, 42 pages	$18–25 $18–25	
519. *BEATLES MOVIE*	Published by *Dig* magazine	$6–8	$5
520. *BEATLES ON BROADWAY*	Published by Whitman, 64 pages, written by Sam Leach, 1964	$6–8	
521. *BEATLES: 1001 PHOTOS & SECRETS*		$10	
522. *BEATLES OPEADIA*	48 pages, 1964 U.K., mail order item, rare, bound in binder	$20	
523. *BEATLES PERSONALITY ALBUM*	Countrywide Pub., "annual" 1964, 66 pages	$9–10	
524. *BEATLES PICTURES SUITABLE FOR FRAMING*	Black-and-white, 1964, Norman Parkman photographs, text by M. Cleave	$15	$8–10
525. *BEATLES PUNCHOUT PORTRAITS*	Whitman, 1964, four standup Beatle portraits and miniature bandstand and mobile	$20+	
526. *BEATLES QUIZ BOOK*	1964, William Collins Sons, U.K., John Freeman photographs, wholesaled in U.S. in 70s, common	$10–12	
527. *BEATLES REVIVAL*	Large format, Australia, color pictures, 1976	$7–10	
528. *BEATLES 'ROUND THE WORLD*	No. 1 Acme, large format with color cover (Pop Pics Special)	$10–15	$8–10
529. *BEATLES 'ROUND THE WORLD NO. 2*	Large format, rare	$15–25	
530. *BEATLES 'ROUND THE WORLD NO. 3*	Elvis vs Beatles	$15–25	

----

*See chapter on Counterfeit Controversy to determine originals from reprints.

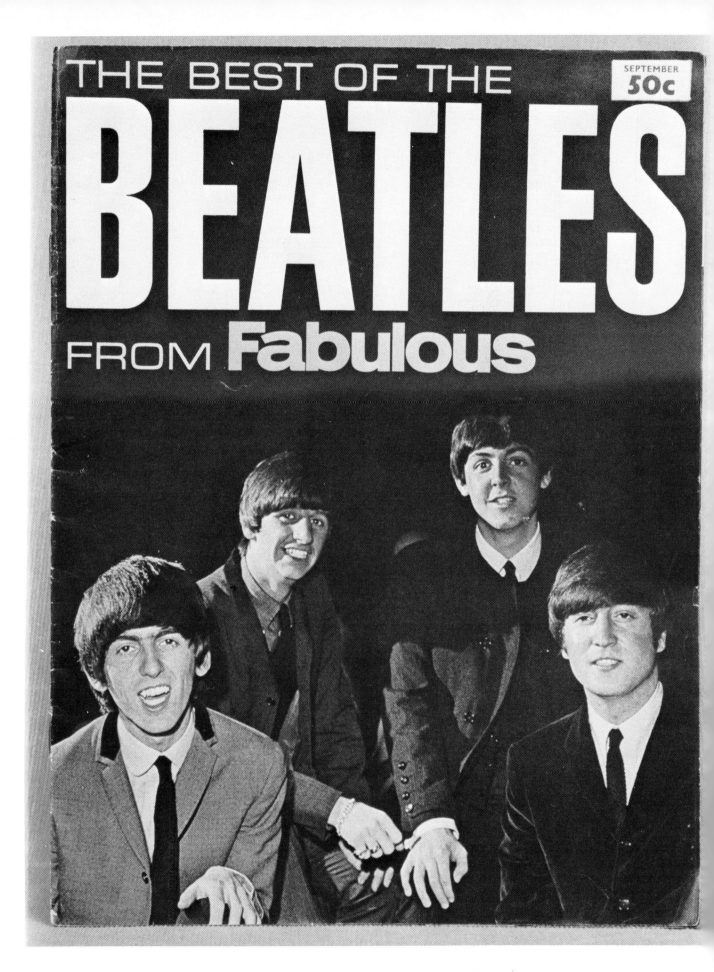

THE BEST OF THE
BEATLES
FROM Fabulous

SEPTEMBER
50c

A U.S. version of a magazine first published in England. Large size with color pin-ups, valued at $15-18. *Price Guide No.: 537*

Title	Description	Condition	
		Near Mint	Very Good
531. *BEATLES STARTED THE BIG SOUND*		$15	$10
532. *BEATLES STORY*	Marvel Super Special	$3.50	
533. *BEATLES TALK*	By *Dig* magazine, 1964	$15	$10
534. *BEATLES U.S.A.*	Large format, Jamie Pub., 16 pages, 1964	$10	
535. *BEATLES VS DAVE CLARK 5*	Tempest Publ., 66 pages, 1964	$10--12	$6--9
536. *BEATLES YESTERDAY & TODAY*	Countywide Pub., 70 pages, 1975	$5	
537. *BEST OF THE BEATLES*	By *Fabulous* magazine, U.K., September, 1964	$15–20	$10--13
538. *BEST OF THE BEATLES*	By McFadden-Bartell, 78 pages, 1964	$10--15	
539. *BIG BEATLES FUN KIT*	Dierdre Publications, 1964, rare	$30–50	
540. *COMPLETE STORY OF THE BEATLES*	Number 7 of 7, "Collectors Edition" 15 cents originally, thin pink newsprint, Charlton Publications	$4	
	Numbers 1--6, Charlton Publications	$3--4 ea.	
541. *COSMOPOLITAN*	December, 1964, John Lennon on cover, color picture, article by Gloria Steinem	$12--15	
542. *DATEBOOK*	Issues with Beatles on cover	$10--12	
	September, 1966, John Lennon's "Beatles more popular than Christ . . . ." statement	$15--25	
543. *EVERY LITTLE THING*	Published by Ticket to Ride, variations listings, 1979	$5	
544. *EYE*	September, 1968, John Lennon on cover, color photograph by Linda Eastman, article by Lilian Roxan. Also article on George Martin, rare	$15–20	
	August, 1968, Yellow Submarine featured	$15	
545. *FAB FOUR COME BACK NEW BEATLES*	*Ideal* magazine, 68 pages, color cover, black-and-white pictures, 1964	$10--15	$7--9
546. *FABULOUS*	*Fabulous* Goes Filming with The Beatles, 6/64	$15	
	Fabulous Goes All Beatles, 2/64 (U.K. weekly pinup magazine with color, large format pictures)	$15	
	Issues which feature Beatles, or wives/ girlfriends, etc.	$9--10	$7–9

Title	Description	Condition	
		Near Mint	Very Good
547. *HULLABALOO*	February, 1969 John and Yoko on cover, six pages, article by Derek Taylor	$9	$7
548. *INSIDE STORY OF YELLOW SUBMARINE*	Souvenir Special, Go Publ., 32 pages, 1968	$25	
549. *JOHN & YOKO: THEIR LOVE BOOK*	1970	$25	$10--15
550. *LIFE*	8/28/64, Beatles cover, seven pages	$15--20	$12--15
	10/23/64, three pages on Beatles	$8	$6
	9/13/68, Beatles cover and article	$15	$10--15
	11/7/69, McCartney on cover	$9--12	$7--9
	4/16/71, McCartneys on cover	$5--7	$5
551. *LIFE WITH THE BEATLES*	Forty-page booklet, U.K., 1964	$18	
552. *LOOK*	12/13/66, John Lennon color cover, "IIow I Won The War"	$10--12	$8--10
	1/9/68, John Lennon color cover, Avedon photographs and poster offer (pull-out poster)	$25--30	$15--20
	3/18/69, John and Yoko color cover and story with pictures	$10--12	$8--10
553. *MEET THE BEATLES*	Souvenir Press black-and-white pictures, compiled by Tony Barrow, U.K., 1963, one of the first magazines on the Beatles, very rare in U.S.	$20	$15--18
	Star Special No. 12, different cover, U.K.	$12--15	
554. *NATIONAL LAMPOON*	Special on Beatles, October, 1977	$6	$4
555. *NEWSWEEK*	Beatles on cover, 2/24/64	$10--15	$7--9
556. *ORIGINAL BEATLES BOOK*	Peterson Publ., Earl Leaf, ed., 1964 (Meet the Beatles LP cover), glossy magazine	$12--20	$9--12
ORIGINAL BEATLES BOOK, TWO	1964 with color cover	$12--20	$9--12
	Both in set	$25--30	$20--25
557. *PAUL McCARTNEY DEAD, THE GREAT HOAX*	1969	$10--12	
	Reprint of original, 1978	$3--5	
558. *PLAYBOY*	February, 1965, famous Beatles interview	$12--15	$10
559. *POST*	3/21/64, Beatles on cover, rare	$20	$10--25
	8/15/64, Beatles on cover	$15	$8--12
	8/27/66, Beatles on cover	$15	$12
	5/4/68, Beatles with Maharishi on cover	$5--10	$5--7

75 NEVER-BEFORE-SEEN PHOTOS OF THE BEATLES

RINGO'S PHOTO-ALBUM

TAKEN BY RINGO
PLUS
PERSONAL PIX OF
THE GIRLS AND GUYS
IN RINGO'S LIFE

A
50c

ALL
PHOTOS
BY
RINGO

EXTRA!
AN
**INTRODUCTORY
LETTER**
WRITTEN BY
RINGO
TO ALL
HIS FANS!

Ringo Starr

RINGO'S CANDID PHOTOS OF GEORGE, JOHN & PAUL

A popular **1964 Beatles** magazine with more pictures than the average. In Near Mint condition, worth $15; this Very Good copy is valued at **$10-12.** *Price Guide No.: 563*

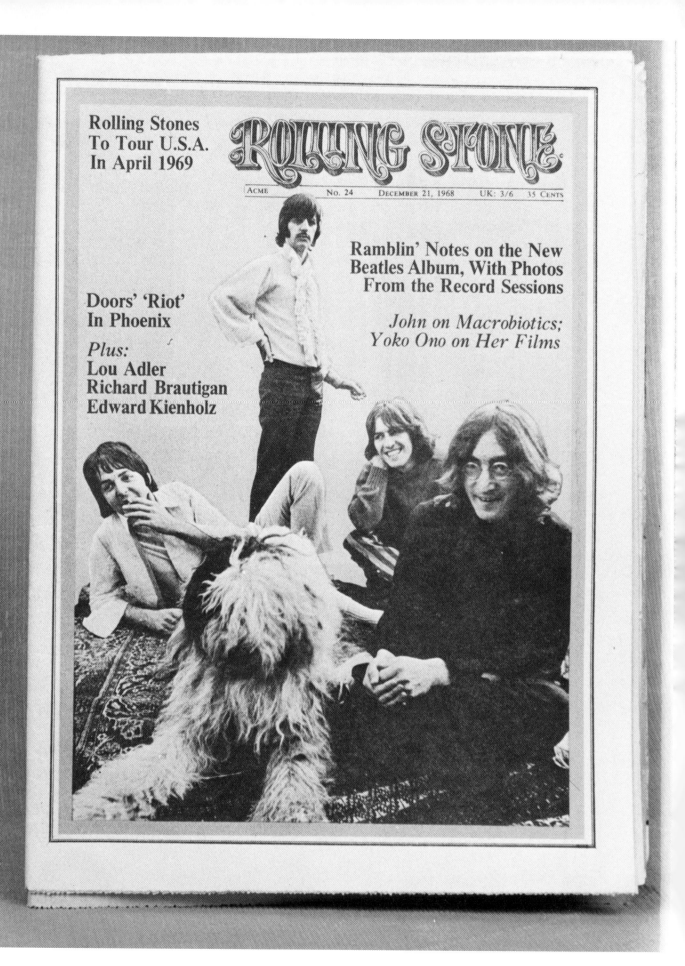

An early issue of *Rolling Stone* magazine with details on the "White Album". Value is increased because the Beatles are on the cover: **$15-20.** *Price Guide No.: 564*

Title	Description	Condition	
		Near Mint	Very Good
560. *RAMPARTS*	John Lennon on cover, color, 1967	$25	
561. *RAVE*	U.K. monthly pop magazine, Beatles on cover issues or issues with lots of pictures	$8--10	$5--7
	No. 10, 11/64, nine pages of Beatles	$10	
	No. 62, 3/69, Beatles color cover and centerfold	$12	
562. *REAL TRUE BEATLES*	Written by Michael Braun, *Love Me Do* book in magazine format for U.S. market, Fawcett Publ., color cover, 96 pages, 1964	$12--15	$9--10
563. *RINGO'S PHOTO ALBUM*	Published by Jamie Publ., New York, 1964, 64 pages, Ringo in color on cover	$13--15	$10--12
564. *ROLLING STONE*	No. 1, John Lennon on cover, HIWTW, rare	$25+	
	With Beatles cover, 1960s	$12--14	$10
	70s cover stories on individuals	$3--5	
565. *ROLLING STONE*	John Lennon interviews, Vol. 1 & 2	$12--15 ea $25 set	
566. *SIXTEEN*	Monthly U.S. magazine, early 60s issues with Beatles features, prices depend on amount of pictures, or if Beatles featured in centerfold and inside color pinups, etc.	$5--10	
567. *SIXTEEN'S: BEATLE MOVIE (AHDN)*	Rare than *16*'s "Help!"	$16–18	$12--14
568. *SIXTEEN'S: BEATLE MOVIE (HELP!)*	Color cover	$15	$12
569. *SIXTEEN'S BEATLES COM- PLETE STORY FROM BIRTH TO NOW*	*16* scoop, seven color pinups, color cover sought after, 1965	$15--20	$10--15
570. *SIXTEEN'S: BEATLES WHOLE TRUE STORY*	1966, sought after	$15--16	$10
571. *STARTIME PRESENTS THE BEATLES*	AAA Pub., 66 pages, 1965	$8--10	
572. *SUPER POP PICS*	U.K., 1964, rare small size color magazine on each Beatle (8½ by 5 inches), 16 pages each	$16–20 ea	
	Set of four	$75	
573. *TALKING PICTURES: SPECIAL BEATLES ISSUE*	No. 1, 1964	$15	$9–12

Three (out of a series of four) U.K. color magazines from 1963; also sold in the U.S. for a limited time in 1964.

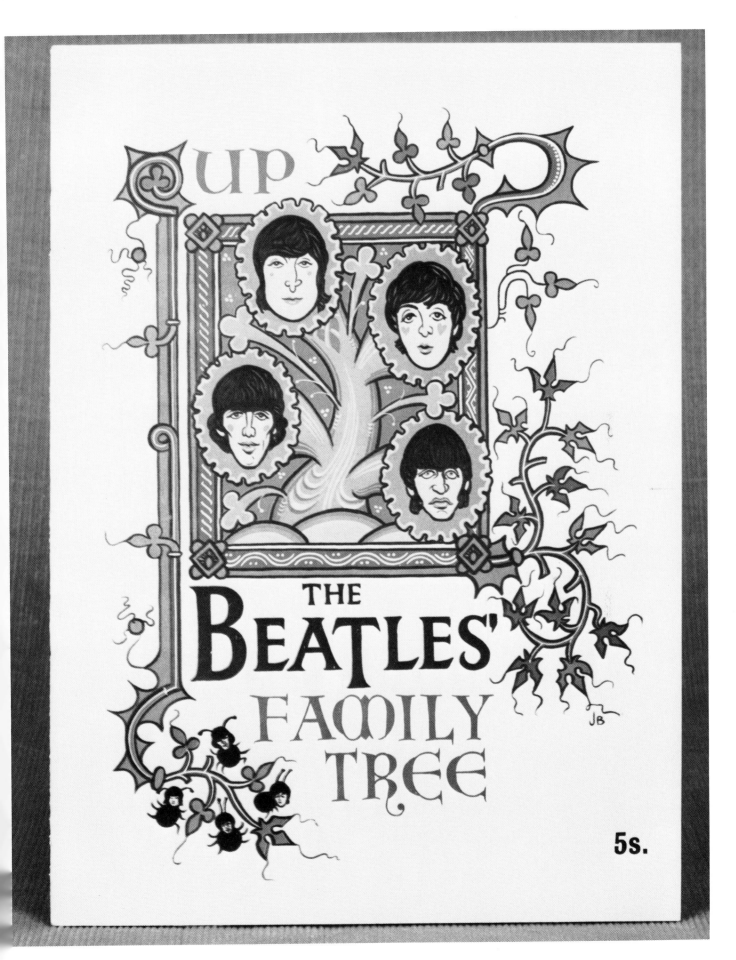

THE **Beatles'** FAMILY TREE

5s.

Published in 1966, this small booklet from the U.K. is now unavailable. Worth at least $10-12. *Price Guide No.:* 585

Title	Description	Condition	
		Near Mint	Very Good
574. *TEEN PIX ALBUM: THE BEATLES*	1964 valuable collectors edition	$18	
	Regular edition	$10	
575. *TEEN SCREEN*	Monthly magazine with features on Beatles, price depends on amount of pictures, if featured on cover, color pinups, etc.	$4--8	
576. *TEEN SCREEN: BEATLES COMPLETE LIFE STORIES*	1964	$15	$10--12
577. *TEEN SCREEN: JOHN, PAUL, GEORGE & RINGO*	Individual specials on each with color covers, lots of pinups, 1964	$10--15 ea.	$8--10 ea.
578. *TEEN SET*	Yellow Sub special, 62 pages, 1968	$10--12	
579. *TEEN TALK: THE BEATLES*	Dezo Hoffman pictures, 1964	$12	$10
580. *TEEN TALK: PICTURE PACKED EDITION*	First U.S. tour	$15	$10
581. *TEENERS SPECIAL: BEATLES*	Welcome Back Beatles, U.S., 1964	$18--20	
582. *TEENVILLE*	More On The Beatles, 66 pages, 1964	$10	
583. *TEN YEARS OF THE BEATLES*	Special Beatles magazine from France, 1975, color cover, color pictures	$10--15	$8--10
584. *TIME*	9/27/67, only cover on Beatles	$10--12	$6--8
585. *UP THE BEATLES FAMILY TREE*	Pamphlet from U.K. Achievements, Ltd., 12 pages, 1966, rare in U.S.	$12--15	$8--12
586. *WHO WILL BEAT THE BEATLES*	Magnum Publ., 1964	$8--12	$8
587. *YELLOW SUBMARINE*	Official magazine, two variations:		
	48 pages, 1968	$15	$10--12
	64 pages, more common	$12--14	$8--10
588. *YELLOW SUBMARINE COMIC*	By Gold Key, original with poster, 1968	$20--35	$16
	Without poster	$9--12	$8--9

Miscellaneous Booklets, Brochures, Pamphlets, Programs & Papers

Title	Description	Condition	
589. *Japanese 1966 Tour Program*	Large format, white cover, booklet	$10	
590. *Japanese Picture Magazine*	Small size, color cover pictures of Beatles' Japanese concerts, pictured in *Beatles Forever* book, much sought after	$20+	

M
A
G
A
Z
I
N
E
S,

P
A
M
P
H
L
E
T
S

&

P
R
O
G
R
A
M
M
E
S

An issue of the Official National Beatles Fan Club bulletin from 1965, valued at $15. *Price Guide No.: 591*

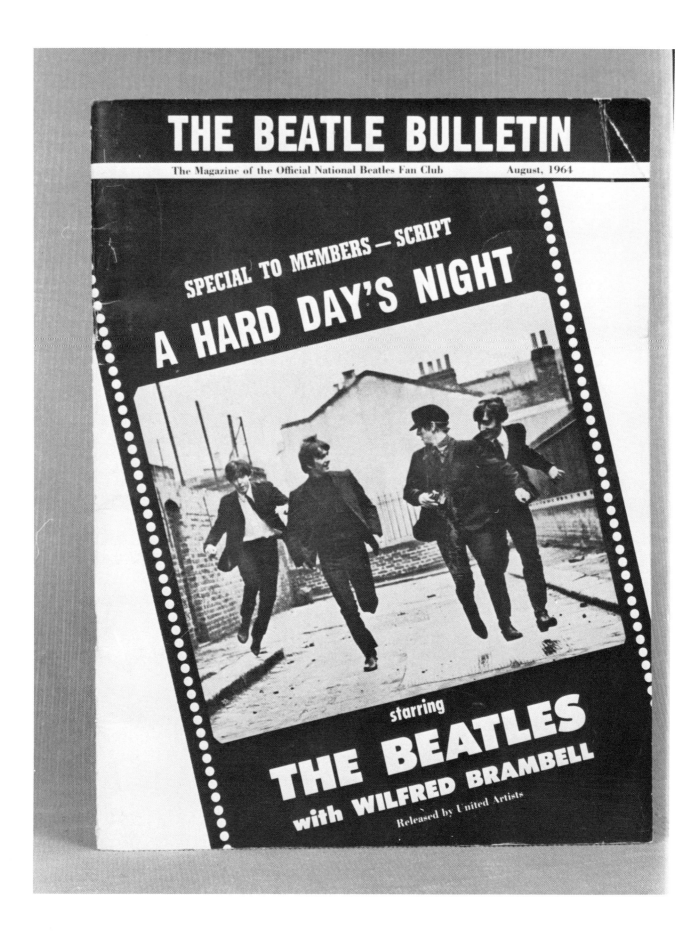

Another special bulletin from the Official National Beatles Fan Club, worth about $25. *Price Guide No.: 592*

Title	Description	Condition Near Mint	Very Good
591. *BEATLE BULLETIN, THE*	Special anniversary album, 1965, mailed to members only	$15--18	
592. *BEATLE BULLETIN, THE*	"A Hard Day's Night" script, August, 1964, mailed to members only	$18--25	
593. *BEATLES LTD – U.K. & BEATLES USA LTD*	Fan club bulletin programs, 4/66, article on cartoon series	$10	
594. *BEATLES USA LTD.: JOHN LENNON ALBUM PAUL McCARTNEY ALBUM RINGO STARR ALBUM GEORGE HARRISON ALBUM*	Black-and-white glossy magazines, eight pages, mailed to members, 1964 Set of all four	$8--10 ea. $28--35	
595. *Fan Club booklets*	1969, 1970, 1971 from Beatles USA Ltd., newsletters and pictures Booklets and membership kit: card, letter, etc.	$8--12 $20	
596. *Concert programs*	From U.S. tours: 1964 with faces in half light* 1965* 1966, rarest	$6–12 $8--10 $20	
597. *U.K. music papers*	Weekly pop newspapers: *Record Mirror, New Musical Express, Disc, Melody Maker, Sounds* 1963 papers featuring the Beatles 1964–1969 1970s (Value determined by amount of Beatles articles, pictures, or color covers or centerfolds used)	$5--10 $3--5 $1--3.50	
598. *1970--80s Beatles reissues, tributes, cash-ins, etc. Special issues, common*		$2--4	
599. *Magazines from 1960s with Beatle articles*	Magazines include: *Circus, Crawdaddy, Creem, Dig, Flip, Hit Parader, Teen Life, Photoplay, Redbook, Rock Scene, Teen World, Teen Set, Tiger Beat,* movie magazines, and more (Price depends on number of pages on Beatles, amount of pictures, interest of articles, etc.)	$2.50–6	
600. *Magazines from 1970s and 1980s with Beatle articles*	Includes: *People, Us, Time, Newsweek, Life,* etc. (exceptions all noted above) (Price depends on same as above)	$2--3	

---

*Large quantities of the 1964 and 1965 U.S. tour programs were found in the 70s and they are now a common item. But the 1966 program is very difficult to locate.

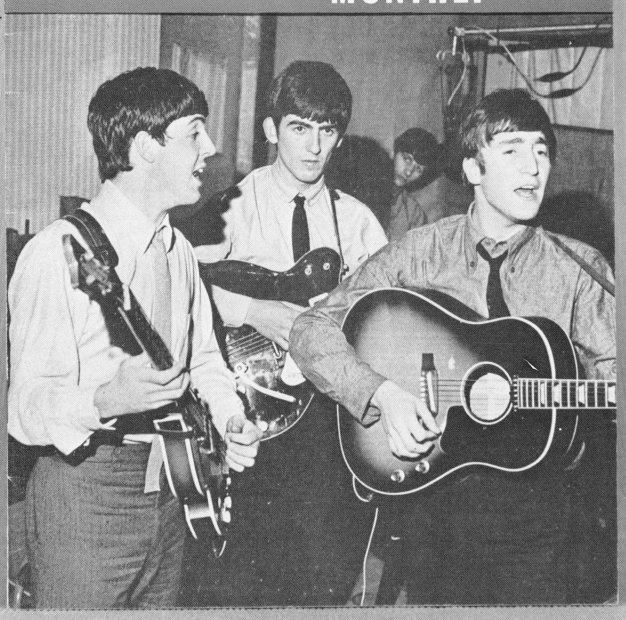

In No. 6 Last Chance to enter 135 gns. AMPLIFIER Competition

· · · POP TEN GROUP & INSTRUMENTAL MAG · · ·

SHADOWS · BEATLES · JET · TONY · JAYWALKERS · PACEMAKERS

Beat No.6

One Shilling & Sixpence   MONTHLY   Oct., 1963

An old and rare U.K. magazine, increased in value by the Beatles' cover picture. Worth approximately $7-10.

Price Guide No.: 599

OFFICIAL SOUVENIR

THE BEATLES

AUSTRALIAN TOUR 1964

There are many different programmes from the Beatles' 1963-66 touring days. This one, from Australia, might sell for $20+. *Price Guide No.: 606*

From the tour that never was: the programme for Wings' Japanese tour, 1980. Currently unavailable commercial-

Title	Description	Condition Near Mint Very Good

Title	Description	Condition
		Near Mint Very Good
601. *Fanzines*	Newsletters issued by fan clubs in 1970s and 1980s, usually offset printing with pictures. Back issues include: *Beatlefan, Beatles Unlimited, Harrison Alliance, Imagine, Inner Light, McCartney Observer, Paperback Writer, Strawberry Fields Forever, With a Little Help from My Friends* and *The Write Thing* (Value depends on number of pages, quality of printing, etc.)	$.50--$3.50
602. *Beatles books (not listed previously)*	Books and magazines still for sale in the stores or very commonly sold for cover price at conventions not listed separately. Price is as marked on jacket or discount may be given. Many Beatles books on remainders tables.	
603. *Carnegie Hall Program*	VERY rare, 1964	$60–100
604. *1963 U.K. Tour Program*		$25--30
605. *1964 U.K. Tour with Mary Wells*		$30
606. *Australian Tour Program*	1964	$20–30
607. *Beatles Christmas Show, U.K. Program*	December, 1964, John Lennon drawing on cover	$30--40
608. *Beatles Christmas Show, U.K. Program*	December, 1963, "Meet The Beatles" on cover	$30–40
609. *WINGS OVER AMERICA Tour Program*	1976	$5
610. *WINGS Japanese Tour Program*	1980 tour that was cancelled, programs sold through MPL/Fun Club First offered at Now out of stock	$8--12 $25--40
611. *DARK HORSE Tour Program*	George Harrison 1974 tour	$5–10

MAGAZINES, PAMPHLETS & PROGRAMMES

Closer view of the Apple wristwatch, a promotional piece from the Beatles' own company, Apple Corps Ltd. Rarely seen (only 50 were made), it has been valued at $300-500. *Price Guide No.: 612*

Item	Description	Condition	
		Near Mint	Very Good

Apple Promotional Items

612. Apple Watch	From Apple Corp. Ltd., square face, extremely rare, one collector was offered $800 but didn't want to sell, only 50 given out	$500	
613. Dartboard	Rare item given as promotional gimmick by Apple to friends and employees	$600	
614. Key Ring	On clear plastic with Apple (green and red)	$25--30	$12--15
615. Matches	Packaged in set of four, black books with green Apple on them Still sealed	$25 ea. $100 set	$7--10
616. Stationery	By the sheet, official company paper	$5 ea.	

Original Memorabilia

617. APRON	U.S. with Beatles faces	$50	
618. ARCADE CARDS	Original form, 1964--65, with writing on back Counterfeit with no writing	$3--5 no value	
619. ASHTRAY	1964 pose, small white	$20	$15--18
620. BALL	Rare	$35--50	
621. BALLOON	Rare, still in package, NEMS	$40--50	$18--25
622. BANJO	NEMS	$700+	
623. BAMBOO TRAY	Six-inch round, made in Taiwan with "A Hard Day's Night" picture Different sizes, 12-inch, 16-inch	$12--15 $15--20	
624. BEACH TOWEL	With picture of Beatles in 20s swimsuits	$50--100	
625. BED SHEETS	From Whittier Hotel, Detroit, 9/6/64, piece of bedsheet that individual Beatle slept on, with letter attesting to authenticity signed by hotel director From hotel in Kansas City, 1964 tour Counterfeit bedsheet and fake letter, current sales price	$15--20 $15--20 $8*	
626. BED SPREAD	Original 1964 item, rare	$200+	

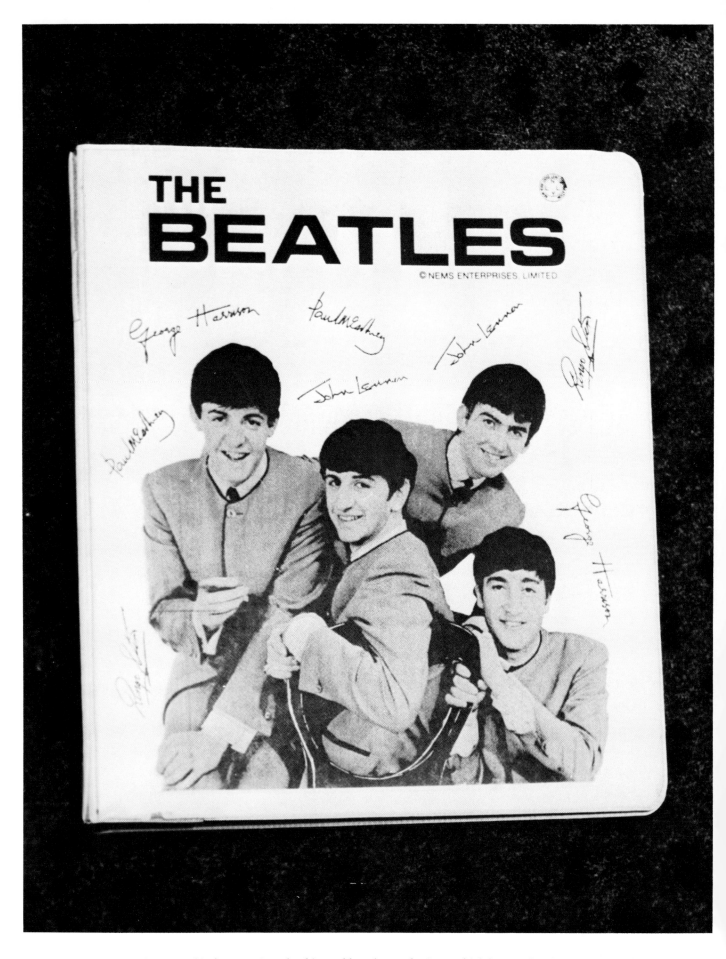

The Beatles three-ring binder came in red, white or blue. A popular item which has escalated in price from $15 to $40 in three years. *Price Guide No.: 627*

Beatles soap bubbles were recently discovered in many different colors, and now sell for about $20 a bottle. *Price Guide No.: 635*

Cake top decorations came in several variations. These are worth more if still in the original packaging. *Price Guide No.: 638*

Item	Description	Condition Near Mint	Very Good
627. BINDER	NEMS '64, 3 & 2 ring, colors	$25–40	
628. BINDER – BEATLE BOOK	Specially made for Beatle Monthlies in 60s, rare	$25–40	
629. BIRTH CERTIFICATES	Original set of four reproductions, 1964, in original envelopes	$35–40	
	Reprinted in 70s, set of four	$5–8	
630. BIRTHDAY CARD	1964	$15–20	
631. BONGOS	1964 – rare	NPA	
632. BOOK COVER	Yellow with black-and-white pictures	$12	
	Hardcover	$20	
633. BOOTS	Original 1964 black boots with Cuban heels like original "Beatle boots"	unknown	
634. BUBBLE BATH	In container, Paul and Ringo (no John or George ones made), U.S., 1965 by Colgate Palmolive Co., plastic with removable head	$30–50 ea.	
635. BUBBLES	1964 NEMS, U.K. item comes in several colors (blow bubbles), value is in bottle even if empty	$20	$12–15
636. BUGLE (MEGAPHONE)	Rare NEMS items with Beatles faces, 1964 –white with black	$25–35	$15–25
	Counterfeit – yellow	$10	
637. BUTTONS	"If I were 21, I'd vote for Paul [John, George, or Ringo]"	$4–6	
	"Official Beatlefan" 1964, 4-inch red and white with Beatles picture	$5–8	
	"I Love the Beatles," "I Love Ringo," "I *Still* Love the Beatles," etc., 3½ inch original from 1964–1966	$4–6.50	
	"I'm a Beatle Booster," one-inch, 1964	$4	
	Gum machine buttons, ½-inch, 1964–1965, "I LUV the Beatles" etc.	$2–4	
	Counterfeited (very hard to tell)	$2	
638. CAKE DECORATIONS	Two-inch models in blue suits, vaguely look like Beatles	$4–5	
	Two and one-half inch in grey suits with instruments and drum kit	$12	
	Still in original box	$15–20	
	Beatles stickpin, plastic, three-inch with heart-shaped flasher	$10	
639. CALENDAR, BEATLES FOREVER	Japanese EMI 1977 color pictures	$8–12	
	Japanese EMI 1978 color pictures	$8–15	
640. CALENDAR, JOHN LENNON	From **Live Peace in Toronto** LP, 1970, came with original release of LP only	$30–40	$20–25

M
E
M
O
R
A
B
I
L
I
A

The Beatles carrying case (or flight bag) from 1964 is another NEMS copyrighted item. This round vinyl model comes in seven colors, but black is the most common. It sells for close to $50 in Mint condition. *Price Guide No.: 643*

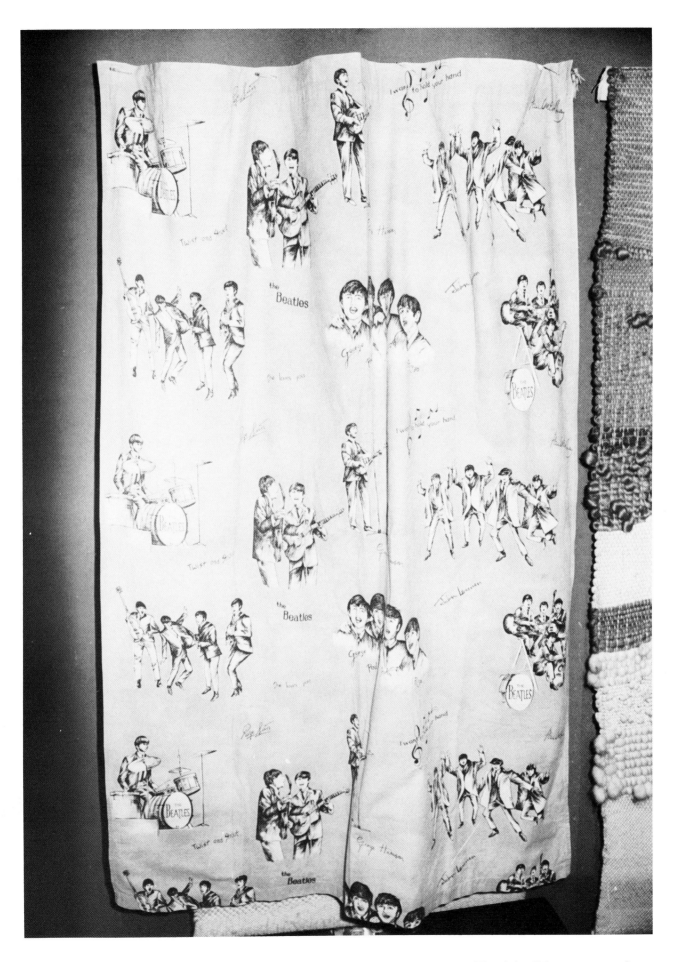

A very rare U.K. Beatles window curtain with a blue background. Displayed at "Beatlefest," but never seen for sale, the estimated value for a complete pair would be **$300-400**. *Price Guide No.: 657*

Item	Description	Condition Near Mint	Very Good
641. CALENDARS, BEATLES	U.K. 1964 by Beat Publications (*Beatles Monthly*), rare in U.S.	$25--35	
642. CAP	With fringe, "Beetle," small, estimated	$15--20	
643. CARRYING CASE, AIR FLIGHT BAG	NEMS 1964 rare item, round vinyl in seven different colors, black most common. Beatles pictures on front	$50–75	$35--50
644. CARRYING CASE, KABOODLE KIT	NEMS 1964, square vinyl small case, Beatles picture on front	$40--50	$35--40
645. CHRISTMAS TREE ORNA-MENT	Rare	unknown	
646. CLOCK	Alarm clock, 1970s, with 60s pictures	$15	
647. CLOTHES LABELS	NEMS 1966 "Beatles authentic mod fashions" to be sewn in clothing	$4 ea.	
648. COIN	Commemorative from 1964 U.S. tour Commemorative from 1964 Canadian tour	$8--10 $10--15	
649. COIN PURSE	Shaped like cartoon Beatle, vinyl purse, 1964, one for each Beatle	$10--20 ea.	
650. COIN PURSE	Small red coin holder with faces and "Beatles" on it Counterfeit	$15 $5	
651. COLORING BOOK	NEMS 1964 If pages are colored	$15--30	 $6--8
652. COLORING SET	U.S. original with crayons and one plastic drawing to color in	$20	
653. COMB	1964 large twelve-inch Beatles faces and signatures	$15--20	
654. COMPACT	For powder	$30+	
655. CUFF LINKS	With Beatles 1963 pose	$20	
656. CUPS	Different styles, men's, women's	$20 ea.	
657. CURTAIN	Beatles playing instruments, song titles, signatures on blue background. Rare, U.K. Estimated value	$200--400	
658. DIARY	Beatles pocket diary from Scotland, 1965, with photographs	$10–15	
659. DICTIONARY	"Beatles Jive Dictionary," 3¾ by 8 inches, from Capitol in Canada	$10	

M
E
M
O
R
A
B
I
L
I
A

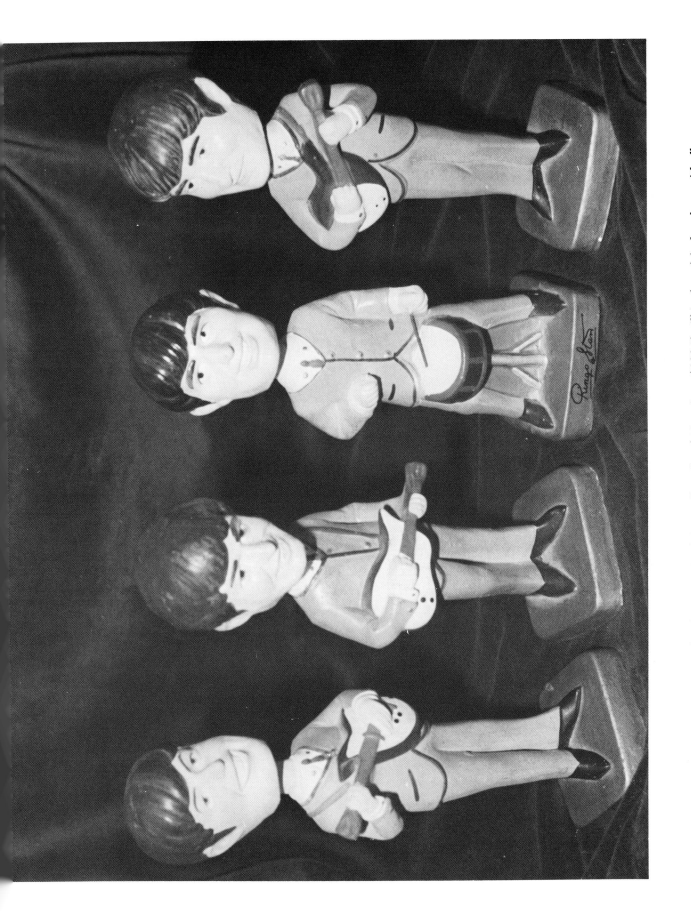

This set of **large size (8")** bobbing head dolls sells well at $40 each, or $200 if still in the original package with all four dolls. *Price Guide No.: 661*

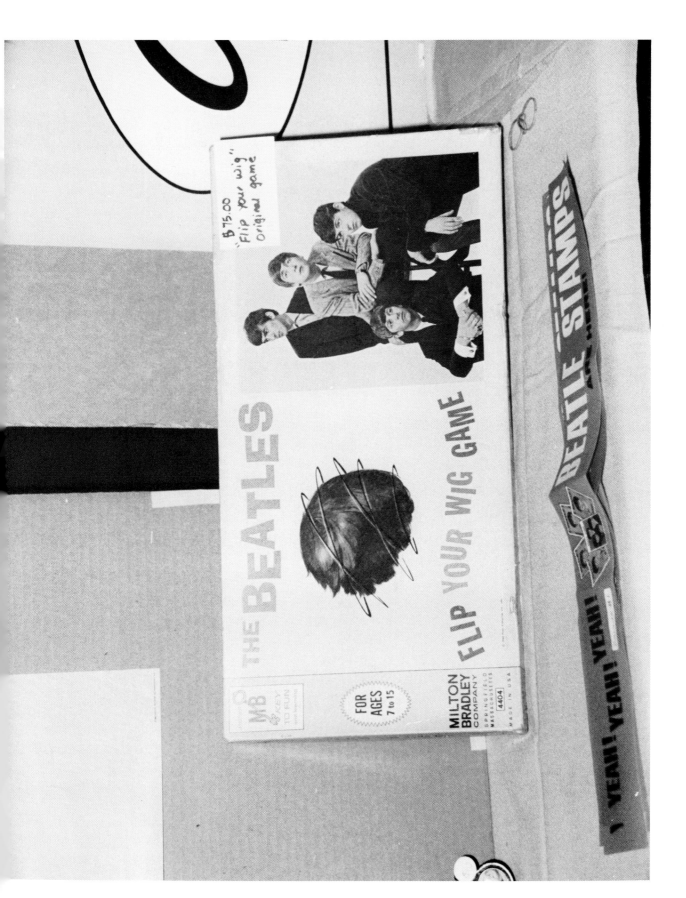

The "Flip Your Wig Game" in its original box usually sells for $50-75. One set brought in $87 in an auction.
Price Guide No.: 668

Item	Description	Condition	
		Near Mint	Very Good
660. DISK-GO-CASE	NEMS 1966 manufactured in many different colors, including yellow, red, purple as three most common, Beatles faces on round 45 record holder, also aqua, bright pink, light blue	$50	$35–45
661. DOLLS, BOBBING HEADS	Eight-inch plaster, hand painted, heads on springs, made in Japan, sold in U.S. by Carmaseat Co., 1964, one for each Beatle, wearing blue/grey collarless suits	$30–40 ea.	
	Set of all four	$160–175	
	In box with original inserts	$200	
662. DOLLS, INFLATABLE	Cartoon characters, 15 inches when inflated of each Beatle	$12–15	
	Set of four	$40	
663. DOLLS, NODDER	Four-inch plastic with moveable instruments of each Beatle	$10–12 ca.	
	Four-inch plastic dolls, nodder heads, instruments do not move, made in Hong Kong	$8–10 ea.	
664. DOLLS, REMCO	*Four and one-half inch rubber dolls with doll hair in black suits, holding instruments with signatures, NEMS 1964 by Remco Co.		
	With instruments	$30–50 ea.	$25–30
	Without instruments	$25–30 ea.	
	Still in original box	$40–60	
	Set of all four still in original boxes	$150–200	
665. DRUM	With Beatles faces, rare	$400+	
666. FLASHER PINS	Two and one-half inch, one of each Beatle, one says "Beattle Booster"	$3.50 ea.	
	Counterfeit	$2 ea.	
667. FLASHER RINGS	One of each Beatle, Beatles face flashes on small plastic ring, set of four	$15 set	
668. FLIP YOUR WIG GAME	By Milton Bradley Co., 1964, in box with all pieces	$50–75**	$25–40
	Individual pieces to complete a set	$2–4 ea.	

M E M O R A B I L I A

----

*George doll hardest to find; two varieties of faces, hard rubber and soft rubber — no value difference.
**Average price. Some dealers have been getting $85 on very good set and over $100 on an almost mint condition box and complete set.

An example of the colored Beatles drinking glasses (yellow or white background) worth about $35. *Price Guide No.: 669*

Beatles drinking glasses came in clear or colored versions. A complete set of four still in the original box would be worth at least $100. *Price Guide No.: 669*

Item	Description	Condition	
		Near Mint	Very Good
669. GLASSES/CUPS	NEMS 1964, different varieties, one of each Beatle, white and rare yellow	$35--200 ea.	
	Clear	$35–40	
670. GUITAR	Small red plastic by Mastro Industries with Beatles faces and signatures, "JR Guitar"	$50–65	
	Medium guitar Beatles "New Sound" Guitar	$65–75	
	With original instruction book	$75--90	
	Large size with faces and signatures, U.K. rare	$75--100	
	Large plastic electric, U.K., with faces and signature, rare	$100+	
671. GUM CARDS	TCG 1964 (Complete Sets):		
	Black-and-white series 1, nos. 1–60	$30–35	
	Black-and-white series 2, nos. 61--115	$30–35	
	Black-and-white series 3, nos. 116–165	$25–30	
	"A Hard Day's Night" series 1–55	$30–40	
	Color cards 1--64	$35–45	
	Color Diary cards 1--60	$35–45	
	Individual cards, black-and-white	$.25--.50 ea.	
	Individual cards, color	$.50–1.00 ea.	
	Still in original wrapper, unopened, five cards and gum	$10–15	
672. GUM CARD WRAPPERS & BOXES, CARTONS	Yellow wrapper from color cards	$10–15 ea.	
	Blue wrapper from black-and-white cards	$10–15 ea.	
	"A Hard Day's Night" wrapper from cards	$10–15 ea.	
	Original carton that held 24 packs of gum cards, 8 by 3½ inches, 1st--3rd editions	$30–50	$15--25
	"A Hard Day's Night" series carton	$50	
	Original box that held 24 cartons, 15½ by 8 by 11½ inches, rare item	$50--75	
673. GUM RINGS & DOLLS	Small flasher rings from gum machines, set of four	$4	
	Small troll-like dolls with "Beatle hair" from gum machines	$1 ea.	
674. HAIR BAND	Still in package	$15	
675. HAIR BRUSH	1964 in original package, three different colors – red, white, blue	$8--12	
676. HAIR SPRAY	NEMS 1964 with Beatles faces on can, rare	$100–125	
677. HALLOWEEN COSTUMES	Beatles, Ben Cooper Costume Co., 1964, one of each Beatle	$60–75	

MEMORABILIA

The large size Beatles guitar, a very rare and valuable item of $100-300 estimated worth. *Price Guide No.: 670*

A version of the small size Beatles guitar, this one from the U.K. There is also a small red U.S. version often called a ukelele; both are valued at $75+. *Price Guide No.: 670*

An extremely rare item: Beatles hair spray. Dating from **1964**, this item might sell for **$100 or more**. *Price Guide No.: 676*

The "Beatles harmonica" by Hohner was an ordinary harmonica distinguished only by the Beatles' portraits on its box (item must therefore include the box to be valuable). *Price Guide No.: 679*

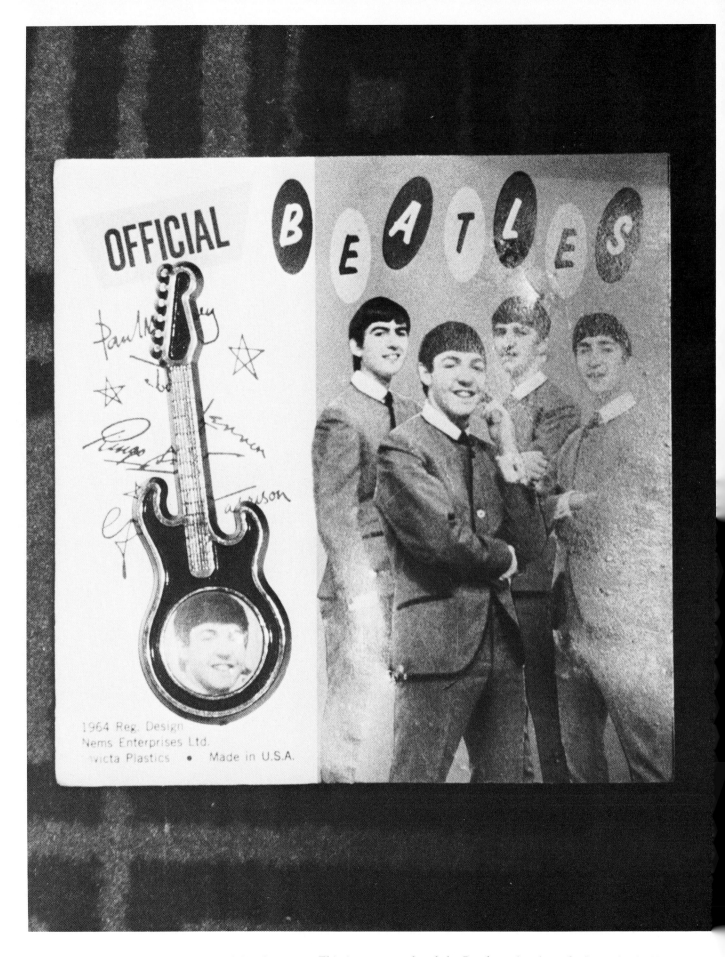

NEMS licensed many official jewelry items. This is an example of the Beatles guitar brooch. *Price Guide No.*
686

Item	Description	Condition Near Mint	Very Good
678. HANGERS	Each Beatle, made by Saunders Ent., U.K.	$25--30 ea.	$15--20 ea.
679. HARMONICA	In box, rare (box mentions Beatles, harmonica is ordinary Hofner)	$50	$35--45
680. HAT	1964 mail order item, red/white or blue/white with Beatles pictures, advertised as "Souvenir of Hollywood Bowl"	$15--30	
	"Surfer" hat, black-and-white	$25	
681. HUMMER	NEMS 1964 with Beatles pictures on blue background, rare item	$35	
682. ICE CREAM WRAPPER & BOX	"Beatle Bars"	NPA	

═══ Jewelry ═══

Item	Description	Near Mint	Very Good
683. Charm Bracelet	(Not NEMS), with painted faces of each individual Beatle hanging separately	$25	
684. Necklace	Made in England, 1 by 1 inch with 11 photographs in leather locket on chain, different colors	$20--25	

Jewelry (NEMS)

Item	Description	Near Mint	Very Good
685. Bracelet	With black-and-white pictures	$35--45	$25--35
686. Brooches	Set of five guitar-shaped pins with individual Beatles and one with group picture, NEMS 1964	$25	
687. Locket	Says Beatles on outside, black-and-white of inside by Randall Co.	$35--50	
688. Medallion	One and one-half inch with all four faces, color	$35	
689. Ring	With all four faces	$30	

Item	Description	Near Mint	Very Good
690. KEY CHAIN	Gold with black-and-white Beatle pictures, NEMS	$25	
691. LAMPSHADE	Rare 1964 U.K., Beatles faces and song titles	$100	
692. LICORICE COVERS	Very rare U.S., 1964, licorice records, one of each Beatle in sleeve	$50--100	
	Original box	$50	

MEMORABILIA

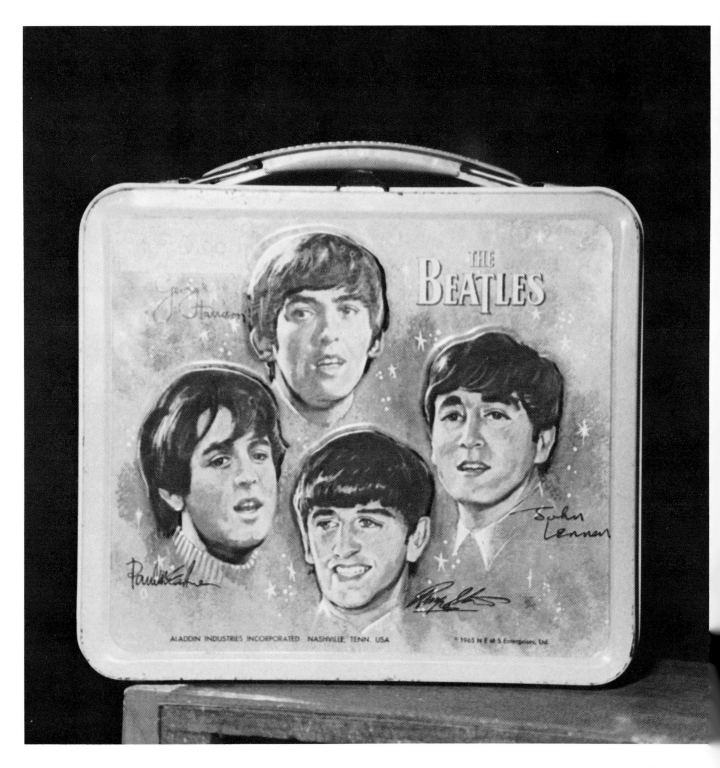

This Beatles (blue metal) lunchbox from 1965 sells for at least $40 in Very Good condition. The matching thermos sells for $35-40. *Price Guide No.: 693*

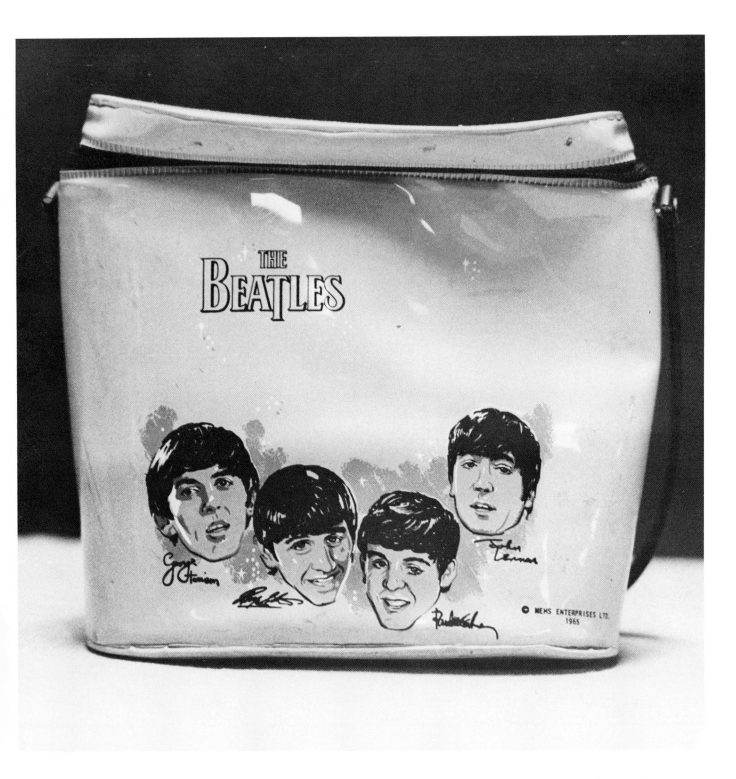

A soft-vinyl example of a Beatles lunchbox. This style, from 1965, came in a light blue and had a matching thermos. *Price Guide No.: 693*

MEMORABILIA

Item	Description	Near Mint	Very Good
693. LUNCH BOX & THERMOS	1964 Alladin Ind. blue box with Beatle pictures, lunchbox alone	$55–100	$35--55
	With matching thermos	$75–100	$45–75
	Thermos alone	$20–40	$25--30
	Soft blue plastic lunch box with Beatle pictures, 1965, lunchbox alone	$50--60	
	With matching thermos	$75–100	
	Thermos alone	$25--35	$20–25
	Yellow Submarine lunchbox and thermos	(see YS)	
694. MIRROR	With picture of Beatles, **Rubber Soul** cover, 32 by 22 inches	$50--75	
	Small size, 8 by 10 inches	$15	
695. MODEL KIT	1964 Revell Co. In U.S. Paul & Ringo models sold In U.K. George & John models sold		
	In box with all pieces, not assembled	$25–45	
	Assembled		$12--15
696. MUG	White ceramic with color photograph of Beatles, NEMS	$35–60	
697. NOTEBOOK	1964 NEMS, London Palladium picture on front cover, five-hold filler paper	$15--25	
698. NYLONS	Manufactured in U.K. and Europe by Carefree, two variations, brown or black, Beatles pictures on nylon stockings, still in original package	$15--30	
699. PAPER WEIGHTS	Original with 1963 picture	$25	
	Counterfeit	$10	
700. PATCH	Original 1964 as advertised in *Beatles Book*, 2½ by 4 inches	$6	
701. PEN	Original 1964 NEMS, white with Beatles signatures, faces on clip	$20–25	
	Also colored and colored Beatles picture	$10	
702. PEN & DESK SET	NEMS 1964 rare item, plain black pen in square white holder, holder has faces and names of each Beatle. Counterfeit is cube shaped.	$25--35	
703. PENCIL CASE	Made in China, rare	$50	
704. PENCILS	One of each, black-and-white picture and date of birth, 1964	$10 ea.	
705. PENNANT	1964 with four faces, came in different colors, different styles.	$5--10	

The 1965 (blue metal) lunchbox with matching thermos sells for at least $75. *Price Guide No.: 693*

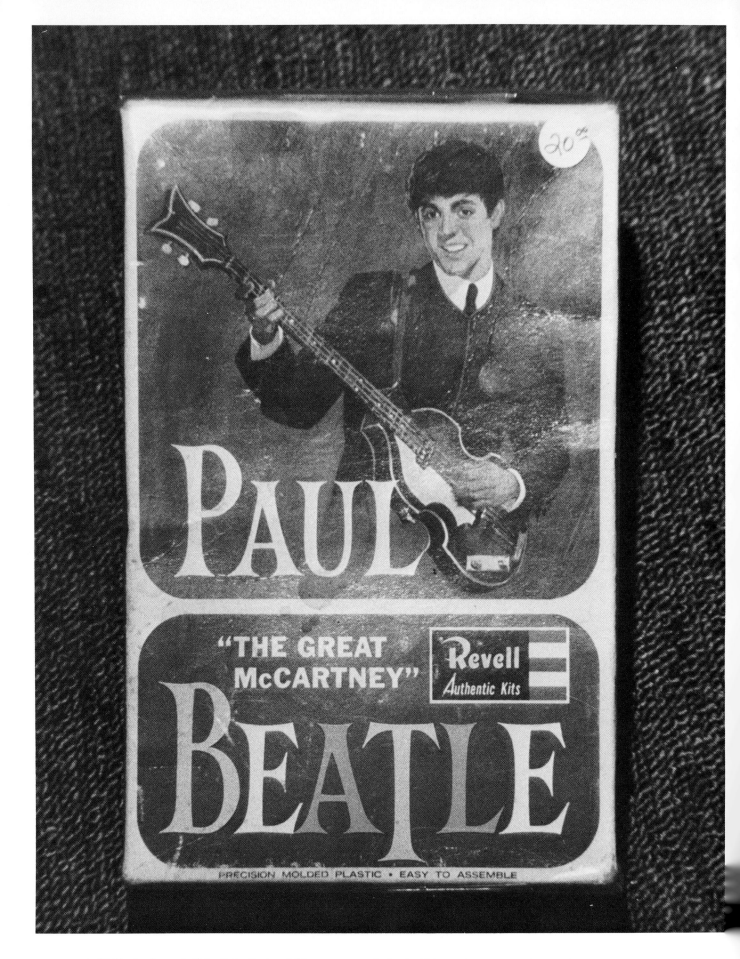

A 1964 plastic model kit. Only Paul and Ringo were made in the U.S., with John and George available in the U.K. Worth twice as much unassembled and complete with kit box. *Price Guide No.: 695*

This desk pen and stand is a popular 1964 item and very collectable. At the first conventions it was priced at a mere $8, but today it sells for $25-35. *Price Guide No.: 702*

Item	Description	Condition Near Mint	Very Good
706. PHONOGRAPH	Blue with Beatles faces in inside cover	$200–500	$100–200
	In box, original packaging	$600	
707. PHOTOGRAPHS	Beatles U.S.A. Ltd. fan club photographs, black-and-white, 8 x 10 inch and 6 by 8 inch	$1--3 ea.	
	In-person snapshots by fans, color	$1--2 ea.	
	In-person snapshots by fans, black-and-white	$.50--1.25 ea.	
	Professional press photographs from news agencies, color transparencies and 8 by 10 inch	$2--5 ea.	
	Black-and-white 4 by 6 inch, 8 by 10 inch, professional	$2--5 ea.	
	Rare in-person photographs of historical value, Cavern Club, Hamburg, early stage shots, etc.	$3 and up negotiable*	
708. PILLOW	NEMS 1964, Beatles faces and blue suits on white background, blue backside (also with red)	$50--75	$25–50
709. PIN-UPS & POSTCARDS	NEMS 1964 stills, color one of each Beatle, one group shot in collarless suits, 8 by 10 inch — common	$1.50--3 ea.	
	Legitimate postcards, various poses, 1960s, European	$1 ea.	
710. PIXERAMA FOLD BOOK	1963, U.K., 12 black-and-white wallet size pictures in folding pocket size booklet	$8--18	
711. PLATE	U.S., rare, faces of all four	$50–100	
712. POSTERS	Dell Poster Nos. 1 & 2, 50 by 20 inch, 1964, U.S.	$10–20	$5–7.50
	Various Beatles posters, 1964, black-and-white	$2--5**	
	1970--80 posters, color and black-and-white	$2--3***	
	Movie posters (see movie items)		
713. POUCH (PENCIL CASE)	Two difference styles, looks like bank money pouch, but is really described as pencil case, 1964 with Beatles faces, various colors — red, gold, blue, black, olive green, aqua	$25–40	
	Counterfeit, in red	$9	

M
E
M
O
R
A
B
I
L
I
A

---

*No set value — dependent upon quality, rarity, etc.

**Value dependent on quality, rarity, interest in picture, etc.

***Some exceptions for poses of high demand — particular interest.

Another variation of the Beatles record carrying case from 1964. This one came in blue or red, with a white top. It can sell for $80 in merely Good condition, and up to $150 in Near Mint condition. *Price Guide No.: 715*

A Beatles Irish linen tablecloth (or wall hanging) is almost never seen for sale in the U.S. It might go for $100 or

Item	Description	Condition	
		Near Mint	Very Good
714. PUZZLE	Illustrated lyrics jigsaw puzzle, 1970s, 800 pieces and poster included Yellow Sub puzzle (see YS items)	$10–25	
715. RECORD CARRYING CASE	Square blue and white top, NEMS 1964, rare (also red and white, rarer) Small size (45) Large size (LP)	 $100–125 $125–150	 $80–100 $100
716. RINGO CAP (also called John Lennon caps)	1965 original with Ringo trademark in gold inside, black leather Corduroy green (as John wore in "Help!"), also has Ringo trademark inside Without trademark — cloth caps	$25–35 $15 $10	
717. RINGO'S TOY DRUM	Sold through magazine ads, 1964, originally $19.95, extremely rare	$100+* est.	
718. RUG	Beatles faces woven, rare	$50+	$25–45
719. SATCHEL	Beatles faces, signatures	$30–45	
720. SCARF, HANDKERCHIEF	NEMS 10 by 10 inch (approximately) scarf with Beatles logo in various colored design Counterfeit (no fringe) Red triangular scarf with tie strings U.K. scarf with Beatles pictures and signatures	$40–50 $8** $10–20 $25–35	
721. SCRAPBOOK	NEMS 1964	$30–40	$20–30
722. STAMPS	NEMS 1964, distributed by Hallmark U.S.A., 100 Beatle stamps in set, one page of each Beatle and one of each individual, originally sold for $.59, color Complete set and cover still intact	$1–2 sheet $8	
723. SUNGLASSES	With Beatles faces pasted on corner, two on each lens, black rounded plastic With original display board	$12–15 $50* est.	$10
724. SWEATSHIRT	Official Beatles NEMS 1964 with Beatles ("I Want To Hold Your Hand" pose), and signatures on white background	$25–50	$15–25
725. TABLE CLOTH or WALL HANGING	U.K., Irish linen, rare Beatles pose	$50–100+	

---

*Never seen offered for sale.
**No collector value.

A rarity seldom seen for sale: Beatles talc (talcum powder). Containers came in blue-gray or yellow. At least a $60 item which, like Beatles hairspray, could probably sell for $100. *Price Guide No.: 726*

Item	Description	Condition	
		Near Mint	Very Good
726. TALC POWDER	Says "with the Beatles" by Margo of Mayfair, U.K., 1964, Beatles poses in collarless suit on one side, faces on the other, one yellow, one blue/grey, rare	$75--100*	$50--75
727. TEA SET	Beatles pictures on each cup and saucer, rare	$300	
728. TENNIS SHOES	By Wing Ding, 1964, box says "Beatles Sneakers by Wing Dings" with Beatles faces and signatures, blue, white, rare pink	$40--50	$30--40
	With original box	$60--100	
	High back style	$100	
729. TICKETS	To Beatles concerts:		
	Shea Stadium	$15--25	
	U.S. Beatles tours, unused	$15--25	
	Stub only	$8--15	
	To movie premieres: "A Hard Day's Night" preview, picture of Beatles on ticket, unused	$12	$10
	Washington, DC, closed-circuit show of first U.S. concert, 3/15/64	$10	
	Other unused movie tickets	$7--10	
730. TIE (Lariat)	NEMS 1964, on original card with Beatles faces on clip around string tie	$30--50	
731. TIE TACS	Set of four original cards, one of each, NEMS, 1964, gold or silver color	$10 ea.	
	Set of all four	$35	
	Guitar pin on 3 by 3 inch card, all four Beatles on guitar shaped tie-tac, bronze color	$25	
732. TILE	Rare U.K. ceramic wall tiles with Beatles poses, black on white background, orange and blue	$15--20 ea.	
733. TOTE BAG	Clear plastic with pictures of Beatles in black suits	$30--35	
	Blue plastic, 1965, designed like lunchbox	$25--30	
734. TOY, BEATLES HAIR NOVELTY	"Create your own hairstyle," 10½ by 8 inch, magnet moves iron fillings to form hair on drawing of head. Made by Merit, NEMS 1964	$15--25	
735. TOY, LIVING BEATLES	"Watch hair grow"		

M
E
M
O
R
A
B
I
L
I
A

---

*Listed for $200 by one dealer.

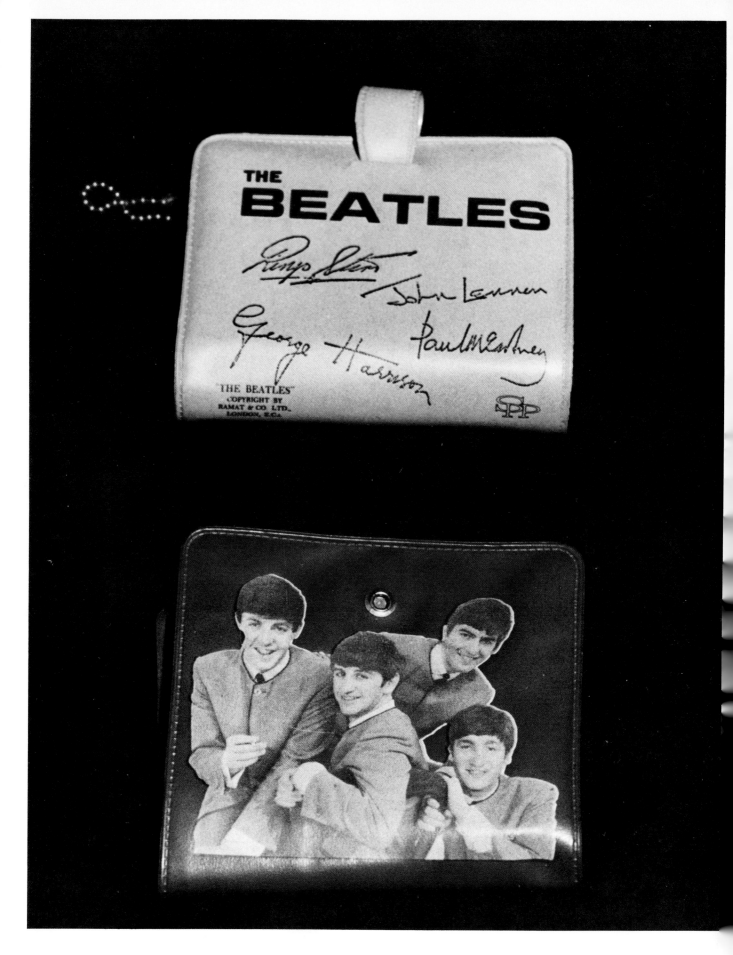

The Beatles wallet (back and front shown) included mirror, nail file, and wallet-size pictures of The Four. Made in several different colors, including the most common — gold and red. *Price Guide No.: 739*

A large display of Beatles wallpaper from 1964. This colorful item is usually sold today in 18 x 22-inch panels for approximately $20-35. A complete eight foot roll might be priced at $80 or more. *Price Guide No.: 741*

M E M O R A B I L I A

Item	Description	Near Mint	Very Good
736. TRAY	1964 U.K., made by Worcester Ware, Beatles faces individually in color on white background, back side is red, 12½ by 12½ inches	$35–50	$30–35
737. T-SHIRT	1964 original, with picture in upper left corner	$25–35	
738. UNDERWEAR	Beatles faces on panties, U.K., rare	$50*	
739. WALLET	Sold through magazine offers, 1964, more than one style, different colors (beige, red, gold, pink), with Beatles pose and signatures		
	Original came with comb, mirror and Beatles pictures	$30–40	$20–30
	Without extras, wallet alone	$20–25	$12–18
740. WALLET PHOTOS BOOKLET	Original 1964 Dell publishing booklet 5 by 3¾ inches, with 20 wallet pictures, black-and-white and Beatles horoscopes, biographies	$10–15	
741. WALLPAPER	1964, with Beatles faces and signatures, full color, complete roll (8 feet)	$50–80	
	In panels (18 by 22 inch sections)	$25–50	$20–25
742. WATCH	Pocket watch, rare, 1960s	$100+	
	Beatles faces, original	$100+	
	Made in 1970s	$25	
743. WIG & WIG CASE	Original packaging says "Beatle wig" black moptop wig doesn't say Beatles NEMS 1964 in original package	$35–50	
	Without package	$10	
	Rare wig case	$60	
	U.K. version, package says "The Beatles Wig"	$25–50	

"Yellow Submarine" Items

Item	Description	Near Mint	Very Good
744. ANIMATION CELLS	Original cells from "Yellow Submarine" movie (sold for $35 in department stores in late 1960s) with Beatle character or important film characters (Blue Meanie, Boob, etc.)	$75–200	
	Less important pieces of film	$15–50**	
745. BANK	Ceramic, of each Beatle	$40–50 ea.	$30–35

---

*Estimated value.

**Value dependent upon interest of picture, amount of color, importance of character, etc.

An uncommon collectible: the "Yellow Submarine" Blue Meanie Halloween costume, which sells for at least $50 these days. *Price Guide No.: 757*

Item	Description	Near Mint	Very Good
746. BOOK MARKER	Shaped like each character	$10	
747. BULLETIN BOARD	Colorful Blue Meanie pin-up boards, 22 by 7 inch, one says "Stamp Out Fun"	$10–15 ea.	
748. BULLETIN BOARD	Set of six, including one group, one each Beatle, one Yellow Submarine -- 2x2 ft.	$20–25 ea. $100 set	
749. CALENDAR	With individual scenes from film, large size 12 by 12 inches, Western Publ. Co., 1968, U.S.	$18–25	$12–18
750. CARTOON KIT	By Colorforms — rare	$75	$50
751. CLOCK	Oris, rare	$300	
752. COASTER SET	Five different, one of each Beatles character, one of Yellow Submarine, in original package	$15--25	
753. CORGI TOY	Yellow Submarine toy made by Corgi Co., metal submarine with Beatles heads and some moving parts	$70--75	
	In original box	$100–125	
754. FIGURINES	By Hummel, of each Yellow Submarine character, rare	$75 ea.	
755. GREETING CARDS	Sunshine Art Studios, 6 by 4½ inch, blank inside with colorful scenes and characters from film on cover	$1.50–2.50 ea.	
	Large cards of individual character with greeting (i.e., "Happy Birthday")	$2--4 ea.	
	Still in original box of 18 cards	$18--30	
756. GUM CARDS	U.K., small-size — 2 by 1 inch — complete set of 60 cards from film, in color	$50–100	
	U.K., rare large cards (same size as U.S. gum cards)	$100–200* est.	
	Rare wrapper, estimated value	$75–100 est.	
757. HALLOWEEN COSTUMES	Blue Meanie by Collegeville Costumes	$50–75	
758. HANGERS	Each Beatle film character on a cardboard clothes hanger (set of 4)	$25--40 ea. $100--150 set	
759. KEY CHAIN	Individual Beatle character on colorful seven-inch metal	$7--8 ea.	
760. LUNCH BOX & THERMOS	Lunchbox alone	$45--50	$25
	Thermos alone	$35	$20
	Set	$70	$40--50

---

*Saw offered for $1,000.00 — $100--200 more realistic.

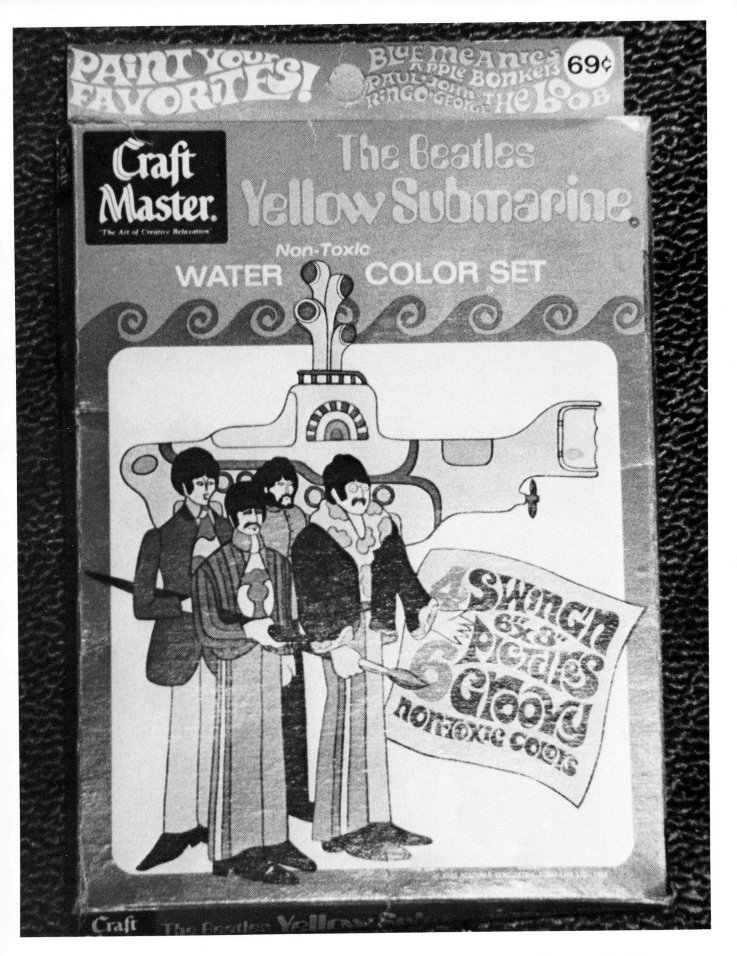

Another "Yellow Submarine" spin-off memorabilia item from 1968 — a set of water colors. *Price Guide No.:* 763

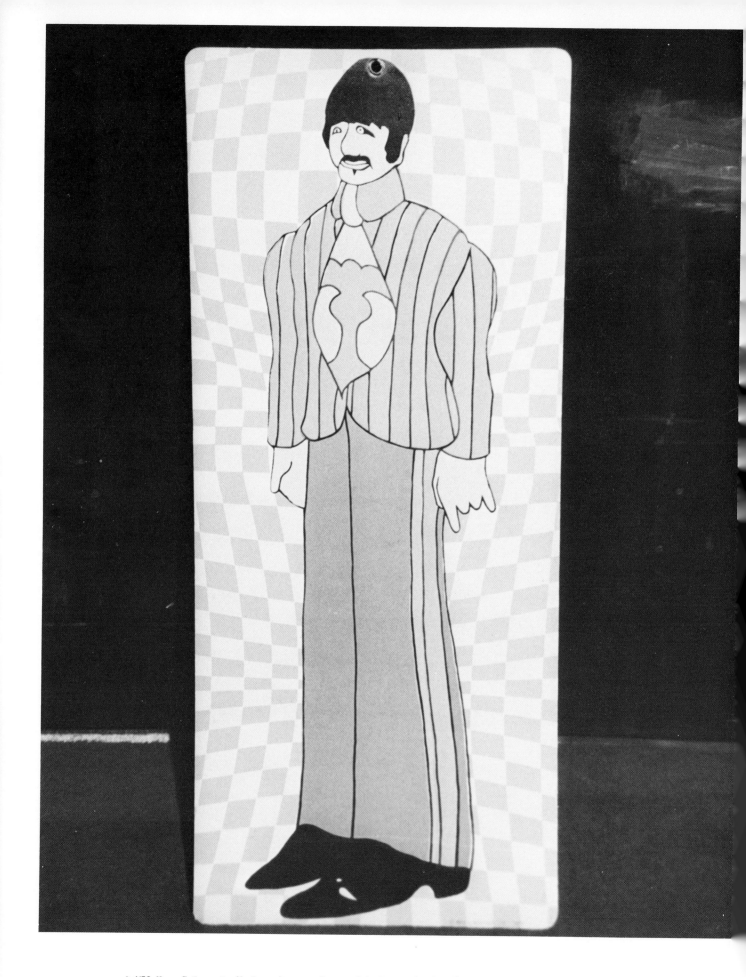

A "Yellow Submarine" placard, one of several designs valued at $15-20 each. *Price Guide No.: 766*

A colorful "Yellow Submarine" poster from 1968. *Price Guide No.: 769*

A "Yellow Submarine" poster still in its original packaging, which makes it worth about $15. *Price Guide No.:* 769

Item	Description	Condition Near Mint	Very Good
761. MOBILE	Yellow Submarine and figures (Blue Meanie, Beatles, etc.) set in packaging	$45	
	Individual cardboard mobile figures	$7–10 ea.	
762. MODEL	Plastic Beatles display, Yellow Submarine and Beatles standups, still in box	$75	
	Already assembled	$50	
763. PAINT SET	Two sizes, large and small, water color set by Craft Master	$20–30 ea.	
764. PHOTO ALBUMS & SCRAPBOOK	Photo album, 9½ by 7½ inches, with plastic sheets for 3 by 5 inch pictures	$30–35	
	Regular large size scrapbook with white construction paper pages	$30–40	
765. PINS	Set of eight character pins, including each Beatle, Lord Mayor, Blue Meanie, Apple Bonker, etc.	$8–16	
	Yellow Submarine stickpin	$16	
766. PLACARDS	Set of four, 9 by 21 inch long, colorful cardboard, day-glow colors	$18–20 set	
767. PLAQUE	Wall hanging of Yellow Submarine	$15	
768. POP OUT DECORATIONS BOOK	Cutouts booklet, 18 by 24 inches	$12–25	
769. POSTER	In box by Craft Master, 15 by 21 inches	$15	
770. PUZZLES	Small size (mini), 10–20 variations	$15	
	Medium size, 8½ by 9½ inches, 10–20 variations	$20–30	
	Large size, 12 by 12 inches (box) makes 19 inch puzzle, 650 pieces, many different designs, all manufactured by Jaymar	$25–40	
771. STATIONERY	Note paper and envelopes, U.S., still in original wrapper of different characters	$10–20	
772. STICK-ONS	Of each Beatle	$10–12	
773. SWITCH PLATES	For lights in different characters	$12–25 ea.	
	Set of four	$50	
774. WRIST WATCH	In original box, still working	$175	

MEMORABILIA

213

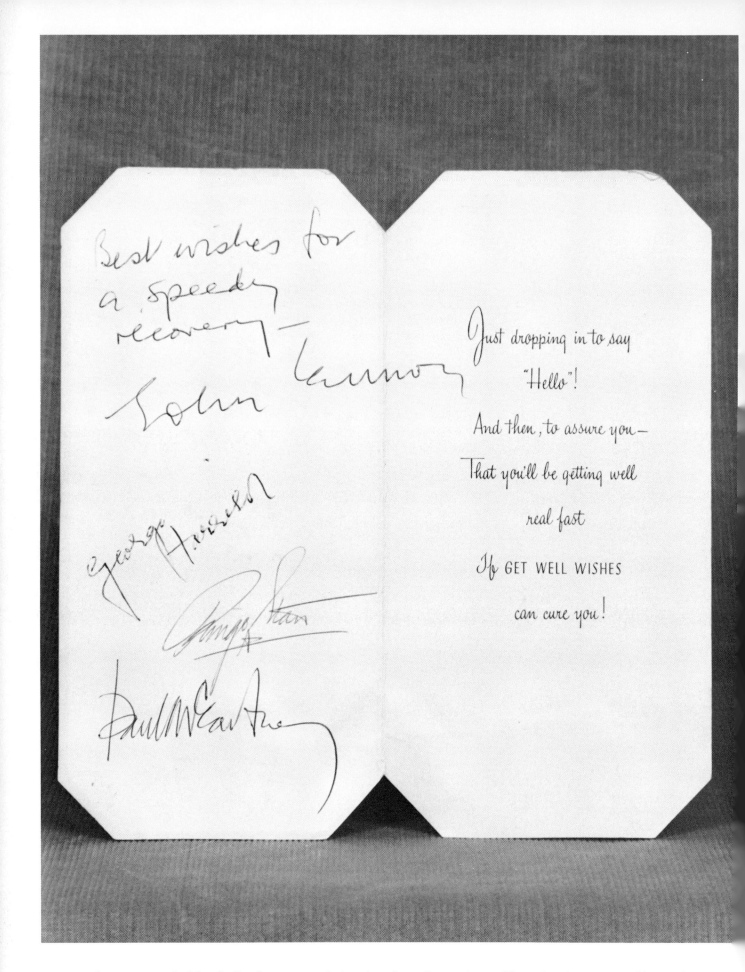

Items autographed by the Beatles vary greatly in value, depending on factors like authenticity, source, historical significance, etc. This one, a get well card, might bring $100 in an auction. *Price Guide No.: 792*

Item	Description	Condition	
		Near Mint	Very Good

Miscellaneous Promo Items

775. SUNGLASSES — Promo by Warner Bros. for George Harrison's **33 1/3** LP, made like glasses George wears on cover of LP — $40–60

776. NEON LIGHT — Promo from Capitol Records, rare, says **WINGS** in neon, sits on base — $200–300

777. BEATLES STYROFOAM DISPLAY — Says "Beatles" in large styrofoam wall hanging with each of the Beatles' faces, released 1974, for ten-year anniversary of Beatles on Capitol, blue and green — $35–50

778. WINGS STYROFOAM DISPLAY — Large blue Wings in styrofoam to hang on wall — $60–75

779. PROMO POSTERS
- **London Town**, U.K., 40 by 60 inch, rare — $15
- **Rotogravure**, LP cover pictured — $8
- **Dark Horse**, LP cover pictured, 24 by 35 inches — $8
- **Love Songs** — $4.50
- Most posters — $3–5

780. PROMO DISPLAYS
- **Ringo The 4th** stand-up — $15
- **Back To The Egg** stand-up, cardboard — $8
- *Starting Over* stand-up, held the single — $15–20
- **Walking On Thin Ice** — $20

781. MOBILES
- Wings **Speed Of Sound** — $15
- Beatles **Rock 'N Roll**, clothesline with jackets — $12–15
- **Hollywood Bowl**, kits contain clothes-line and 20 LP cover slicks to hang from it — $15

782. PROMO PHOTOS
- Still from Apple — $3 ea.
- Press photographs from record company — $1–3 ea.

783. PRESS KITS — For:
- **Dark Horse** with biography — $8
- **Venus & Mars** — $12
- John Lennon **Rock & Roll** — $12–15
- **London Town**, pictures and post-cards, etc. — $12–15

784. FRISBEE
- Beatles **Rock & Roll Music**, 1976 — $10–15
- Wings **Venus & Mars**, 1975 — $5

785. FAN CLUB ITEMS — From Beatles USA Ltd., put together cube, 1969 — $10–12

OTHER SPECIAL & PROMOTIONAL ITEMS

OTHER SPECIAL & PROMOTIONAL ITEMS

786. PROMO T-SHIRTS

No set price, depends on number made, how widely distributed, how much demand, etc. Many promo shirts have been counterfeited are are now common, i.e., *Walls & Bridges* and *Dark Horse*

Venus & Mars, "It's All Balls," U.K. version — $15

Back To The Egg, from press party, original — $15

787. PROMO JACKETS

No set price, as above. Many fakes** — $50–75

788. DISPLAY BOXES

For special Collectors issue of 45s — $10

Original shipping box for Apple records for singles with Apple logo on it — $81*

789. PROMO TOYS

Wings bus, **London Town** promo, with box — $35

790. PROMO ACCESSORIES

Mending packet for **Walls & Bridges** with John Lennon's eyes — $6.50

Four-inch comb for John Lennon's **Rock & Roll** — $6.50

791. PROMO BUTTONS

Two-inch "Listen to this Badge," shows John Lennon's face — $4.50

"You Should Have Been There" from John Lennon's **Rock & Roll** — $4.50

"Ohnothimagain" George Harrison, one-inch — $2.50

Ruttles 1½ inch — $2.50

Most buttons — $2.50–4.50

Other Collectibles

792. AUTOGRAPHS

Highly variable value, dependent upon what it is signed on, historical value, authenticity guarantee, etc.

Some examples:

Beatles photo 1962 with Pete Best, given to George's girlfriend, with xxx's from Paul and George — $175

Ringo's autograph on in-person framed photograph (showing Ringo and Paul at L.A. concert, Wings, 1976) — $91

Ringo's on *Blindman* single — $35

George's on *Ding Dong* single — $35

Paul's on sheet music to *Wonderful Xmas* — $118

John's autograph on Hunter Davies Beatles biography — $75

---

*Brought this much in an open auction at Los Angeles Beatlefest in 1980.
**Beware of Beatles "tour jackets". They never existed. Not authentic.

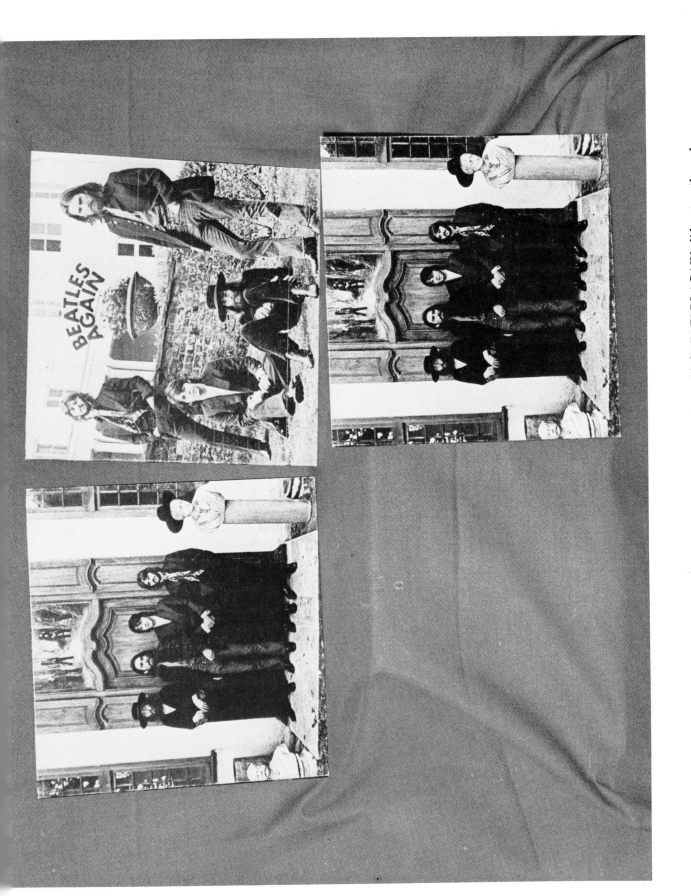

The front covers of the HEY JUDE album, originally to have been titled BEATLES AGAIN, did not go through as many changes as the LP's back cover art work.

Four different back cover slicks for this U.S. Beatles' album. Before official release, Capitol Records experimented with different jacket art work, but these versions were never commercially released and no price has been

Item	Description	Condition Near Mint Very Good
	John and Yoko's on *In His Own Write*	$110
	John's on *Starting Over* 45	$125
	Original **Please Please Me** LP, U.K., autographed by all four	$150–200
	Autographed fan club photographs signed by all four, 1964 (genuine** autographs only)	$130
	Most genuine autographs by an individual Beatle will bring (at least in an auction and open bidding)	$50–100
	By all four Beatles	$100--150
	With historic value, on rare record, program, sheet music, etc.	$150–500+
	Beatles USA Ltd. fan club photographs, autograph is stamped on, common, looks like signed, one for each year of the club	$5–10
793. BEATLES COLLECTION	Boxed set, 12 LPs and **Rarities**, 3,000 pressed, U.S., still sealed	$300--400
	Japanese	$100–125
794. BUTCHER COVER POSTER	Original promo from 1966 by Capitol, full color picture, rare, 18 by 24 inches	$200–350
	Remake from 1973	$6
	Fake jacket slicks (texture wrong)	$3
	Original slicks — pebbly feel	$100
795. CHINA IMPORTS	**Beatles vs Tom Jones LP**	$100
	My Bonnie 10-inch	$600
	Rubber Soul red vinyl	$125
796. COVERS	*Somewhere in England* original art	$100–250
	Counterfeit	$3
797. FRENCH RECORDS	*Why* and three EP on Polydor	$200
798. GOLD RECORDS	Many different ones exist, for every Beatles and solo record and LP made there exists at least half a dozen gold records, each of the Beatles received one, plus the company and several more may have gone to branch offices, etc.	
	No one set value, dependent on which record it is for, demand for that particular one, historical value, guarantee of authenticity, etc.*	
	Some examples seen sold:	
	Let It Be platinum award for two million sold	$450
	Wings Over America presented to Paul	$450

------

*Counterfeit gold records are common at conventions. Exact duplications right down to RIAA seal, frames, even gold plated. But never belonged to the Beatles or record company. Very good homemade jobs. Still have value as wall hangings but not as a collectible. (Real worth should be $200, not $400–500.)

**All fan club members received "autographed" photos, but signatures were stamped on — not real.

		Near Mint	Very Good

Item	Description	Near Mint	Very Good
	With The Beatles on Parlophone presented to the Beatles with notarized statement of authenticity, minimum bid	$400	
	Hey Jude, original presented to Beatles	$300	
799. GUM CARD PLATES	Original plates from which the Topps trading cards were printed	$500*	
800. INDIAN 78s	Rare singles on 78 rpm from India	$200--400	
801. ITALIAN JOHN LENNON ANTHOLOGY	10 LP set promo, only 1,000 pressed	$350	
802. LABELS	"Girl/You're Gonna Lose That Girl" set of six unused labels still on 8 by 11 inch sheet, uncut	$2	
	Set of two for *Getting Closer* promo	$2	
803. LITHOGRAPHS	Bag 1 limited edition set released in Holland in late 70s (originally in Amsterdam, 1970, but confiscated by police)		
	Numbered box set	$50–80	
	One of the original lithos, framed, personally autographed by John	$1500–3500**	
	One of limited edition (300) complete Bag 1 sets, contains 14 original lithos, all signed by John	$25,000	
	Original Bag 1 bag, white	$300--500	
	Reproduced booklet sold by Lee Nordness Gallery in 1980–81, pictures all 14 lithos	$8	
804. LOOK POSTERS	Photographed by Richard Avendon, 1968, offered through *Look* Magazine, set of five	$70	
	Individually of each Beatle	$25--35	
805. PAUL'S HAT	The one he wore in "A Hard Day's Night"	$400***	
806. POLAND EPs	Fold-open color covers double EPs	$15–25	
807. POLAND POSTCARD RECORDS	On flexi-disc square cardboard solos	$6	
	Rare pink square with picture unrelated to Beatles, 1968	$25	
808. RINGO'S TIE	Given to fan along with photograph of Ringo wearing it	$41****	

---

*Went for this amount in an auction at L.A. Beatlefest in 1980.

**One seen in San Francisco art gallery in 1980 for $500, after John's death price rose immediately to

***In auction in Boston, 1976.

****In auction at New Jersey Beatlefest, 1980.

A Polish "postcard 45," this one for *Sally G* by Wings. *Price Guide No.: 807*

Item	Description	Condition	
		Near Mint	Very Good
809. ROADIE SHIRTS/PINS/ BACKSTAGE PASSES	Shirts from tours	$10+	
	Official tour pins	$5+	
	Backstage passes	$1+	
810. RUSSIAN EPs & LPs	With picture jacket, includes: *Penny Lane, Can't Buy Me Love, Something, Here Comes The Sun, Carry That Weight, Let It Be*	$20--35 ea.	
	Imagine LP, import, common	$14--16	
811. SCRAPBOOK, CLIPPINGS	Complete old scrapbook of assorted clippings (not in Beatles scrapbook)	$8--25*	
	Individual clippings:		
	Pin-ups, color	$1	
	Black-and-white	$.50	
	Articles	$.50+	
	Often sold in packages on each individual Beatle	$3--5*	
812. SHEET MUSIC	Most old Beatles sheet music sells in the range of	$3--7	
	Some exceptions seen include:		
	Strawberry Fields Forever with color Beatles picture on front	$8	
	Please Please Me, old picture of Beatles on front cover	$15	
	I Want To Hold Your Hand, Help!, Eight Days A Week	$10 ea.	
813. UK RECORDS	Some special cases:		
	Please Please Me LP on Parlophone, monophonic, original black and gold label, rare	$200	
	My Bonnie EP, green sleeve, Polydor, rare	$350	
	Love Me Do "Not for sale" white label promo	$290	
	I Want To Hold Your Hand/This Boy, Parlophone demo R 5084	$200+	$150
	From Me To You "Not for sale" white label promo	$140	

---

*Value very dependent on quality of clippings, historic value, demand on particular items, condition clip are in, rarity of clippings, etc.

Item	Description	Condition Near Mint	Very Good
814. FILMS	8mm silent sold through teen and movie magazines, 50 ft.	$20–25	$15
	Super 8mm sound		
	7 minute film	$35–40	
	1 hour film	$125–200	
	16mm full length film	NPA	
815. LOBBY CARDS	For Beatles movies in color, usually eight to a set	$4–10 ea.	
	"How I Won The War" set	$20–25	
	"A Hard Day's Night" counterfeits, no collector value		
816. POSTER CARDS (window cards)	For window of movie theater:		
	"A Hard Day's Night"	$12–20	
	"Yellow Submarine" set of four in color	$16–20	
	Poster and poster cards for "Let It Be" with press book	$150	
	Counterfeits, no true collector value		
817. POSTERS	"A Hard Day's Night" large size comes in two sections	$35–50	
	Regular size, one sheet	$35–50	
	"Blindman" in French	$15	
	"Family Way" 1967	$20–40	
	"A Hard Day's Night" and "Help!" combination	$75	
	"Help!" – three sheets	$75–80	
	"Help!" – one sheet	$30–50	
	"How I Won The War"	$8–100	
	"Let It Be"	$30–50	
	"Live & Let Die" in French	$30	
	"Son Of Dracula"	$12	$10
	"Yellow Submarine" (one sheet)	$30–50*	
	"Yellow Submarine" (six sheets)	$100	
	"Blindman"	$20	
	"Magical Mystery Tour" U.K. & U.S., rare, estimated value	$50	
	"Bangladesh" (one sheet)	$10–15	
	"Beatles Come To Town" (one sheet)	$20	
	"Around The Beatles"	$20	
	Various foreign posters for Beatles films	$25–75	
818. PRESS BOOKS	"Yellow Submarine" eight pages, 13 by 18 inches, shows the posters available, list of companies that sold "Yellow Submarine" merchandise	$25	$18
	"Magic Christian," 28 pages	$10	
	"Caveman" with biographies and 20 black-and-white stills, color transparencies	$20+	

---

*Has gone for $95 at Beatles convention.

Item	Description	Condition	
		Near Mint	**Very Good**
819. PROGRAMS	"A Hard Day's Night" — rare	$35+	
	"How I Won The War"	$12--16	
820. SOUVENIRS	Bandaid from "Help!" — rare	$10–15	
	Paper badge	$5	
821. STILLS	Wide variety of shots, black-and-white, most from 1964--65		
	"A Hard Day's Night" shots, common	$1--3	
	"How I Won The War"	$3--5	
	Jane Asher film stills:		
	Black-and-white	$2–4	
	Color	$3–4	
822. TICKETS	Special preview to "A Hard Day's Night," August 24, 1964	$10	$7
	Special preview sourvenir ticket with picture of Beatles on it	$15	$10
	"Help!" souvenir ticket, August 23, 1965	$4	
823. VIDEOS	One hour length, illegal	$45--60	
	Commercial (i.e., "Let It Be")	$65–75	

M O V I E   I T E M S

The Beatles As Merchandise:
A List of Licensed Manufacturers & Their Products

Following the death of Brian Epstein and the setting up of offices for Apple Corps Ltd., mounting friction between The Beatles and Nemperor Holdings resulted in an extended dispute culminating in the transfer of all merchandising rights to Apple Corps Ltd. What follows is the text of a document prepared for The Beatles' holding company at the time of the transfer. The original document was typed in small, ordinary typewriter face, and has been reset for this book (preserving typographical errors). The list of manufacturers is probably incomplete, and is largely confined to firms in the U.K. It is also not known how many of the items licensed were actually manufactured.

Exclusive Licences

NAME AND ADDRESS	DATE OF AGREEMENT	TERM	LICENCE FOR:	TERRITORY
A. & B.C. Chewing Gum Ltd. Harold Hill Estate, Spilsby Road, Romford, Essex.	1st Nov. 1963	3 years	Chewing gum and bubble gum. Trading/Hobby cards.	World.
	6th Feb. 1964.	3 years	Confectionery excluding Chocolate, Rock and rock products, lollipops, humbugs and fondants. Stickers.	World.
Daniel Buckley Enterprises Ltd. 1–5 Poland Street, London, W.1.	Nov. 1963.	5 years.	Gonk Toy Models Men's slacks and casual jackets, suits, ties, shirts. Women's suits, casual jackets, slacks, skirts, shirts, nylon stockings, blouses. Socks, Pyjamas, T. Shirts, Salt & Pepper Pots. Containers for Easter eggs, Fans, Balloons, Lighters, Mechanical toys, Watches, Book Matches, Soft Drinks, Swimwear, Cuff links, Biscuits, Rubber Toys, Egg cups (not glass), Hair bands including hair bows, hair ribbons, hair clips.) Hair shampoo, Towels, Pillow Cases, Sheets, Chocolate.	United Kingdom.
Barrow Hepburn & Gale Ltd. Grange Mills, Bermondsey, London, S.E.1.	4th Dec. 1963.	2 years. Option to renew.	Waist belts of all materials.	U.K. Eire. U.S.A. Western Germany. Australia. New Zealand.
R.D. Blackwood & Son (Production) Ltd. 30a, Elizabeth Street, Blackpool.	10th Feb. 1964.	2 years. Option to renew.	All lettered rock and rock novelties (excluding an imitation rock disc record) lollipops, humbugs.	U.K. N.I.
Bell Toys Ltd. Primus House, Willow Street, London, E.C.2.	27th Nov. 1963.	2 years. Option to renew.	Plastic wig.	U.K.
C. Kendall Clapp, John Cottrell and Charles W. Schillings, 310 Sansome Street, San Francisco.	2nd Mar. 1964.	5 years.	Pompon.	World.
Centro Carpets (Sales) Ltd. Winchester House, Old Broad Street, E.C.2.	9th Mar. 1964.	12 months.	Floor covering and textile velour wall hanging.	U.K. N.I. U.S.A. Canada. Germany. France. Benelux Countries.
P.B. Cow (Li-Lo) Ltd. Liverpool Road, Trading Estate, Slough, Bucks.	18th March 1964.	2 years.	Airbeds.	World.
Louis F. Dow Co. 2242, University Avenue, St. Paul 14, Minnesota.	26th Feb. 1964.	5 years.	Calendars, Lithographic Posters, Murals.	World.
Robert Dunn Ltd. 7 Wilton Square South, Belfast, 13.	13th Mar. 1964.	2 years.	Bedheads.	U.K. N.I. Eire. U.S.A.

NAME AND ADDRESS	DATE OF AGREEMENT	TERM	LICENCE FOR:	TERRITORY
European Travel Goods Ltd. 172–174, Albion Road, London, N.19.	5th Dec. 1963.	2 years. Option to renew.	Travelling bags.	World.
Charles Early & Marriott (Witney) Ltd. Witney Mills, Oxfordshire.	3rd March 1964.	2 years.	Blanket.	World.
Excel Fancy Goods Ltd. Bk. St. Heliers Road, Blackpool, Lancs.	8th Jan. 1964.	1 year. Option to renew.	T.V. Lamps of 3-dimensional design.	Germany, Holland, Canada, U.S.A.
Gordon Dunn Ltd. 7, Highfield Road, Doncaster.	6th Jan. 1964.	Amended to 1 year from 6th Mar. 1964.	Curtain fabric.	World.
Thomas Hope and Sankey Hudson Ltd. Crusader Works, Chapeltown Street, Manchester 1.	7th Nov. 1963.		Writing Pad, Jigsaw Puzzle, Scrapbook.	World.
Industrial Gifts Ltd. Saxone House, 74a, Regent Street, London W.1.	27th Nov. 1963.	6 months. Option to renew.	Lipsticks.	U.K. Eire.
Kangolone Ltd. Kangol House, Fitzroy Square, London, W.1.	22nd Nov. 1963.		Hats and Berets.	World.
Kigu Limited, Waldo Works, Waldo Road, London, N.W.10.	29th Nov. 1963.	2 years. Option to renew.	Compacts.	World.
Lau-Kee & Co. Ltd. 2 Lower Ormond Quay, Dublin, 1.	3rd Mar. 1964.	2 years. Option to renew.	Cutlery, Spectacles.	U.S.A. Canada.
Joseph Lang & Co. Ltd. Bath House, 57–60, Holborn Viaduct, London, E.C.1.	19th Nov. 1963.	2 years from 1st Dec. 1963 with option on 2 further years.	Glass Tumblers.	World.
Lester Belliston, c/o Froerer, Horowitz, Parker, Richards & Thornley, Suite 200, Kiesel Building, Ogden, Utah, U.S.A.	12th Mar. 1964.		Pocket brush.	World excluding U.K. Eire. C.I.
Littlewoods Mail Order Stores Ltd. Waterloo Buildings, Liverpool.	18th Nov. 1963.	7 years with 1 year option.	Dresses.	U.K. N.I.
Sidney Margolis Ltd., Margo House, Hemp Row, London, S.E.17.	27th Nov. 1963.	2 years. Option to renew.	Talcum Powder.	World.
Maddocks & Dick Ltd. Sandeman House, 13 High Street, Edinburgh 1.	4th Dec. 1963. 6th Dec. 1963.	2 years. 2 years. Option to renew.	Handkerchiefs, Pennants. Headsquares.	United Kingdom.
David Marsh (Manchester) Ltd. Irk Rubber Works, Queen's Road, Collyhurst, Manchester 9.	10th Dec. 1963.	2 years. Option to renew.	Vinyl Playballs.	U.K.
Olive Adair Ltd. 32, Hope Street, Liverpool 1.	23rd Jan. 1964.	2 years. Option to renew.	Perfume.	World.
Paton Advertising Service Pty Ltd. for Mobil Oil Australia Ltd. — Melbourne, Australia.	5th Mar. 1964.	Until 31st Dec. 1964.	Photographs to be given away from all service stations and right to advertise such.	Australia.
The Metal Box Company Ltd. 37, Baker Street, London, W.1.	6th Dec. 1963. 6th Jan. 1964.	2 years. Option to renew.	Metal trays of all sizes. Table drink mats.	World excluding Japan.

NAME AND ADDRESS	DATE OF AGREEMENT	TERM	LICENCE FOR:	TERRITORY
The Palace Rock Co. Ltd. 22, Birley Street, Blackpool, Lancs.	14th Feb. 1964.	5 years–continuing unless determined.	Sugar confectionery in the shape of a rock disc imitation record.	World.
Leonard, Page & Co. (Leather Goods) Limited, 127, Mill Road, Burgess Hill, Sussex.	12th Mar. 1964.	2 years.	Ladies fancy garter with locket.	~~U.K. N.I. U.S.A. Europe.~~ World.
Raymond, 286/295 Brick Lane, London, E.2.	18th Dec. 1963.	2 years.	Bat and Ball Games, Shuttlecock Sets, Coat Hangers.	U.K.
Frank Ross & Co. (London) Ltd. 7a, Grafton Street, London, W.1.	28th Nov. 1963.	5 years. Extendable on 6 months notice.	Wall Plaques and Plates.	World.
L. Rosenthal & Co. Nokeener House, 623/5/7, Holloway Road, London N.19.	1st Jan. 1964.	2 years. Option of further year.	Wigs.	World excluding U.K.
Rudolf Stein Ltd. 93, Great Titchfield Street, London, W.1.	8th Nov. 1963.	To 31st Dec. 1965. Automatically renewed to Dec. 1967.	Anod. Aluminum Locket to slide open on chain.	U.K. N.I.
Regis Shoes Ltd. 134E, Kingsland Road, Shoreditch, E.2.	12th Mar. 1964.	2 years.	Ringo Boots.	U.K.
Ramat & Co. Ltd. Parksworth House, 30, City Road, London, E.C.1.	21st Nov. 1963.	3 years. Option to renew.	Handbags, Shopping Bags, Vanity Cases, Purses, Wallets, Basketware, Key-purses, Foam Goods (Bath mats, sponges), Plastic Toilet Bags, Mirrors, Scarves, Transferers. Christmas Cards.	World.
N.V. Stoomweverij Nijverheid, Postaug 51, Enschade, Holland.	5th Mar. 1964.	12 months with option to renew.	Printed fabric to be made up into dresses.	Holland, Belgium, Germany, France, Italy, Luxembourg, Switzerland, Norway, Sweden, Denmark.
R. Slocombe & Sons Ltd. Monmouth Street, Bridgwater, Somerset.	19th Mar.1964.	1 year.	Room Tidy, Ottoman, Linen Baskets, Record Cabinets on legs, Chairs.	U.K. N.I. Eire.
Sharene Creations Pty Ltd. 24, Victoria Street, Carlton N.3. Melbourne, Australia.	27th Feb. 1964.	2 years.	Dresses in all materials.	Australia. Japan.
Subbuteo Limited, Langton Green, Tunbridge Wells, Kent.	30th Dec. 1963.	2 years. Option to renew.	P.V.C. Plastic mouldings of figures 2¼" high.	World.
Thomas Scott & Sons (Bakers) Ltd. Sunblest Bakery, Dunnings Bridge Road, Netherton, Liverpool 10.	5th Feb. 1964.	2 years. Option to renew.	Ringo Roll (Loaf).	U.K.
Sayers (Confectioners) Ltd. The Ideal Bakery, Lorenzo Drive, West Derby, Liverpool 11.	2nd Jan. 1964.		Cake. Fondants.	U.K.
Searchlight Electric (Lancs) Ltd. Searchlight House, Middlewood Street, Salford 5, Manchester.	28th Nov. 1963.	2 years. Option to renew.	Table lamp.	U.K.
Sto-Rose Toys Ltd. 113, Coldsmith Row, Hackney Road, E.2.	18th Dec. 1963.	2 years. Option to renew.	Cotton Jockey Hats and Felt and Plastic Hats.	U.K. Channel Islands. Eire. South Africa. Sweden.

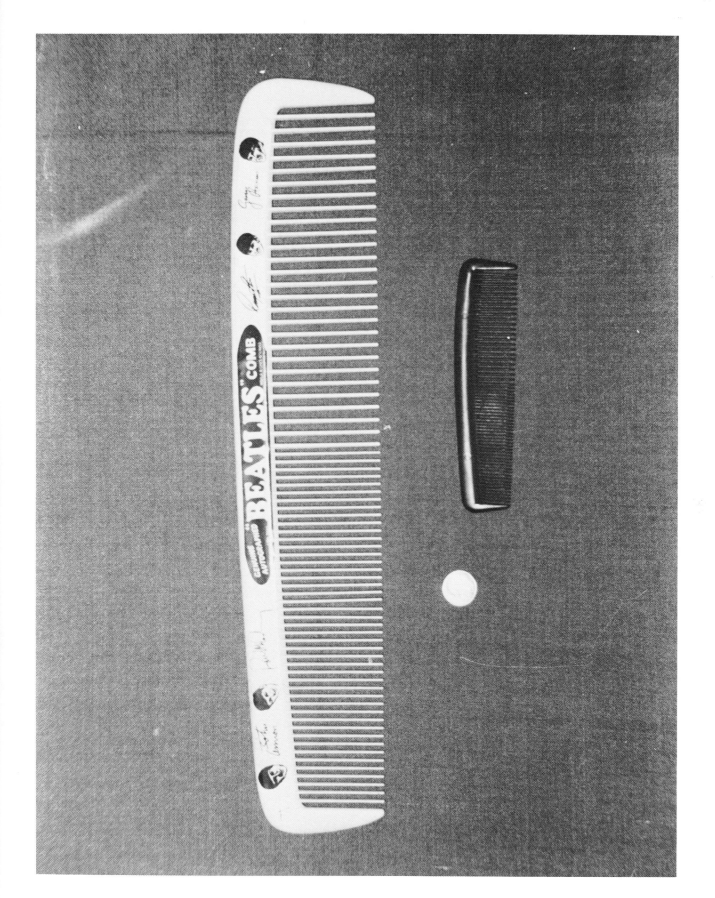

The outsized Beatles comb from 1964, its exaggerated size here contrasted with an ordinary pocket comb and a

NAME AND ADDRESS	DATE OF AGREEMENT	TERM	LICENCE FOR:	TERRITORY
Seagull Products, Seidners Limited, Empire Hall Building, Egremont, Cumberland.	21st Nov. 1963.		Diary, Record Carrier, Autograph Book, Pencil Case, Treasure Box, Carry All, Secrets 'N Such, Notes & Numbers, Deskette, Picnic Case, Telephone Address Book, Sewing Basket Set, Dolls Travelling Cabin & Trunk, Dolls luggage.	World.
Selcol Products Limited, 114--116, Charing Cross Road, London, W.C.2.	22nd Nov. 1963. 16th Dec. 1963. 12th Feb. 1964. 13th Mar. 1964.	2 years, with option of further year. 3 years.	Money Bank. Different types of guitars. Drums. "Combo" – guitar and snare drum. Tom-Toms. Record racks. Musical Greeting cards and non-musical greeting cards excluding Christmas Cards.	World.
Travtrac Films Limited, 125, Pall Mall, London, S.W.1.	18th Feb. 1964.		Life-size photograph 60" x 40".	World.
Toy Works Ltd. Court Gardens, Pound Lane, Marlow, Bucks.	1st Jan. 1964.	12 months with option of further 12 months.	Beatle Bingo (Boxed game).	World.
L. & C. Vincent Industries Pty Ltd. 25, Atchison Street, Crows Nest, New South Wales.	11th Mar. 1964.	2 years.	Female briefs.	Australia.
George Wostenholm & Son Ltd. Washington Works, Wellington Street, Sheffield, 1.	3rd Dec. 1963.	3 years. Option to renew.	Stainless steel bracelets and amulets.	World.
Wells-Brimtsy Ltd. Progress Works, Stirling Road, Walthamstow, E.17.	11th Dec. 1963.	1 year. Option to renew.	Perpetual desk calendar on support.	World.
R.B. Weldon, 144, Rye Lane, Peckham, S.E.15.	Confirmed 31st Jan. 1964.		Official Beatles Sweater incorporating official Beatles badge in form of Beatles fan club badge. Official Beatles badge excluding metal badges.	World.
Washington Pottery (Staffordshire) Ltd. 121–125, Park Street, Marble Arch, London, W.1.	15th Nov. 1963.		Earthenware plates, mugs, television sets (being round tray with mug), saucers and sets of 4 fruit dishes.	World.
Smiths Clocks & Watches Ltd. Sectric House, Waterloo Road, CRicklewood, N.W.2.	24th Dec. 1963.	2 years. Option to renew.	Fob watch in shape of Beatle.	World.
Barton's Agencies (Glasgow) Ltd. 3, Miller Street, Glasgow, C.1.	8th Jan. 1964.	2 years. Option to renew.	Dolls, Pyjama Dolls, Hand Puppets, Metal Badges.	U.K. Europe.
The Wallpaper Manufacturers Ltd. King's House, King Street West, Manchester 3.	19th Nov. 1963.	12 months from 1st Dec. 1963. Option to renew.	Wallpaper	U.K. N.I. Channel Islands. Isle of Man.
Beatle Twig. Inc. U.S.A.	17th Mar. 1964.	2 years and continuing yearly.	The Beatle Twig.	World.

Non Exclusive Licences

NAME AND ADDRESS	DATE OF AGREEMENT	TERM	LICENCE FOR:	TERRITORY
Anglo American Jewellery Ltd. 63, Glenthorne Road, Hammersmith, W.6.	29th Nov. 1963.		Artificial jewellery.	World.

NAME AND ADDRESS	DATE OF AGREEMENT	TERM	LICENCE FOR:	TERRITORY
Allan & Co., 38, Merkland Street, Glasgow, W.1.	22nd Nov. 1963.		Medallion.	U.K.
Belt Manufacturing Company of Canada Limited, 1425, Weston Road, Toronto, Canada	13th Feb. 1964. 11th Mar. 1964.	2 years. 2 years.	Children's Satchels, Open Ring Binders, Schoolbags, Briefcases. School Exercise Book — Plain, School Exercise Book — Ruled, Wire Bound Note Book — Ruled, School Refill — Plain and Ruled.	Canada and North America. Canada and U.S.A.
Bailey's Agencies (1953) Ltd. 51, Farringdon Road, London, E.C.1.	30th Dec, 1963.	2 years. Option to renew.	Lead pencils, Propelling pencils, Ball point pens.	World.
A. & R. Coffer Ltd. 100, Wardour Street, London, W.1.	18th Nov. 1963.	3 years.	Pendants on chain. Brooches. Rings. Bracelets.	World.
Clarke Bros. (Liverpool) Ltd. Speke, Liverpool 24.	23rd Jan. 1964.	2 years.	Leather watch straps on card.	U.K.
Studio Jon Douglas, 30, Chichele Road, London, N.W.2.	12th Feb. 1964.	2 years.	Sculptured Panels.	World.
Dorincourt Potters, (Disabled) Oaklawn Road, Leatherhead, Surrey.	17th Dec. 1963.		Tiles.	World.
The Excel Press, 302, Ilord Lane, Ilford, Essex.	17th Jan. 1964.		Photographs.	World.
Exquisite Jewellery Ltd. Lode Lane Industrial Estate, Solihull, Warwickshire.	29th Nov. 1963.	2 years. Option to renew.	Brooch.	U.K. U.S.A.
Fancy Jewellery Ltd. 403, St. Johns Street, London, E.C.1.	29th Nov. 1963.	2 years. Option to renew.	Pendant.	U.K.
Fleetway Publications Ltd. Fleetway House, Farringdon Street, London, E.C.4.	5th Dec. 1963.	Offer with magazine.	Bracelet.	World.
William Foster (Wigan) Ltd. Rainford, St. Helens, Lancs.	3rd Jan. 1964.	2 years. Option to renew.	Ornament in shape of Golden Disc Record.	U.K.
Florex Manufacturing Co. Ltd. Chalk Farm Tube, Adelaide, Road, N.W.3.	20th Dec. 1963.	2 years.	3-dimensional pictures.	U.K.
L. Hilton & Co. Ltd. Mount Pleasant Street, Ashton-under-Lyne, Lancs.	10th Mar. 1964.	12 months. Option to renew.	Candlewick bedspreads.	U.K. N.I.
Invicta Plastics Ltd. Cadby, Leicester.	17th Dec. 1963.	3 years. Option to renew.	Brooch.	World.
Lau-Kee & Co. Ltd. 2 Lower Ormond Quay, Dublin, 1.	9th Jan. 1964.	2 years. Option to renew.	Bracelets, Rings, Pendants, Brooches, Earrings.	World.
Lido Toys Ltd. 125 Tycos Drive, Toronto. Lido Corp. 1340, Viele, New York.	12th Feb. 1964.		Comb 15" long, 3" wide. Plastic Wig.	World. World excluding U.K.
Emanuel Langsam, Plastic Products. 174 Cannon Street Road, London, E.1.	28th Jan. 1964.	1 year. Option to renew.	Hair slides.	U.K.

NAME AND ADDRESS	DATE OF AGREEMENT	TERM	LICENCE FOR:	TERRITORY
Meadway Manufacturing Co. Ltd. 144–148, Lee High Road, London, S.E.13.	12th Feb. 1964.	2 years. Option to renew.	Plastic Tray Mats.	World.
Proudholme Products, Groveway House, 20, Elm Grove, Brighton.	18th Dec. 1963.	2 years. Option to renew.	Table mats.	U.K. U.S.A. Sweden. Australia. New Zealand. South Africa.
Rudolf Stein Ltd. 93 Great Titchfield Street, London, W.1.	8th Nov. 1963.	2 years. Automatically renewed to Dec. 1967.	Pendants, Brooches, Necklets.	U.K.
J. & L. Randall Ltd. Merit House, Cranborne Road, Potters Bar, Middx.	24th Dec. 1963.	2 years. Option to renew.	Magnetic Drawing Cards. Magic Slate.	World.
Sachet Production Ltd. Shapley Industrial Estate, Rudenshaw, Nr. Manchester.	4th Mar. 1964.	2 years.	Bubble bath.	World.
Starstats Ltd. 86a, Bold Street, Liverpool 1.	19th Dec. 1963.	2 years. Option to renew.	Busts. Statuettes.	World. U.K.
Shallwin Fashions Limited, Metropole Works, Waltham Abbey, Essex.	28th Nov. 1963.	2 years.	Imitation jewellery.	World.
Spa Brushes Limited, Alma Road, Chesham, Bucks.	18th Nov. 1963.	3 years.	Hairbrushes, Toothbrushes, Nailbrushes, Clothes Brushes, Combs.	U.K. N.I. Eire. C.I.
Ulster Weaving Co. Ltd. Silver House, 31–35, Beak Street, W.1.	27th Nov. 1963. 20th Feb. 1964.	2 years. 2 years, with option on further 2 years.	Printed Linen Teacloth. Printed Tablecloth;	U.K. Eire. Europe. U.S.A. Canada. South Africa. New Zealand. Australia.
Unitrend Limited, 8, Cavendish Road, Woking, Surrey.	18th Dec. 1963.	3 years. Option to renew.	Cushions. Cushion covers.	World.
Leon J. Mitchell Ltd. 74, Forest Road, Dalston, London, E.8.	4th Dec. 1963.		3-d formed process.	U.K.
Invincible Industries, P.O. Box 35, Elsies River, Cape, South Africa.	16th Mar. 1964.	1 year.	Photograph albums, brief cases.	South Africa.
The Wallpaper Manufacturers Ltd. King's House, King Street West, Manchester 3.	16th Jan. 1964.	12 months. Option to renew.	Wallpaper.	World excluding U.K. N.I. C.I. Isle of Man.
7-Kay Enterprises, 577 Washington Avenue, Belleville, N. Jersey, U.S.A.	13th Feb. 1964.	2 years.	Booster Pins.	U.S.A.
Cotswold Plastics Limited, Cotswold House, 7, Crawford Passage, Farringdon Road, London E.C.1.	25th Mar. 1964.	2 years.	Moving Panoramic and Photographic Ball Point Pens.	U.K. N.I.
Freevy Limited, Alucraft Works, Gatehouse Industrial Estate, Aylesbury, Bucks.	3rd Jan. 1964.	2 years.	Costume Jewellery.	World but excluding the United States of America.

Current Merchandising Licences

NAME AND ADDRESS	DATE OF AGREEMENT	RATE	LICENCE FOR:	TERRITORY
Hallmark Cards			Hallmark Cards	
Cavendish Exports Ltd	March, 1967		Head and shoulder models of The Beatles	
Fomisa, Via Berna 2, Lugana, Switzerland	February, 1966		Beatle phones	
Simpack A/S Denmark	26th May, 1965	10% on gross payable quarterly.	Safe adhesive punched names	Europe.
Metalimport Ltd	19th November, 1965	6/– per medal.	Silver medals	World.
Bellaplast Africa (Pty) Ltd	23rd December, 1965	5% on gross receipts.	Plastic disposal drinking cups	Republic of South Africa South West Africa, Rhodesia.
Dunn & Co. Ltd	20th January, 1966	10% on gross receipts.	Locket, bracelet, and tie pin	World excl. U.S.A.
Saunders Enterprises Ltd	February, 1968		Beatle Coathangers.	

Merchandising Licences

All Contracts Supplied to Apple Corps Limited on 8–8–68 by Wright, Webb & Co.

Anglo-American Jewellery
Allan & Co.
Albert Fischer & Co.
The American Flag Co.
J. & I. Arbiter Limited
Beatle, Twig Inc.
Bookcovers Inc.
Bachmann Brothers Inc.
Colorcraft, Lithographers Inc.
C. Kendall, Clapp, John Cotterell and
Childs W. Schillings
Cray Randall Manufacturing Co. Inc.
Car Mascots Inc.
Daniel Buckley Enterprises Limited

Dezo Hoffman Limited
Dorincourt Potters
Dame Belt & Bag Co.
Dannenberger Vorrichtungsbau Stellamans
Eric Potter & Clarkson
Filtral GMBH
Green Duck Metal Stamping Co.
Holland Hill Products Inc.
M. Hohner Incorporated
Lido Toys Limited
Milton Bradley Co.
Oak Manufacturing Co. Inc.
Park Lane Neckwear Co.
Permalgraph Inc.

The Palace Rock Co. Ltd.
Paul Clark Designs
Pop Colour Portraits Limited
R.B. Weldon Limited
Rudin & Roth Inc.
Remco Industries Inc.
Revell Inc.
Travtrac Films Limited
Trivus – Sportswear
Sidney Margolies Limited
Mr. Donald Leroy Spence
Sayers (Confectioners) Limited
Windsor Textile Co.
Washington Pottery (Staffordshire) Limited

The Beatles On The Block

Beyond the universe of "ordinary" mass-produced Beatles collectibles encountered at "Beatlefests" and other large fan gatherings, there exists the more rarified world of one-of-a-kind collectibles offered up at "auction galleries" or "auction houses," located principally in London and New York, a world which very few average collectors know about, much less experience on a first-hand basis.

Professional auctioneers act as agents for a seller or consignor, and are intermediaries who publicize and conduct public auctions to realise a profit for their clients (and for themselves, inasmuch as the auctioneer generally receives both a premium from the buyer and a commission from the seller).

The very first such auction involving Beatles items apparently occurred in New York City. In the sale catalog of September 30th, 1965, Charles Hamilton Autographs, Inc., offered for bid a Beatles "Program, sgd, 24 Dec 1964. 12pp, 4to. hn9 (6)" and valued it at "$55.00". It is not known what the item eventually sold for, or whether it was even sold at all.

The auctioning of Beatles memorabilia has come a long way since the meager debut of a single autographed program in 1965. The news that an enormous rock 'n' roll auction (the first of its kind) was held in London in December 1981, and that the high point of the proceedings were the lots devoted to Beatles items, is fairly well known to most Beatles fans at this point. Less well known is the fact that smaller gatherings of similar items have been put up for auction with some regularity since the late seventies. (There seems to have been a hiatus of nearly fifteen years between the 1965 sale and the next gallery auction, as far as can be determined.) Information about the items offered for bid, along with the auctioneer's suggested price or price range, are normally printed in a sale catalog prior to the auction, in order to advertise the sale. After the sale occurs, a list of final selling prices is also made available, sometimes indicating the name of the buyer.

Foremost among such auctioneers is Sotheby Parke Bernet & Co., headquartered in London but with overseas representatives worldwide. The December 1981 rock 'n' roll sale was actually Sotheby's seventh London auction featuring Beatles memorabilia, and there will undoubtedly be many more both at Sotheby's and elsewhere. (London's Phillips galleries offered several Beatles lots for bid in a June 1981 sale, for example).

The good news is that the average collector *can* participate in such auctions even if unable to journey to places like London or New York to attend in person. Sale catalogs can be obtained on a subscription basis from Sotheby's (write to: Catalogue Subscription Department, Sotheby Parke Bernet & Co., 34/35 New Bond Street, London W1A 2AA, England) for £20 per year (around $40.00) postpaid. The catalogs should reach you several weeks in advance of the auction date(s), so you can examine what might be available in the way of Beatles items. (Note: There is *no guarantee* that your subscription will result in sale catalogs filled with Beatles memorabilia. Though there have been seven such sales (and sale catalogs) from late 1979 to late 1981, there is no assurance that a certain number of sales will occur in a given year. There may be none at all.)

Should a sale catalog arrive detailing a number of Beatles lots in which you are interested, however, you *can* place a bid for them by mail or by phone. The bad news about such absentee participation in an auction of this type, apart from the ever escalating prices involved, is that your mail-order or phoned-in bid can be bettered by someone on the scene, unless you pay for an open phone line so you can participate further during the sale.

Nevertheless, you can take your best shot by mail, and maybe no one will decide to outbid you. Special photographs of the items you might be interested in can often be arranged for (at cost to you) if you'd like to get a closer look before bidding.

A note of caution: auctions are governed by strict rules of business and conditions of sale; these are printed in detail in each of Sotheby's catalogs. You should probably obtain a sample catalog before placing a subscription; in fact, you might still be able to obtain a copy of the beautiful December 1981 rock 'n' roll catalog (the Beatles section is reproduced in this Appendix, although the color pictures appear here in black-and-white), which costs £3 (about $6.00). You might inquire after this particular catalog, but indicate that you will accept any other sample catalog if this one is no longer available. Sotheby's catalogs all have code names, both because the formal catalog titles are often very similar and because the only other identifying feature of such catalogs – the date(s) of sale – may not be known to a prospective catalog buyer. The rock 'n' roll catalog was aptly dubbed with the code name of "BOOGIE," which is how you should ask for it.

Should you bid on an item and win, you would be required to pay promptly in pounds sterling or with an international money order before your property would be shipped to you (you would also have to pay the shipping charges). Sotheby's does not guarantee the authenticity or genuineness of the items it sells, although a refund is available for up to five years from purchase for items which can be proven, to Sotheby's satisfaction, to be a "deliberate forgery".

What follows are several pages of photographs of one-of-a-kind, original autograph letters and cards from the early Beatles period of the type often found for sale at such auctions. All are from the collection of David J. Smith, who graciously allowed us to reproduce them here. Next, there appears a descriptive listing of all the Beatles lots sold since 1979 at Sotheby's in London (copied from the original catalogs with Sotheby's permission), together with the asking prices and the prices finally realised. The "withdrawn" lots are those for which only unacceptably low bids were made, and the seller simply refused a sale. Lastly, this section concludes with a photo-graphic reproduction of the twenty-three pages from the December 1981 sale catalog ("BOOGIE") which featured many Beatles items (again reproduced with permission from Sotheby's), along with a listing of the final "gavel" prices for each lot.

A great deal of information can be culled from these listings, including both price trends over a period of years and comparative prices for similar types of autograph items. To determine the U.S. dollar values for the figures listed in British pounds, a serviceable rule of thumb is simply to multiply by two (£10 = $20, £20 = $40, etc.). The exchange rate for the British pound versus the U.S. dollar changes daily, fluctuating from £1 = $2.30+ a few years ago to the current £1 = $1.80+. Exact current rates can be determined by calling any large bank and asking to speak to the person who can advise you about foreign currency exchange rates. As a handy yardstick, however, simply double the pound figure and you have the dollar figure, more or less. **Tom Schultheiss**

Photo courtesy of David J. Smith

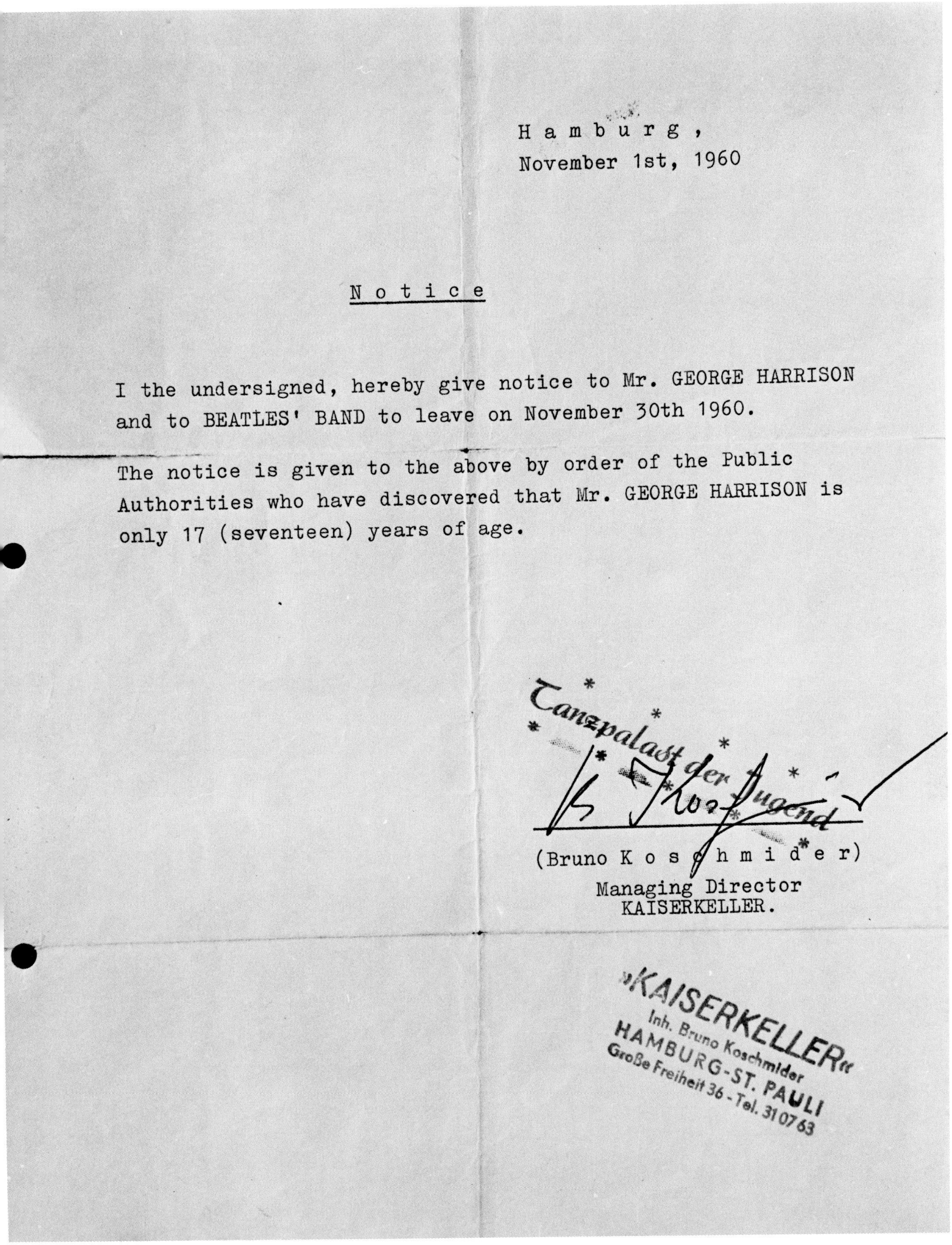

H a m b u r g ,
November 1st, 1960

N o t i c e

I the undersigned, hereby give notice to Mr. GEORGE HARRISON and to BEATLES' BAND to leave on November 30th 1960.

The notice is given to the above by order of the Public Authorities who have discovered that Mr. GEORGE HARRISON is only 17 (seventeen) years of age.

Tanzpalast der Jugend

(Bruno K o s c h m i d e r)
Managing Director
KAISERKELLER.

»KAISERKELLER«
Inh. Bruno Koschmider
HAMBURG-ST. PAULI
Große Freiheit 36 - Tel. 31 07 63

Bruno Koschmider's notice expelling the Beatles from the Kaiserkeller (November 1960).

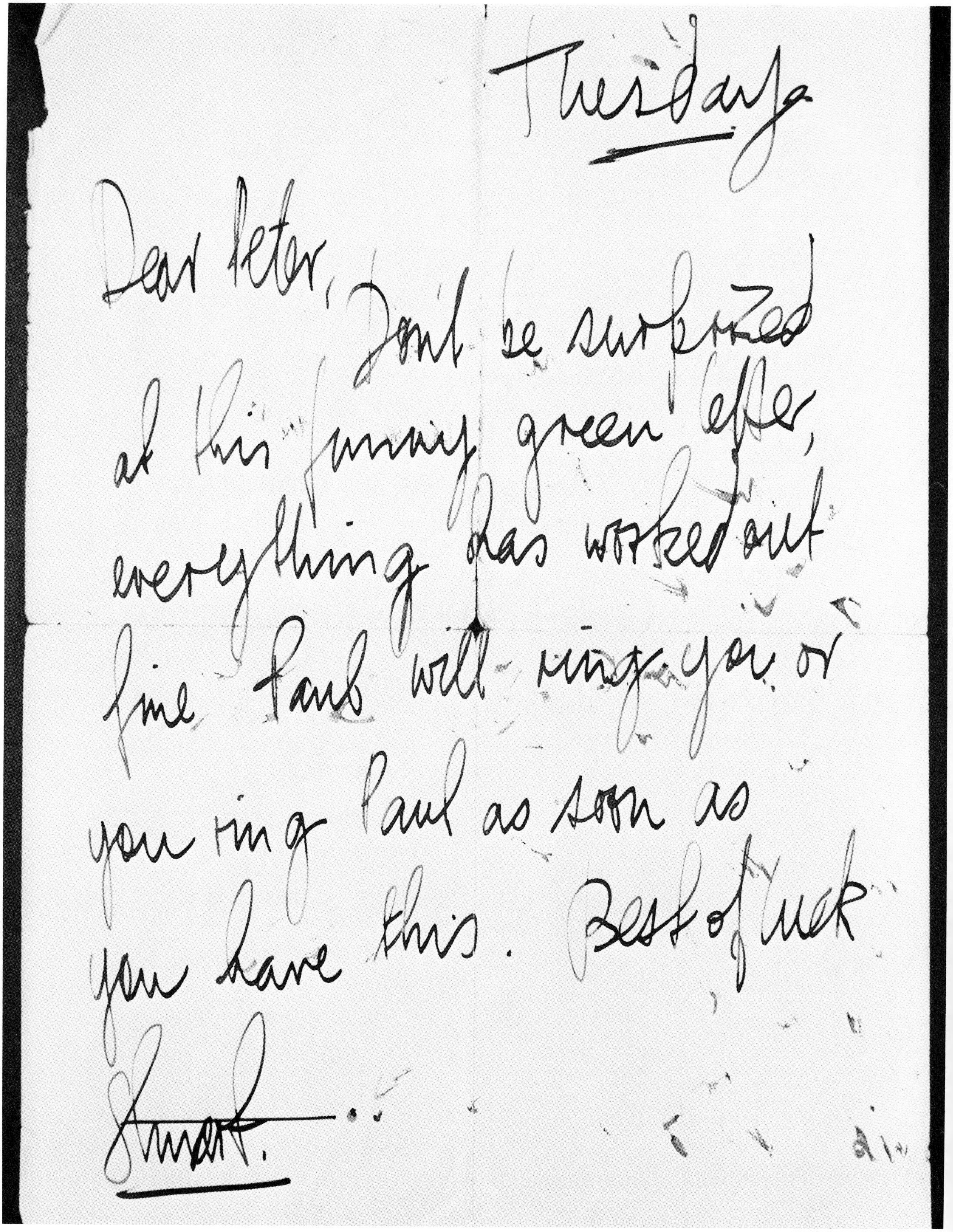

Thursday

Dear Peter,

Don't be surprised at this "funny green efte," everything has worked out fine. Paul will ring you, or you ring Paul as soon as you have this. Best of luck

Stuart.

Stu Sutcliffe's two-page note to Pete Best advising him that the Beatles can return to Germany (early 1961).

One thing I forgot to tell Paul, and that is that you both must pay Peter Eglorn 79 D.M (each) this the cost of sending you home.

The lifting of the deportation ban is only valid for 1 year, then you can have it renewed. One thing they made clear, if you have any trouble with the Police, no matter how small then you've had it forever. (Drunkeness, fighting, women etc).

bye bye.

Stuart.

A. R. Williams

jacaranda enterprises

23 SLATER STREET   LIVERPOOL 1 / **ROYAL 6544**

20th April, 1961.

Dear All,

I am very distressed to hear you are contemplating not paying my commission out of your pay as was agreed in our contract for your engagement at the Top Ten Club.

May I remind you, seeing you are all appearing to get more than a little swollen-headed, that you would not even have smelled Hamburg if I had not made the contacts, and by Law it is illegal for any person under contract to make a contract through the first contract.

I would also point out that the only reason you are there is through the work that I did and ifyou had tried yourselves to play at the Top Ten without a bonafide contract and working through a British Government approved Agency you would not be in Germany now.

Remember in your last contract under Koschmider you agreed not to play 30 weeks from terminating that contract, the only reason you managed to get out of that was again through myself. So far as you are concerned hekept the contract.

So you see Lads, I'm very annoyed you should welsh out of your agreed contract. If you decide not to pay I promise you that I shall have you out of Germany inside two weeks through several legal ways and don't you think I'm bluffing.

I will also submit a full report of your behaviour to the Agency Members Association of which I am a full member, and every Agent in England is a member, to protect Agents from artistes who misbehave and welsh out of agreements.

So if you want to play in Liverpool for all the local boys you go straight ahead and welsh on your contract. Don't underestimate my ability to carry out what I have written.

-continued-

Allan Williams' two-page letter to "The Beetles" demanding payment of his commission (April 1961).

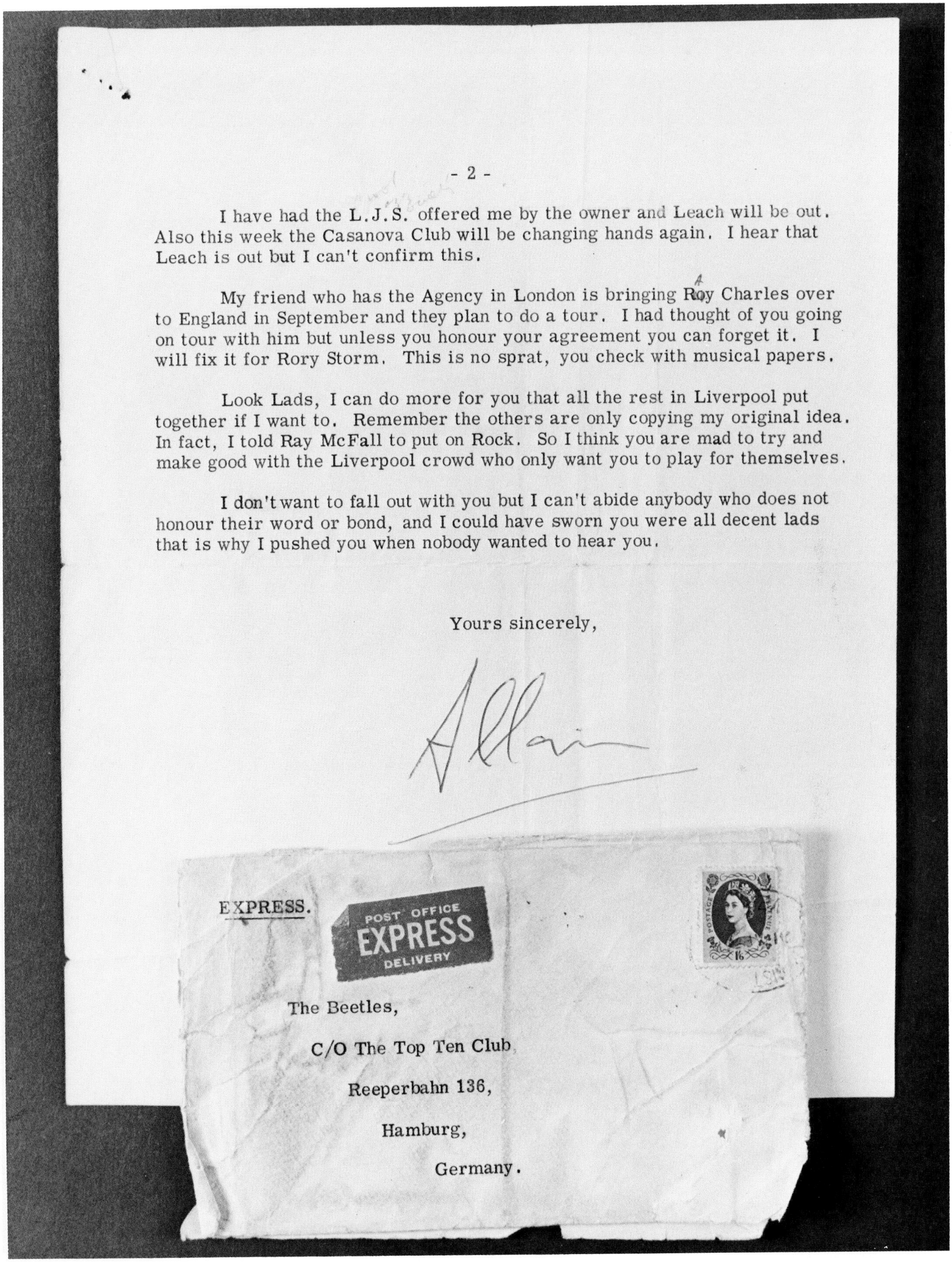

I have had the L.J.S. offered me by the owner and Leach will be out. Also this week the Casanova Club will be changing hands again. I hear that Leach is out but I can't confirm this.

My friend who has the Agency in London is bringing Roy Charles over to England in September and they plan to do a tour. I had thought of you going on tour with him but unless you honour your agreement you can forget it. I will fix it for Rory Storm. This is no sprat, you check with musical papers.

Look Lads, I can do more for you that all the rest in Liverpool put together if I want to. Remember the others are only copying my original idea. In fact, I told Ray McFall to put on Rock. So I think you are mad to try and make good with the Liverpool crowd who only want you to play for themselves.

I don't want to fall out with you but I can't abide anybody who does not honour their word or bond, and I could have sworn you were all decent lads that is why I pushed you when nobody wanted to hear you.

Yours sincerely,

EXPRESS.

POST OFFICE
EXPRESS
DELIVERY

The Beetles,

C/O The Top Ten Club,

Reeperbahn 136,

Hamburg,

Germany.

B/A/1485

7 Dec 1961

Dear Mr McCartney

Re: **Yourself and Allen Williams**

As this claim made against you by the above named gentleman appears to have lapsed I take this opportunity of enclosing my statement of account and receipted bill of costs, and my cheque in your favour in the sum of £2.13.0. representing the balance due to you after payment of my legal charges.

Please acknowledge safe receipt of this cheque at your convenience.

Yours truly

CHARLES D MUNRO

J P McCartney Esq
20 Forthlin Road
LIVERPOOL 18

PA

RECEIVED
1 5 DEC 1961

JPMcCartney
20 Forthlin Rd.
L'pool 18.

Dear Sir,
I received your cheque for £2.13.0,
on the 9th December '61.
Yours Truly,
JPMcCartney.

A note to Paul McCartney from his solicitor about Allan Williams' claim, and Paul's post card reply (December 1961).

The Auctions At
Sotheby Parke Bernet & Co., London

SALE OF MONDAY, JUNE 18, 1979 ("CAT")

Lot Number/Description	Asking price	Sold for
196 BEATLES (THE). Letter signed by Paul McCartney, John Lennon, George Harrison and Ringo Starr, *1 page, 4to, no place or date,* to "Dear Stella," thanking her for her letter (" . . . I hope the clover brings us luck . . . ."), *the letter written on the verso of Stella's letter*	£50/100	£140
197 BEATLES (THE). Four American dollar bills, each with an autograph dedication signed by a different member of the Beatles: George Harrison, Paul McCartney, John Lennon and Ringo Starr, *narrow oblong 8vo*	£280/350	Withdrawn

SALE OF MONDAY, MARCH 3, 1980 ("TRINKET")

	Asking price	Sold for
153 THE BEATLES. Collection of 14 early photographs of the group and individual members, signed and inscribed by them on the front or reverse, one photograph showing the group with Pete Best still a member (his signature included on reverse), others showing them on their Hamburg tour etc., with an autograph postcard by Ringo Starr written while on the tour (" . . . Arrived here OK The club is great We are with Little Richard he is fat See you Sunday . . . . "), *creased, trimmed or marked with adhesive tape* *Included in the lot are two signed gramophone records of their first successes, "Love Me Do" and "Please Please Me" *(scratched)*	£300/400	£480
154 THE BEATLES. Photograph of the Beatles signed by each of them, inscribed on reverse "Odeon Lewisham Sunday December 8th 1963," *8 x 10 inches*	£60/80	£120
155 THE BEATLES. Reproduction of a photograph of Paul McCartney, signed and inscribed by him, with separate signatures of the other three Beatles.	£30/40	£60
156 THE BEATLES. Photograph of the Beatles drinking tea, signed by all four, *8½ x 6½ inches*	£40/60	£160
157 THE BEATLES. Four American dollar bills, each with an autograph dedication signed by a different member of the Beatles: George Harrison, Paul McCartney, John Lennon and Ringo Starr, *narrow oblong 8vo*	£60/80	£220

SALE OF WEDNESDAY, JUNE 4 1980 ("RAWLINS")

	Asking price	Sold for
913 THE BEATLES. Photograph of the Beatles drinking tea, signed by all four f them, *8½ x 6½ inches*	£100/150	£240
914 THE BEATLES. Photograph signed by Ringo Starr, issued by the Official Beatles Fan Club, *4½ x 5½ inches*	£30/40	£8

Lot Number/Description	Asking price	Sold for
351 THE BEATLES. Large Christmas card reproducing a drawing by John Lennon, with autograph inscription by Brian Epstein "& many belated congratulations Brian"	£40/60	Withdrawn
352 THE BEATLES. Long-playing gramophone record entitled "With the Beatles," signed on the sleeve by all four of them	£50/80	£35
353 THE BEATLES. Memorabilia, including the V.A.B.F. certificate of congratulations to Paul McCartney on his selection for the Royal Variety Performance on 4 November 1963, a family photograph of Paul and his brother as infants, an A.L.s. by Paul to his family (" . . . better late than negroid . . . ."), seven other photographs of him, a menu for the Dorchester supper following the premiere of "A Hard Day's Night" on 6 July 1964 signed by Paul and by John Lennon, two photographs of the group, a ticket for their show on 28 December 1964, and 16 colour transparencies of the Beatles and their party on board a yacht and elsewhere about February 1964	£100/200	£90
354 THE BEATLES. Photograph of the Beatles, signed by all four of them, *slightly crumpled, 4to*	£60/80	£45
355 THE BEATLES. Photograph signed by all four of them, *4¼ x 5½ inches, creased*	£40/60	Withdrawn
356 THE BEATLES. Photograph signed in ballpoint by all four of them, *c. 4¼ x 5½ inches, creases, traces of mount, with five other photographs of them*	£40/60	£50
357 THE BEATLES. Photograph signed by all four of them, *top edge slightly frayed c. 7¾ x 9½ inches*	£40/60	£45
358 THE BEATLES. Photograph signed by all four of them, *c. 6¼ x 8¼ inches*	£40/60	£45
359 THE BEATLES. Photograph of the Beatles, signed on verso by all four of them, *creased, 3½ x 6 inches*	£60/80	Withdrawn
360 THE BEATLES. Photograph signed and inscribed on the back by all four of them, *3¼ x 5 inches, creased*	£40/60	£30
361 THE BEATLES. Photographic portrait, signed by all four of them, *postcard size*	£40/50	£35
362 THE BEATLES. Photograph signed by all four of them, *postcard*	£80/100	Withdrawn
363 THE BEATLES. Photograph signed on the back by all four of them, *3½ x 5¼ inches, slight creases*	£40/50	Withdrawn
364 THE BEATLES. Postcard-sized photograph signed on the back by all four	£40/50	£34
365 THE BEATLES. Programme of a Beatles show at the Odeon, Weston-Super-Mare, signed by all four, also signed by Gerry and the Pacemakers, *worn*	£50/80	£55

Lot Number/Description	Asking price	Sold for
366 THE BEATLES. Programmes of the premieres of the films "A Hard Day's Night" (1964) and "Help" (1965) both signed by all four members of the group	£50/80	£80
367 THE BEATLES. Programme of "The Beatles' Show," signed by all four of them	£40/60	£40
368 THE BEATLES. Record of "Please Please Me" signed by all four	£40/50	Withdrawn
369 THE BEATLES. Series of five autograph postcards signed by Paul McCartney to his father and family in Liverpool and Heswall, TWO WRITTEN FROM HAMBURG, three from Paris and Indianapolis, *postmarks 1 April 1961 to 3 September 1964*	£300/400	Withdrawn
370 THE BEATLES. Signatures of the four Beatles on the back of a letter from the Central Chancery of the Orders of Knighthood to Major Firminger, concerning his investiture as M.B.E., 1 October 1965 *Signed when the Beatles were at Buckingham Palace for their investitures.	£50/60	£30
371 THE BEATLES. Wooden breadboard signed by the Beatles and (?) Brian Epstein, *signatures of Harrison and Epstein indistinct, others slightly faded, the board circular, 12 inches across* *Inscribed "Joes Caff" (near the Cavern Club, Liverpool), where the board was signed.	£50/60	Withdrawn

SALE OF MONDAY, MARCH 23, 1981 ("SPRINT")

Lot Number/Description	Asking price	Sold for
170 THE BEATLES. Large Christmas card reproducing a drawing by John Lennon, with autograph inscription by Brian Epstein "& many belated congratulations Brian"	£20/25	£10
171 THE BEATLES. Original contract with General Artists Corporation for the two Beatles' concerts at the Hollywood Bowl, California, on 29 and 30 August 1965, signed twice by Brian Epstein, Robert Eubanks and Michael Brown, the copy retained by Epstein, *4 pages, folio, 24 March 1965* *The contract specifies total payment of $19,000, the extensive conditions including police protection of not less than 150 officers, a platform of 10 x 6 x 4 feet for Ringo Starr and his drums, a non-segregated audience, strict control over sale of souvenirs, and use by Epstein of two Cadillacs with chauffeurs.	£600/800	Withdrawn
172 THE BEATLES. Series of five autograph postcards signed by Paul McCartney to his father and family in Liverpool and Heswall, TWO WRITTEN FROM HAMBURG, three from Paris and Indianapolis, *postmarks 1 April 1961 to 3 September 1964*	£80/100	£100
173 THE BEATLES. Photograph of the group with Mike and Bernie Winters, signed on the back by the Beatles, *c. 4¾ x 6½ inches, creased*	£40/60	£60
174 THE BEATLES. Fine photograph signed by all four of them, with others	£100/150	£200
175 THE BEATLES. Photograph signed by all four of them, *framed and glazed, overall size c. 7 x 8½ inches*	£60/80	£180

Lot Number/Description	Asking price	Sold for
176 THE BEATLES. Postcard signed on verso by all four of them, *4 x 4¾ inches, trimmed*	£50/60	Withdrawn
177 THE BEATLES. Printed copy of "Penny Lane," signed on the front cover photograph by all four of them, *creased*	£80/120	£210
198 McCARTNEY (PAUL). Two autograph letters signed, *3 pages [1962],* to Pat Powell, referring to his coming back from Germany and recording for George Martin, *autograph envelope, with photograph of the early Beatles signed by McCartney*	£80/120	£120

SALE OF TUESDAY, OCTOBER 27, 1981 ("AMPERSAND")

270 THE BEATLES. Original contract with General Artists Corporation for the two Beatles' concerts at the Hollywood Bowl, California, on 29 and 30 August 1965, signed twice by Brian Epstein, Robert Eubanks and Michael Brown, the copy retained by Epstein, *4 pages, folio, 24 March 1965* *The contract specifies total payment of $90,000, the extensive conditions including police protection of not less than 150 officers, a platform of 10 x 6 x 4 feet for Ringo Starr and his drums, a non-segregated audience, strict control over sale of souvenirs, and use by Epstein of two Cadillacs with chauffeurs.	£200/220	Withdrawn
271 THE BEATLES. Photograph signed by all four on the back, *c. 7¾ x 9¾ inches*	£100/150	£88
272 THE BEATLES. Two photographs signed by all four of them (one on verso), *c. 6½ x 8½ inches each, framed and glazed*	£100/150	£110
273 THE BEATLES. Photograph of the group on stage, signed by all four of them, *6½ x 8½ inches, with another bearing facsimile signatures*	£80/100	£93.50
274 THE BEATLES. Fine photograph of the group in casual clothes, signed by all four of them and inscribed by Lennon "for Sally Morris," *10 x 8 inches*	£100/150	£176
292 LENNON (JOHN). *In His Own Write,* signed by Lennon, Cynthia and others, *slightly worn*	£80/100	£121

Lot No.	Sold for
69	£352
70	Withdrawn
71	Withdrawn
72	£27
73	£176
74	£93

THE BEATLES

69 £80/120

AN AUTOGRAPHED BEATLE LP, the album cover of 'With the Beatles' autographed on the back cover by the four members of the Beatles group, with LP record within (2)

70† £80/120

THE BEATLES' HISTORY, comprising The Savage Young Beatles (Hamburg 1961), The Beatles' First, The Beatles' Story, and I Apologise by John Lennon (4)

71† £150/250

THE BEATLES, eight LP's comprising With the Beatles, Beatles VI, Rubber Soul, Please Please Me, The Beatles Beat, and a Collection of Beatles Oldies (2) (8)

72† £15/20

BRIAN EPSTEIN, a postcard to Mr Epstein from a girl-friend in Madrid

73† £80/120

THE BEATLES, demo discs and promotional singles, comprising Strawberry Fields Forever, Help!, All You Need is Love (3), Got to Get You into My Life, Paperback Writer (7)

74† £40/60

THE BEATLES' FAN CLUB ISSUES, comprising Everywhere It's Christmas, and the third Christmas record (2)

BUDDY HOLLY

A photograph by Harry Hammond

◉ **67** £80/120

BUDDY HOLLY & THE CRICKETS, Buddy Holly, Joe Maudlin and Jerry Allison, who were photographed during their trip to England in 1958, mounted in card

67

68 £2500/3500

BUDDY HOLLY, a most unusual letter addressed to Mr Paul Cohen of Decca Records, Inc., detailing a brief autobiography: . . . *'During the seventh grade my interest in western music was aroused and I started to learn to play the guitar . . . and started to sing duets . . . won several contests'* . . . and asking for a release date for his records, dated March 2, 1956, and signed, 7¼ by 11in; 18.5 by 28cm

SALE OF TUESDAY, DECEMBER 22, 1981 ("BOOGIE")

Lot No.	Sold for
75	£28
76	£187
77	£33
78	£286
79	£286
80	£242
81	£60
82	£2420
83	£231

80

75†
£60/100
THE BEATLES, twelve singles, comprising Help! (2), Ain't She Sweet, Love Me Do (2), Can't Buy Me Love, She's a Woman, A Hard Day's Night, Paperback Writer (2), Strawberry Fields Forever, Day Tripper (12)

76†
£150/250
THE BEATLES, eight red vinyl foreign issue LPs on Odeon, comprising The Beatles' second album (2), A Hard Day's Night, Beatles For Sale (2), Meet the Beatles, Please, Please Me, and Rubber Soul (8)

77
£30/50
FOURTEEN BEATLES SINGLES on Parlophone, comprising: Long Tall Sally, Twist and Shout, I Saw Her Standing There, Can't Buy Me Love, Daytripper, Help!, Paperback Writer, Ticket to Ride, I Feel Fine, From Me To You, I Want To Hold Your Hand, Please, Please Me, She Loves You and Love Me Do, in original covers (14)

78
£60/80
A COLLECTION OF BEATLES FAN CLUB MATERIAL, comprising: thirty-three monthly magazines, Beatles concert programmes, calendars, photograph books and other related publications dating from c. 1963 (qty)

79
£60/100
THE BEATLES, three photographs of the Beatles rehearsing in the Cavern Club (one duplicated), a Fan Club photograph signed by the four members of the group on the reverse, and a card similarly signed on the front (5)

◉ 80
£80/150
THE BEATLES FOR THEIR FANS, a hand-out leaflet illustrating 'John, George, Paul and Pete', and detailing a concert at the Cavern on 5th April, 1962, the reverse in Paul McCartney's hand giving his forwarding address at 'The Twist Club' in Hamburg, 6 by 9in; 15 by 23cm, c. 1961

81
£30/50
THE CAVERN CLUB, printed material related to the Mersey Sound music venue in Liverpool, comprising a booklet detailing the club's history, a photograph of Mannfred Mann, a signed postcard of Billy J. Kramer, a Christmas card signed by members of the Merseybeats, and a Christmas card signed by Ray McFall and Bob Wooler of the Cavern Club, c. 1963 (4)

82
£180/250
PAUL McCARTNEY, a letter in ink to a fan from the Star Club, Hamburg, detailing life in the city and the cost of living there . . . 'I think we'll be making some records soon, and we'll get them released in Liverpool as soon as possible' . . ., 11½ by 8¼in; 29 by 21cm, c. 1961

83
£25/35
A SIGNED PHOTOGRAPH OF THE BEATLES, depicting the group with three guitars, framed and glazed, 14½ by 11½in; 37 by 29cm, c. 1965

21

SALE OF TUESDAY, DECEMBER 22, 1981 ("BOOGIE")

Lot No.	Sold for
84	£165
85	£605
86	£297
87	£264
88	£385
89	£176

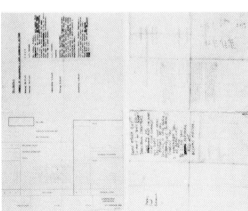

84

◉ **84** £60/100
A N.E.M.S. ENTERPRISES ARTIST ACCOUNT STATEMENT, for The Beatles, week ending 27th July, 1962, detailing appearances at the Cavern Club and other venues, the reverse in ink (presumably Paul McCartney) detailing nineteen songs as a programme for a concert, including Love Me Do, PS I Love You, Postman, and others, 8 by 10in; 20 by 25.5cm, and details of engagements for week commencing 29th July, 1962 (carbon copy) (2)

85 £300/500
THE BEATLES, a collection of twenty-four stock transfer forms relating to Triumph Investment Trust Limited signed by Lennon (6), McCartney (6), Harrison (6) and Richard Starkey (*viz. Ringo Starr*) (6), 1969 (24)

86 and 87

◉ **86** £150/200
THE BEATLES, six official documents and stock transfers relating to N.E.M. Enterprises Ltd, signed by John Lennon (2), Paul McCartney (2), George Harrison (1) and Brian Epstein (1), 1967-1968 (6)

◉ **87** £100/180
THE BEATLES, six official documents and stock transfers relating to N.E.M. Enterprises Ltd, signed by John Lennon (2), Paul McCartney (2), and George Harrison (2), 1967-1968 (6)

88 £150/200
AN INTERESTING SCRAP BOOK RELATING TO THE BEATLES FROM 1961, comprising photographs and cuttings of the Beatles (with Peter Best) in the Cavern Club and Liverpool, with signatures of Pete Best, Paul McCartney, John Lennon and George Harrison, compiled by an employee of the Cavern Club, and contained in 'self-adhesive' photograph album, dating from c. 1961

89 £60/100
THE BEATLES, a photograph of the group, including Pete Best, signed on the reverse by John Lennon, Paul McCartney, George Harrison and Ringo Starr, 6¼ by 8¼in; 15.5 by 21.5cm, c. 1962

**SALE OF TUESDAY,
DECEMBER 22, 1981
("BOOGIE")**

Lot No.	Sold for
90	£8800
91	£396
92	£1155
93	£220
94	£187

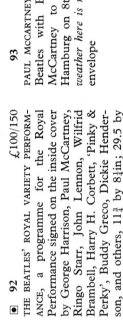

92

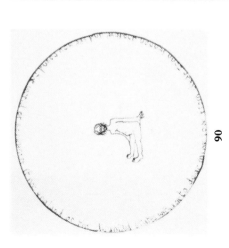

90

◉ **90**
JOHN LENNON, pen-and-ink self-portrait seated within a circle bearing the message 'to dear mike love from dear john lennon goodbye and see you round the world or somewhere if not england or the disunited states with a ★★★', 3¾in; 9.5cm diameter

£100/150

91
£80/120
THE CAVERN CLUB MEMBERSHIP CARD, 1963, the small booklet with card cover and four leaves within, bearing signatures of John Lennon, Paul McCartney, Ringo Starr and George Harrison, 4 by 2½in; 10 by 6.5cm, 1963

◉ **92**
£100/150
THE BEATLES' ROYAL VARIETY PERFORMANCE, a programme for the Royal Performance signed on the inside cover by George Harrison, Paul McCartney, Ringo Starr, John Lennon, Wilfrid Brambell, Harry H. Corbett, 'Pinky & Perky', Buddy Greco, Dickie Henderson, and others, 11¾ by 8¼in; 29.5 by 21cm, 1963

93
£100/150
PAUL McCARTNEY, a photograph of the Beatles with Pete Best from Paul McCartney to a fan posted from Hamburg on 8th May, 1962 . . . 'the weather here is not too bad' . . ., with envelope (2)

94
£15/20
JOHN LENNON, a signed photograph of John Lennon taken in the Cavern Club, 1962

23

SALE OF TUESDAY,
DECEMBER 22, 1981
("BOOGIE")

Lot No.	Sold for
95	£935
96	£1100
97	£1045
98	£770
99	£88
100	£33
101	£132
102	£198
103	£187
104	£110

99

A COLLECTION OF BEATLES SOUVENIRS, including a Lowell Toy Authentic Beatle Wig, in original wraps, seven badges in wraps, an unused diary for 1965, four plastic figures, two cut-out tickets, a plastic ring, and other printed material, c. 1965 (qty)

£20/40

100

A COLLECTION OF POP MAGAZINES, including Volume 1 of Teen Camera, 1965, Pop Weekly, No. 29, 'Get off My Cloud' record sleeve, The Rolling Stones publicity magazine and three 'giant colour pic's' of the Beatles, and six copies of Disc (qty)

£20/40

101

THE BEATLES. Richard Avedon photographic poster for 'Look' magazine, 15 by 40in; 38 by 102cm

£20/40

102

JOHN LENNON. Photographic coloured poster by Richard Avedon, 30 by 22in; 70 by 56cm

£30/50

103

YELLOW SUBMARINE, FILM POSTER in two sections, 78 by 41in; 198 by 104cm, 1968 (2)

£50/75

104

HELP!, FILM POSTER in two sections, 78 by 41in; 198 by 104cm, 1965 (2)

£50/75

95

■ **95**

THE BEATLES WORLD PREMIERE of HELP!, a programme for the première at the London Pavilion, autographed on the back outside cover by Paul McCartney, Jane Asher, John Lennon, Cynthia Lennon, George Harrison, Pattie Boyd, Ringo Starr, and others, 11 by 8½in; 28 by 21.5cm, 1965

£150/200

96

GEORGE HARRISON, a hand-written letter dated 24/8/62 to 'Jenny', including references to the introduction of Ringo Starr into The Beatles '. . Ringo is a much better drummer, and he can smile, which is a bit more than Pete could do. It will seem different for a few weeks . . . but I think that the majority of our fans will soon be taking Ringo for granted . . .'; signed '. . . lots of love from George . . .'; two sheets with envelope, 1962 (3)

£150/200

97

GEORGE HARRISON, a hand-written letter to 'Jenny', including references to his delayed departure to Germany and enclosing his address there, signed '. . lots of love from George . . .', one sheet with envelope postmarked 11th April, 1962

£100/150

98

GEORGE HARRISON, a hand-written letter to 'Jenny', including descriptions of the Star Club in Hamburg '. . The Club is gear and very. Big with a balcony and. Things . . .'; signed '. . love from George . . .', one sheet with envelope postmarked 26th April, 1962 (2)

£100/150

24

105 £60/80
TWO ETCHED COPPER PRINTERS' PHOTOGRAPHIC BLOCKS, depicting John Lennon and Yoko Ono holding hands against a background of strewn clothes and newspapers, each 7 by 5¼in; 17.8 by 13.3cm, c. 1969 (2)

106 £25/50
'A HARD DAY'S NIGHT', film script, 28th June, 1964

107 £20/40
'LET IT BE', United Artists film poster, 30 by 40in; 76 by 102cm, a French Yellow Submarine handbill and a Let It Be hand-out

108 £30/40
YELLOW SUBMARINE, eight front-of-house stills from the cartoon film of the Beatles, each 8 by 10in; 20.5 by 25.5cm, c. 1968 (8)

109 £30/50
YELLOW SUBMARINE, an Italian advertising poster for the film, 54½ by 39in; 138.5 by 99cm, c. 1968

110 £40/60
HELP!, a poster advertising the feature film, 30 by 20in; 76 by 51cm

111 £40/60
THE BEATLES, a signed photograph taken whilst travelling and filming 'The Magical Mystery Tour', 6½ by 8½in; 16.5 by 21.5cm

112 £150/200
THE BEATLES, autograph letter signed by John Lennon, 1 page, *quarto*, thanking John Balduin Bass for his 'piece' ('...*it hangs*...'), counter-signed by Yoko Ono, and envelope (2)

113 £80/120
THE BEATLES SHOW PROGRAMME, for the Odeon, Southport, autographed by George Harrison, Ringo Starr, Paul McCartney, John Lennon, Tommy Quickly, members of the 'Sons of the Piltdown Men', and by all members of 'Gerry and the Pacemakers', 10½ by 8in; 26.5 by 20.5cm, c. 1963 (3)

114 £60/100
THE BEATLES, a ticket to the Christmas Concert at the Gaumont, Bradford, with signatures by George Harrison, John Lennon, Ringo Starr, and Paul McCartney, contained in autograph book including the signatures by members of the Baron-Knights, Tornados, King-Size Taylor and the Dominoes, Joe Brown, Pirates, Hollies, Bachelors, Dave Clarke Five, and the Downbeats, c. 1963 (8)

115 £40/70
WITH THE BEATLES, an LP record with back outside cover signed with messages by John Lennon, Paul McCartney, George Harrison and George Harrison, Senior, c. 1963

116 £150/250
A SHOOTING SCRIPT FOR THE FILM 'MAGICAL MYSTERY TOUR', the photocopied seventeen-page script with annotations in coloured felt-tip pen by Paul McCartney, with four pre-release Beatles pressings on Emidisc of The Magical Mystery Tour, Blue Jay Way, Your Mother Should Know, and Ariel Instrumental, each in cardboard sleeve (21)

The vendor of this lot was the chief cameraman involved with the shooting and making of the film 'Magical Mystery Tour'

117 £20/30
BORN TO BOOGIE, a poster advertising the feature film starring Marc Bolan, Ringo Starr and Elton John, 30 by 40in; 76 by 101.5cm

118 £60/100
THE BEATLES, mounted and framed copy photographs from the Beatles 'White' album, with signatures of the four members of the group in red ballpoint pen below, 32½ by 21½in; 82.5 by 54.5cm, c. 1967

119 £30/50
THIRTEEN ASSORTED LP RECORDS, including Mary Hopkin, Lon and Derek, Van Eaton, Ravi Shankar, Badfinger, John Tavener, and others (some duplicates), each in original cover (13)

SALE OF TUESDAY, DECEMBER 22, 1981 ("BOOGIE")

Lot No.	Sold for
105	£35
106	£154
107	£110
108	£198
109	£52
110	£52
111	£209
112	£550
113	£264
114	£385
115	£440
116	£495
117	£46
118	£1210
119	£52

25

SALE OF TUESDAY, DECEMBER 22, 1981 ("BOOGIE")

Lot No.	Sold for
120	£17
121	£30
122	£46
123	£22
124	£44
125	£33
126	£71
127	£35
128	£44

123 £20/30
JOHN LENNON, YOKO ONO AND THE PLASTIC ONO BAND 33⅓-RPM RECORDS, comprising Approximately Infinite Universe (Sapdo 1001), Feeling the Space (Apple Sapcor 26) (×2), and Fly Yoko Ono (Saptu 101/102), in covers (6)

124 £20/30
SIX BEATLES LP'S, comprising Rock 'N' Roll Music, Abbey Road, The White Album, 1967-1970, Sergeant Pepper, and Yellow Submarine, each in original sleeve (6)

125 £20/25
FIVE BEATLES LP'S, comprising The White Album, With the Beatles, Please, Please Me, A Hard Day's Night, and Sergeant Pepper, each in original sleeve (5)

126 £50/80
PAUL MCCARTNEY AND WINGS, THE BEATLES, GEORGE HARRISON, RINGO STARR LP's, comprising Elephant's Memory, Beatles for Sale, Band on the Run (2), McCartney (2), Electronic Sound, All Things Must Pass, Sentimental Journey, Ringo (3) and Let It Be (3), each in original sleeve (15)

127 £40/60
TWENTY-FOUR BEATLE RE-ISSUED SINGLES, each contained in original sleeve, in cardboard box (25)

128 £40/60
THIRTY-SEVEN ASSORTED BEATLE AND OTHER 45-RPM SINGLES AND E.P.'S, on Parlophone and other labels, each in original sleeves (37)

120 121 122 123

122 £20/25
JOHN LENNON, YOKO ONO AND THE PLASTIC ONO BAND 33⅓-RPM RECORDS, comprising Live Peace in Toronto 1969 (Core 2001), Unfinished Music No. 2: Life with the Lions (Zapple 01), Feeling the Space (Apple Sapcor 26) and Fly Yoko Ono (Saptu 101/102), in covers (5)

120 121 122 123

120 £15/20
THREE JOHN LENNON 33⅓-RPM RECORDS, comprising Rock 'N' Roll (PCS 7169), Imagine (PAS 10004) and Mind Games (PCS 7165), in covers (3)

121 £20/25
FOUR JOHN LENNON 33⅓-RPM RECORDS, comprising Rock 'N' Roll (PCS 7169), Walls and Bridges (PCTC 253) and Mind Games (2), (PCS 7165), in covers (4)

27

129 £50/80
SIXTY-SIX VARIOUS APPLE 45-RPM SINGLES, by a number of artists including the Plastic Ono Band and John Lennon (66)

130 £15/30
THE BEATLES, three books by Hunter Davies, published by Heinemann, 1968 (3)

131 £50/80
BEATLES FAN CLUB MATERIAL, comprising thirty-four posters, the majority in original envelopes, seventy-five photographs with imitation signatures, and seventy-three copies of the Beatles Monthly, The Beatles News and The Beatles Newsletter, *various dates* (qty)

132 £50/80
BEATLES FAN CLUB CHRISTMAS RECORDS, forty-one records in original sleeves (41)

133 £120/200
JOLLY WHAT, The Beatles and Frank Ifield on stage, a Vee-Jay LP (VJLP 1085), *c.* 1964

134 £60/90
BEATLE RECORDS, nine 33- and 45-rpm gramophone records, comprising Please, Please Me (Parlophone PMC 1202), signed on the reverse by the four members of the group, The Magical Mystery Tour (two records), five fan club Christmas records, and My Bonnie/The Saints (Polydor NH66833) (9)

135 £40/60
THE BEATLES PRINTED MATERIAL, comprising John Lennon 'In His Own Write', third edition, fan club photographs and literature, eight black-and-white amateur snapshots of the group, five concert programmes, six booklets, and a calendar for 1964 (qty)

136 £30/50
TWO SIGNED RECORD ALBUMS, comprising McCartney II, and Ringo, each signed on the outside cover by the recording artist, *dating from c.* 1970 *and c.* 1973 (2)

137 £60/100
NINE PHOTOGRAPHIC REPRODUCTIONS OF JOHN LENNON LITHOGRAPHS, including studies of Yoko Ono, pictures of the Bed for Peace protest, a poem, and portraits of Lennon and Ono, various sizes, the largest 30 by 23in; 76 by 58.5cm (9)

138 £200/300
THE BEATLES POSTERS, the four members of the group photographed by Richard Avedon for 'Look' magazine, each brightly coloured and measuring 29¾ by 21¼in; 75.5 by 54cm, *c.* 1968 (4)

139 £50/80

◉ **139**
OUR FIRST FOUR, Apple Records Ltd first four 45-rpm records, each contained in explanatory folder and comprising Hey Jude by the Beatles, Thingumybob by the Black Dyke Mills Band, Those Were the Days by Mary Hopkin and Sour Milk Sea by Jackie Lomax, all contained in presentation folder, 13½ by 9¼in; 34.5 by 24cm (5)

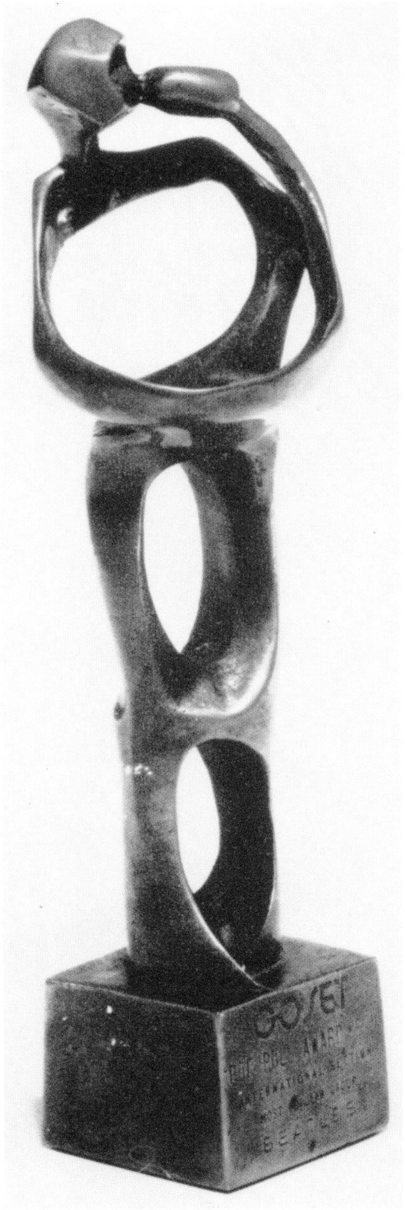

**SALE OF TUESDAY,
DECEMBER 22, 1981
("BOOGIE")**

Lot No.	Sold for
140	£352
141	£682
142	£99
143	£242
144	£176
145	£220

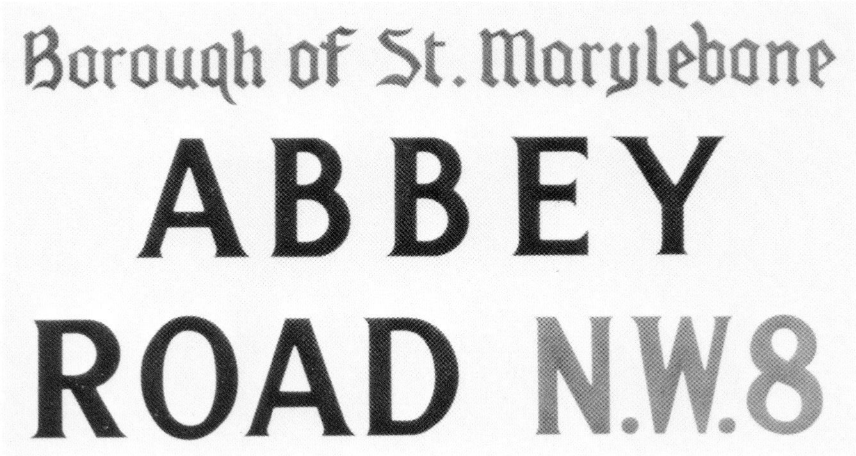

Borough of St. Marylebone
ABBEY ROAD N.W.8

140

⊙ **140**
ABBEY ROAD, the Borough of St Marylebone enamelled street sign, 30 by 18in; 76.5 by 45.5cm £120/180

⊙ **141**
THE COSET POP POLL AWARD 1970, presented to The Beatles as the most popular group in the International Section, bronze, 10in; 25.5cm high £200/300

142
YOKO AT INDICA, an illustrated catalogue of an exhibition held in 1966, 11in; 28cm high £40/50

143
'IN HIS OWN WRITE', by John Lennon, 4th edition, published by Jonathan Cape, bearing the signatures of John Lennon, Paul McCartney, George Harrison and Ringo Starr, 7 by 5¼in; 17.5 by 14cm, 1964 £80/120

144
JOHN LENNON. 'IN HIS OWN WRITE', first edition, published by Jonathan Cape in 1964, signed £50/80

145
THE BEATLES, four painted plastic models of the group playing guitars and drum, 9in; 23cm high, c. 1965 (4) £30/50

141

SALE OF TUESDAY,
DECEMBER 22, 1981
("BOOGIE")

Lot No.	Sold for
146	£935
147	£286
148	£242
149	£198
150	£253
151	£121
152	£3850
153	£1870

152

153

● **146**   £180/250
JOHN LENNON, a poster signed by the
photographer *Avedon* (Richard Avedon)
and dated '68, framed and glazed, 30¼
by 22¼in; 77 by 56.5cm

See colour illustration on front cover

● **147**   £170/250
PAUL McCARTNEY, a poster signed by the
photographer *Avedon* (Richard Avedon)
and dated '68, framed and glazed, 30¼
by 22¼in; 77 by 56.5cm

See colour illustration on front cover

● **148**   £180/250
RINGO STARR, a poster signed by the
photographer *Avedon* (Richard Avedon)
and dated '68, framed and glazed, 30¼
by 22¼in; 77 by 56.5cm

See colour illustration on front cover

● **149**   £180/250
GEORGE HARRISON, a poster signed by the
photographer *Avedon* (Richard Avedon)
and dated '68, framed and glazed, 30¼
by 22¼in; 77 by 56.5cm

See colour illustration on front cover

150   £40/60
'IN HIS OWN WRITE', by John Lennon,
7th edition, published by Jonathan
Cape, bearing the signatures of John
Lennon, Paul McCartney, Ringo Starr
and George Harrison, 7 by 5½in; 17.5
by 14cm, 1964

151   £50/80
THE BEATLES BOOK, twenty-seven copies
numbered 1-27, dating from August
1963 to October 1965   (27)

● **152**   £3000/4000
A GOLD DISC, to the Beatles for 'The
Beatles' Story' (Capitol TBO-2222),
to commemorate one million dollars'
worth of sales, framed and glazed, 21½
by 17¾in; 54.5 by 44.5cm

● **153**   £2000/3000
A GOLD BEATLES DISC, commemorating
the sale of one million dollars' worth of
'Meet the Beatles', framed and glazed,
21 by 16¾in; 53.5 by 42.5cm

29

SALE OF TUESDAY, DECEMBER 22, 1981 ("BOOGIE")

Lot No.	Sold for
154	£154
155	£462
156	£264
157	£60
158	£52
159	£451
160	£198
161	£330

The Property of Alistair Taylor, Esq.

158 £15/20

A TWA FLIGHT BAG, one of a limited edition named for members of the Beatles' tour to America, *c.* 1965

159 £120/180

JOHN LENNON POSTCARD, CHRISTMAS CARD AND LIST, the postcard sent from India during the meditation expedition and signed . . . '*love John/Cyn and the rest.*', 1968, a Christmas card signed '*love to you two too John + Yoko x*' and on the reverse '*I'm a pigaloonee rooooeeee*', and a list in John Lennon's handwriting given to Alistair Taylor describing the type of farmhouse for which he was seeking, *c.* 1968   (3)

160 £80/120

JOHN LENNON, 'A SPANIARD IN THE WORKS', published by Jonathan Cape in 1965, and signed by the author 'To Alistair lots of work from John Lennon'

161 £100/150

PAUL MCCARTNEY POSTCARDS AND CARD, one of Miyajima posted in London and signed . . . '*love from No. 7*', 1968, a postcard from India during the meditation expedition signed by '*Paul + Jane*', 1968, and another three-dimensional folding card from Lagos signed '*Paul Linda + Heather*', posted in Lagos in 1968 (in Hairy Heart envelope)   (4)

154 (detail)

The certificate was found in a second-hand furniture shop in Liverpool, where it had been taped beneath a drawer

156 £100/150

JOHN LENNON, 'IN HIS OWN WRITE', first edition, hard back, autographed '*John Lennon with love to J.M.*', 1964

157 £40/70

'A SPANIARD IN THE WORKS', John Lennon, first edition, hard back, 1965

154

■ **154** £30/50

A PAIR OF BEATLE WOVEN NYLON STOCKINGS, the stocking tops printed with caricature portraits of the Beatles, the stockings woven with motifs of a guitar and a smiling face with a Beatle haircut, *c.* 1965   (2)

155 Refer to Dept.

THE MARRIAGE CERTIFICATE OF JOHN LENNON AND CYNTHIA POWELL, at Liverpool South Register Office, on 23rd August, 1962, witnessed by James Paul McCartney and Marjorie Joyce Powell, and signed by Eric Williams on behalf of the borough, framed and glazed, 1962

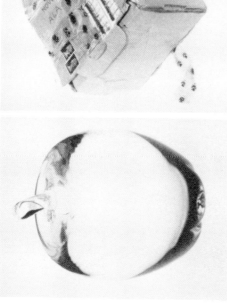

162

163

162 £180/250

A STEUBEN GLASSWORKS GLASS APPLE, presented by Paul McCartney to Alistair Taylor, signed by the manufacturer on the base, 4¼in; 10.5cm high, contained in cardboard box partially wrapped in dog-paw printed sticky tape, with Paul McCartney's handwriting *'Paul's once now Alastair's'*

(2)

163 £100/150

A CELLULOID FROM THE CARTOON FILM YELLOW SUBMARINE, depicting the four Beatles with their instruments, 14 by 10¼in; 35.5 by 26cm

164 £120/180

GEORGE HARRISON, LETTER, CHRISTMAS CARDS AND SIGNED PHOTOGRAPH, the letter written to Alistair Taylor from America requesting a photographic enlargement of a photograph of George Harrison, . . . *'its the funniest picture I have seen for sometime and I couldn't resist a big one for my front door!'* (two sheets), a photographic enlargement signed with the message *'To Alistair why dont you—. . . . . .!!! George (Harrison)'*, a Christmas card with the same photograph, signed *'Without whom it would not have been possible George + Patti'*, and another signed *'From George and Pattie'*, the largest 13¼ by 8¼in; 33.5 by 21.5cm, *dating from c. 1965*

(5)

165 £60/80

BRIAN EPSTEIN CHRISTMAS CARDS AND POSTCARD, the postcard from Acapulco dated 1967 and signed, and two signed Christmas cards, the largest 9¾in; 24.7cm high

(3)

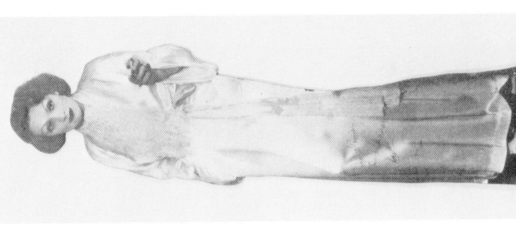

173

171

166 £60/80
PAUL McCARTNEY AND JANE ASHER IN SCOTLAND, six black-and-white photographs showing Miss Asher at the sink, Paul McCartney sweeping the front step with his dog, Martha, and others, each 3½in; 9cm square, c. 1968 (6)

167 £25/30
NEMS PRINTED AND WRITTEN MATERIAL, comprising a programme for the 3rd Anniversary in 1965, an envelope sent from Maine in 1964, a handwritten letter from Cilla Black, and a postcard from Ringo Starr and Maureen (4)

168 £60/100
TWO BEATLE DEMO DISCS, one on Dick James Music Limited, TEM 1687/8 'Bad To Me' and 'Goodbye', each in slip cover (2)

169 £30/50
AN APPLE PUBLISHING CO. LTD PSYCHEDELIC MULTI-COLOURED POSTER designed by Simon & Marijke of 'The Fool', *three tears and small section missing*, 25 by 18in; 63.5 by 46cm, c. 1968

170 £25/35
AN APPLE PUBLISHING CO. LTD MULTI-COLOURED POSTER designed by Simon & Marijke of 'The Fool', 24 by 23in; 61 by 58.5cm, c. 1968

171 £40/60
AN APPLE PUBLISHING CO. LTD DREAM POSTER designed by Simon & Marijke of 'The Fool', signed and dated '67, 24 by 18in; 61 by 46cm, c. 1967

172 £25/35
AN APPLE PUBLISHING CO. LTD DREAM POSTER designed by Simon & Marijke of 'The Fool', 23½in; 60cm square, c. 1967; AND A BILL POSTER FOR THE DOORS, 20 by 14in; 51 by 36cm (2)

173 £200/300
SERGEANT PEPPER'S LONELY HEARTS CLUB BAND, a life-size hand-tinted cut-out photographic enlargement of Marlene Dietrich, used with others on the cover to the album, and signed by each member of The Beatles, 69¾in; 117cm high

SALE OF TUESDAY, DECEMBER 22, 1981 ("BOOGIE")

Lot No.	Sold for
174	£242
175	£4620
176	£82

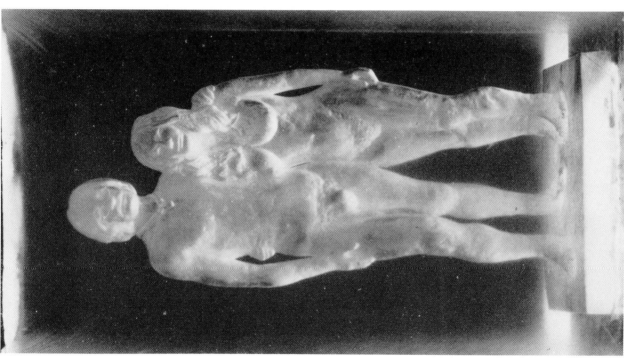

175

174

Photograph by Harry Hammond

◉ **174** £80/120
THE BEATLES, photographed with Roy Orbison and Gerry and the Pacemakers in the dressing room during the first British tour by the Beatles in 1963, mounted in card

Various Properties

◉ **175** £1000/1500
THE TWO VIRGINS, commissioned by Lennon and one of only two made, a perspex and plastic sculpture of the nude figures of John Lennon and Yoko Ono, 13½in; 34cm high

176 £60/120
JOHN LENNON AND YOKO ONO, oil on board, framed, portrait heads against a representation of a revolver blast, 19½ by 15¼in; 49.5 by 38.5cm, 1980

179

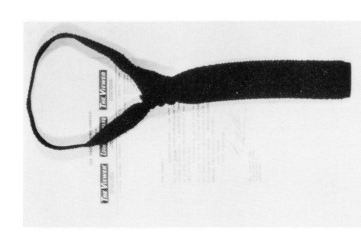

177

Lot No.	Sold for
177	£264
178	£308
179	£99
180	£88
181	£550

◉ **177**   £120/150
RINGO STARR'S NECKTIE, the black hand-stitched knitted silk necktie, 50 by 2in; 127 by 5cm, together with a letter of authenticity signed by Ringo Starr, 1964   (2)

The Property of Templering Ltd, printers for Apple Corps

178   £40/80
APPLE EPHEMERA, including an interest-ing sample book of compliment slips, memo pads, and booklets, two copies of Beatles . . . a little book, 1975 and 1973 catalogues, The Beatles Get Back, Apple Christmas card, John and Yoko calendar, ten copies of Fresh from Apple, and other printed material (qty)

◉ **179**   £80/120
THE BEATLES, photographed in 1963 on the BBC Radio 'Pop Inn' programme whilst promoting their first single, 'Love Me Do', mounted in card   (2)

The Property of D. Millings & Son, Show Business Tailors

180   £100/150
AN INTERESTING SHOW BUSINESS SCRAP-BOOK, containing photographs, cuttings, Christmas cards (*one signed by George Harrison*), orders for stage suits for a large number of personalities, and many other items, the majority con-tained in a large album, some loose   (qty)

181   £350/450
TWO CONTRACTS FOR THE BEATLES CONCERT AT THE HOLLYWOOD BOWL, between General Artists Corporation (*signed by Robert L. Eubanks and Michael Brown on their behalf*) and Nems Enterprises Ltd (*signed by Brian Epstein on their behalf*), in the form of a carbon copy contract concerning a con-cert to be held in America on July 28th, 1965, and the fee, and three photocopies of pages of a contract between Nems and GAC, similarly signed, each 8½ by 11in; 21.5 by 28cm   (4)

Various Properties

◉ **182**　　　£300/400
APPLE, designed by 'The Fool', a brightly painted panel depicting a semi-reclining figure with exotic birds, sun and clouds, oil on board, 28½ by 48in; 72.5 by 122cm, *c.* 1971

This was removed from the Apple retail shop in Baker Street during its closing sale

◉ **183**　　　£250/400
JOHN LENNON. 'OPEN & SHUT', a wooden sculpture in the form of a painted wooden cupboard, framed, 31 by 45in; 79 by 114cm, with exhibition catalogue
(2)

This was made by John Lennon, and donated to raise money for the 'Oz' obscenity trials on 21st April, 1971

182

183

**SALE OF TUESDAY,
DECEMBER 22, 1981
("BOOGIE")**

Lot No.	Sold for
182	Withdrawn
183	£1430

184

185

SALE OF TUESDAY,
DECEMBER 22, 1981
("BOOGIE")

Lot No.   Sold for
184   £3300
185   £2530

◉ 184   £600/900
GEORGE   HARRISON'S   TWELVE-STRING
HARPTONE GUITAR, Model L/12NC,
Serial No. 2004/27, the blond guitar
used by George Harrison for several
years, contained in blue velvet-lined
rexine case, 46in; 117cm long, together
with letter of authenticity from Harold
J. Harrison, Director of Harrisongs
Ltd   (3)

The Property of D. A. Millings & Son,
Show Business Tailors

◉ 185   £200/300
JOHN LENNON'S STAGE SUIT, the collar-
less tan silk jacket edged with brown
velvet, buff lining and small pocket at
one side holding plastic plectrum, and
inner pocket bearing tailor's label and
written 'John Lennon' label, with
matching trousers, c. 1964   (2)

36

SALE OF TUESDAY, DECEMBER 22, 1981 ("BOOGIE")

Lot No.	Sold for
186	£715
187	£572
188	£605

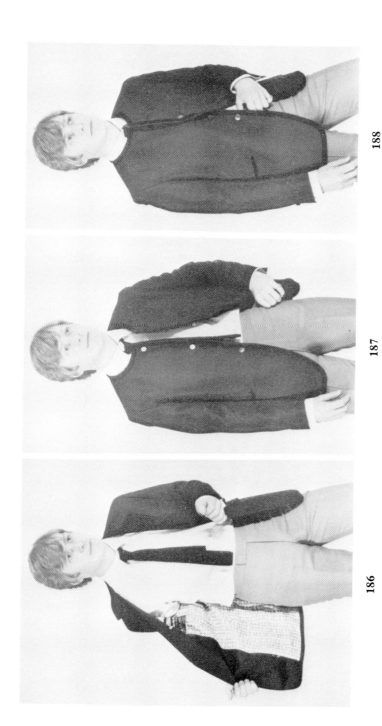

186

187

188

◉ **186**　　　　　*£*180/250
JOHN LENNON'S JACKET, the black jacket, satin finished, green and cream lining and inner pocket bearing tailor's label and written 'John Lennon' label, *c.* 1967

◉ **187**　　　　　*£*180/250
JOHN LENNON'S STAGE JACKET, the collar-less self-striped black jacket edged with black velvet, maroon lining and small pocket at one side holding plastic plectrum, and inner pocket bearing tailor's label and written 'John Lennon' label, *c.* 1964

◉ **188**　　　　　*£*180/250
JOHN LENNON'S STAGE JACKET, the collarless black silk jacket edged in black velvet, the lining of sky blue, with small pocket at one side holding plastic plectrum, and inner pocket bearing tailor's label and written 'John Lennon' label, *c.* 1964

189

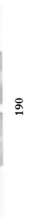

190

191

189　£180/250

JOHN LENNON'S STAGE JACKET, the grey silk jacket with black velvet collar and lining of sky blue, with small pocket at one side holding plastic plectrum, and inner pocket bearing tailor's label and written 'John Lennon' label, *c.* 1964

The Property of Mrs E. Keane

190　£150/200

JOHN LENNON'S JACKET, a black gaberdine semi-frock jacket with acetate lining, *c.* 1963

The authenticity of this jacket has been confirmed by the Beatle tailor who made it for John Lennon, based on jackets worn by the Everly Brothers in one of their concerts

Various Owners

191　£300/400

JOHN LENNON'S BLACK KNITTED SILK TIE, 46in; 117cm long, AND AN AUTOGRAPHED LETTER OF AUTHENTICITY, signed by John Lennon, 1964　(2)

This tie was the first prize in a National competition held by 'The Viewer' magazine with only one winner for this original John Lennon tie

192　£300/500

A RALEIGH SUPER 50 MOPED, *once owned by John Lennon*, the vehicle finished in black with canvas pannier bags, and complete with registration book detailing the ownership of the vehicle by Brian Epstein Automobiles, and then by John Winston Lennon in 1967 and 1968, 69in; 175cm long, *c.* 1965　(2)

SALE OF TUESDAY, DECEMBER 22, 1981 ("BOOGIE")

Lot No.   **Sold for**
192A   £418

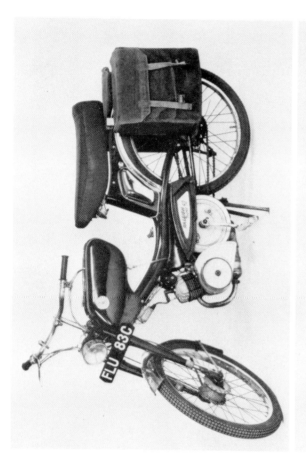

192
192a

192 (log book)

◉ **192a**   £150/300
A RADIOGRAM, the teak-veneered unit with four hinged sections and the top opening to reveal Stereo 30 amplifier controls, Garrard record deck and two storage compartments, the four lower sections for record storage, 35½ by 72½ by 21in; 90 by 183.5 by 53.5cm, *English, c.* 1960

This radiogram originally included a tape deck and was used by John Lennon in the early 60's at the house of Mrs Mimi Smith, to record songs that were then played back over the telephone to Paul McCartney for his comments

193

194

JOHN LENNON'S PIANO

◉ **193**   Refer to Dept.

AN UPRIGHT PIANO by Steinway & Sons, Hamburg, 1970, inscribed on the name-board *Steinway & Sons* and on the frame *Steinway Maker, Germany*, bearing the serial number 417139, the case of teak, the seven-octave keyboard, AAA to c⁵, with ivory naturals and ebony accidentals, two pedals controlling forte and piano stops, height 44¾in; 113.5cm, width 57¼in; 145.5cm

See illustration on page 40

◉ **194**   £1500/2500

PAUL MCCARTNEY's CHAPPELL & CO. LTD UPRIGHT PIANO, *No. 38567*, the ebonised case with seven octave keyboard (AAA-a⁴) with ivory naturals and ebony accidentals, two pedals beneath (forte and piano), 56 by 50 by 24¾in; 142 by 127 by 61.5cm, *English, c. 1902*

This piano was sold to the present owner by J. McCartney in 1955 and will be auctioned with a document to this effect

See illustration on page 41

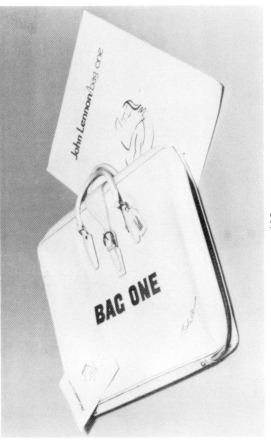

195

◉ **195**   £500/700

'BAG ONE' BY JOHN LENNON, *No. 292 from a limited edition of 300*, comprising fourteen erotic and other lithographs, each signed in pencil by John Lennon, contained in white plastic portfolio with catalogue, from the exhibition at the Lee Nordness Galleries, New York, *dated 1970*, the lithographs 30 by 23in; 76 by 58.5cm   (qty)

For Sale by Private Treaty

A LARGE AND COMPREHENSIVE COLLECTION OF RECORDS comprising over 2000 singles, E.P.'s and L.P.'s of popular music of the period 1964-1981

A detailed card index file of the collection is available for interested parties to view at Sotheby's Belgravia between the 19th and 22nd December, 9 am to 4 pm. Telephone 01-235 4311 for appointment

SALE OF TUESDAY, DECEMBER 22, 1981 ("BOOGIE")

Lot No.	Sold for
193	£8250
194	£9900
195	£5060

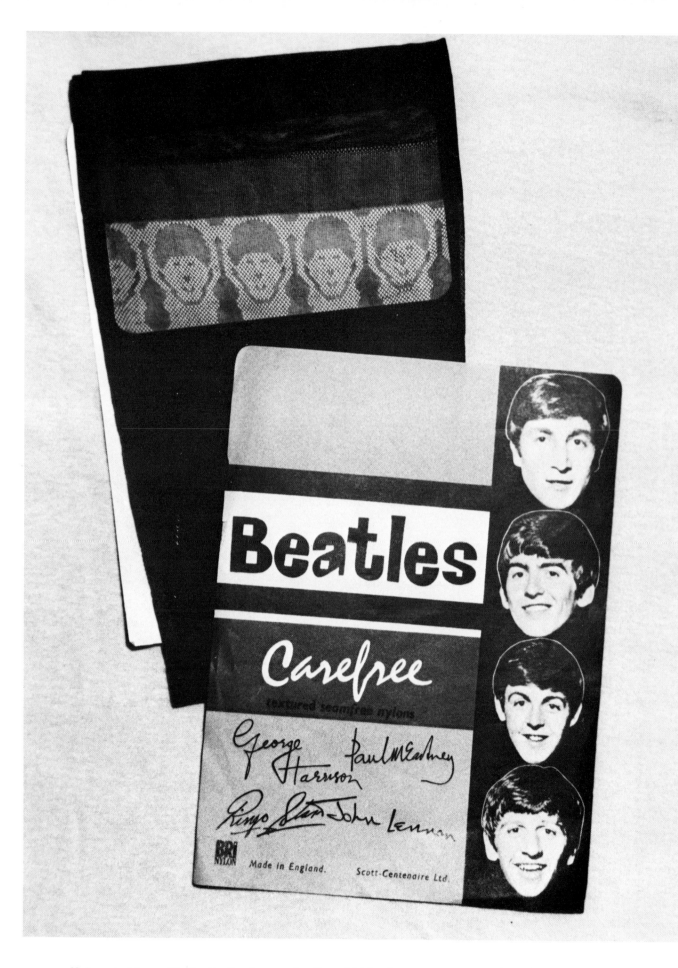

Nylon stockings with the Beatles faces and guitars right in the pattern are a rare item from England. Complete with original packaging, they may sell for $25-30 for the pair. *Price Guide No.: 698*

Additions to the Price Guide

This supplemental list is made up of items for which prices were obtained too late for inclusion in the main Price Guide, as well as a few things which were known but were inadvertently left out during the preparation of the text. The category and relative position of each item is indicated in a way which corresponds to the arrangement of the main listing.

BEATLES ALBUMS

Description	Title	Condition		
		Near Mint	Very Good	Good
69a. Picture Discs	Band On The Run	$20		

PROMO RECORDS

Label and Record Number	Title	Description	Condition		
			Near Mint	Very Good	Good
182a. Capitol SpRo 9758/59	*BEATLES MOVIE MEDLEY*/With interview B-side	Twelve-inch with black jacket	$35–50		
182b. Capitol PRO 2598	*BEATLES OPEN END INTERVIEW* for **BEATLES SECOND ALBUM**	Rare 7-inch to DJs with jacket	$200		
202a. Columbia AS 1444	*McCARTNEY SAMPLER* Selections from **TUG OF WAR**	Twelve-inch on white vinyl	$50		
205a Capitol	*REEL MUSIC*	Promo on gold vinyl, numbered. Only 10,000	$50+		
231a. VJ 581	*PLEASE PLEASE ME/ FROM ME TO YOU* With picture sleeve "the record that started Beatlemania"	Rare white label promo with sleeve Record alone	$100–175 $75		
283a.	Italian jukebox promos		$30–50		

BEATLES-RELATED & NOVELTY RECORDS

Label and Record Number	Title	Description	Condition		
			Near Mint	Very Good	Good
375a. United Artists	MARTIN, GEORGE (Orchestra) *A HARD DAY'S NIGHT/ I SHOULD HAVE KNOWN BETTER*	With picture sleeve of Beatles	$50		
375b. United Artists 745	MARTIN, GEORGE (Orchestra) *RINGO'S THEME/AND I LOVE HER*	With picture sleeve of Beatles	$30–50		

Label and Record Number		Title	Description	Condition Near Mint Very Good Good		
375c.	United Artists	MARTIN, GEORGE (Orchestra)	LPs of instrumentals			
	3377	**OFF THE BEATLES TRACK**		$20–25		
	6383	**A HARD DAYS NIGHT**		$20–25		
	6448	**HELP!**		$15–20		
	3539	**THE BEATLES GIRLS**		$15–20		
375d.	Parlophone R 5135	MARTIN, GEORGE (Orchestra) *ALL MY LOVING/I SAW HER STANDING THERE*	U.K. 45	$5–10		
375e.	Parlophone G EP 8930	MARTIN, GEORGE (Orchestra) **MUSIC FROM A HARD DAYS NIGHT**	U.K. EP	$30		
405a.	Tower 5000	**SING ALONG WITH THE BEATLES**	Instrumental backgrounds. Beatles on jacket.	$15–25		

BOOKS

Publisher		Year	Title	Description	Condition Near Mint Very Good Good		
441a.	Scholastic Books	1974	*BEATLES YESTERDAY, TODAY... TOMORROW* by Rochelle Larkin	Paperback Reissue	$7–8 $2		
472a.	Doubleday	1971	*WE LOVE YOU BEATLES* by Margaret Sutton	Hardcover with dust jacket	$12–15		

MEMORABILIA

Item		Description	Condition Near Mint Very Good Good		
745a.	Yellow Submarine Binder	Colorful "Yellow Submarine" characters on cover	NPA		
762a.	Yellow Submarine Notebook	Cover matches Binder (above). Two sizes.	NPA		

Glossary of Terms
(Or, A Guide to the Jargon of the Beatles Collecting Scene)

GRADING TERMS RELATING TO CONDITION

STILL SEALED (S.S.) Any item (usually an LP or EP) still in its original, unbroken, cellophane wrap. So rarely encountered that it can sometimes *double* the value of an item. (Any item can be fraudulently re-sealed, or shrink-wrapped to pass as an original S.S. item with a high price tag. Some dealers may therefore use the term *factory sealed* (F.S.) instead.)

MINT (M.) Any item uncirculated; never played, never read, never used, etc. Shows *no* sign of wear. All contents including original packaging, inserts, etc., must still be intact. May be valued at 25--50 percent above Near Mint.

NEAR MINT OR EXCELLENT (NR.M. or EX.) The usual top grading. Anything which shows only minimal signs of use. Almost pristine, but *has* been circulated. Records must be free of dirt, scratches, or any markings. Sleeves must be clean; no writing, water marks, ring wear, etc. All memorabilia clean; no rust, chips, or other defacement.

VERY GOOD OR FINE (V.G. or F.) Any item showing some signs of use or wear. May have minimal markings, or writing, dirt or rust, but nothing that interferes with play, use, or appearance. Value is usually 25--50 percent less than Near Mint.

GOOD (G.) Any item that shows heavy use and interfering signs of wear and tear; markings, dirt, heavy ring wear, seam splits, defacement, parts missing, etc. Value may be 25--50 percent less than Very Good.

FAIR OR POOR (F. or P.) Usually not in a collectable state. Any item so defaced that it is almost unusable or ruined. Heavy writing, soil, water damage, warp, broken, etc. Value may be near zero, and certainly less than original selling price.

Pluses (+), double pluses (++), and also minuses (-) are commonly used to denote slight gradations between items which do not fit neatly into any one category. The difference between a V.G.+ and a Nr.M.- may be almost imperceptible.

These terms are the ones most commonly used by "professional" dealers. The definitions are my own, but most dealers would concur. However, every dealer looks on an item with a slightly different reference point and may grade up or down according to individual prejudice and measure.

OTHER HANDY TERMS

ACETATE A type of recording cut on a special lathe with a metal center. A studio may make one from a tape just to hear how it sounds. An *acetate* may exist for a recording that was never even officially released, and these would be the most valuable.

Since few production steps are required, anyone can cut one, and fakes may exist which purport to be genuine, rare Beatles recordings.

APPLE PROMOS Any items distributed or given away by the Beatles own company, Apple Corp., from 1968 on, as a promotional piece to advertise a new Beatles product, the company itself, or the Beatles in general. Value is especially high on those items, as they were never commercially sold, and were instead generally given to only a select few and are consequently very rare today.

BOOTLEG (BOOT) OR UNDERGROUND RECORD A newly created item (usually a recording — LP, EP, 45 — but referring also to record sleeves) which has never existed in this form as an official, original item. Any item that was never legitimately released in its present form. These are illegal materials, usually pressed by fans themselves from material otherwise not available on commercial recordings.

COLLECTIBLE Any item that sells for more than it originally cost, is usually hard to find, and the demand for which exceeds the supply. Most collectibles are out-of-print and no longer for sale commercially.

CONVENTION (CON.) A gathering, usually on a large scale, of fans and collectors in one place. Activities may include films, speakers, live bands, contests, auctions, and most often a merchandise room (*Dealers'* room) full of Beatles items for sale.

COUNTERFEIT Any item which is not original, but which is made to look exactly like the original. An item which intentionally tries to pass as the original. Beatles records, picture sleeves, even memorabilia have all been counterfeited. A counterfeit is an illegal remake of a (usually) valuable collectible.

COVER VERSION A recording of a song by someone other than the original artist who recorded it first (and presumably turned the song into a hit and is associated with it as a result). Thousands of recordings by other performers have "covered" songs first recorded by the Beatles. Similarly, the Beatles "covered" songs originally associated with Chuck Berry, Carl Perkins, Larry Williams, etc. Cover versions of Beatles' songs are not generally sought after as collectibles.

DEALERS Those people who make a living (or at least engage in a money-making hobby) out of selling Beatles items. Beatles dealers are found at conventions, and many also put out their own mail-order sales lists. A few even run specialized record and/or collectibles stores.

DEMOS Demonstration discs. Legitimately cut recordings containing outtakes, alternate versions, etc., which may "get out" to the public, but weren't meant to be sold commercially. Recording studios may manufacture dozens or hundreds of copies simply to circulate the material to test the possible reception it might be given if it were released.

FANDOM Beatle fans who identify with their fellow fans, who participate in fan activities (fan clubs, fan magazines, conventions, etc.).

FANZINE Usually refers to any small-circulation, independent magazine written by fans (of the Beatles, or other performers) for fans, and not ordinarily sold in stores. May range in size from a couple of xeroxed pages to over thirty pages of typeset material. Subscribers may range from a dozen to thousands, and may be locally based or internationally distributed. Some fanzines have been publishing since the sixties, while others have only begun in recent years. The life-span on the average is only a few years, but several have existed for a half dozen years or more.

FIRST EDITION/FIRST PRESSING The original manufacturer's first version of an item. Books may have many printings as part of their first edition. Changes in label, jacket, and even sound quality may exist in different pressings of records, so collectors distinguish between them.

FIRST STATE Principally used to refer to the first cover (or "Butcher cover") of the *original* press-

ing of the **Yesterday and Today** LP. It indicates that the Butcher cover picture (the Beatles wearing butchers' smocks) was *never* covered over with the second "trunk" cover (the Beatles posed around an open trunk). A *first state* Butcher cover is *very* rare, and value would be several times above the usual peeled/unpeeled versions.

JACKET Usually refers to the cardboard covering of an album or EP. Value as a collectible lies in the record *and* jacket combined. Value of one without the other may be diminished by 50 percent or more. A jacket or LP/EP alone may be valueless to a collector.

MARKET PRICE Refers (in this guide) to the top price charged by Beatles dealers who specialize in Beatles items. Usually the price listed in sales lists and at conventions. The prices given in this guide are *top* market prices.

MEMORABILIA Refers to items that came out of the sixties at the height of Beatlemania, mostly from the 1963--66 period. Also, the "Yellow Submarine" inspired items from 1968. "New memorabilia" items are usually promos from record companies, book publishers, etc. Most other newly created items, manufactured just to cash-in on the current collecting craze, are not legitimate memorabilia. All legitimate memorabilia are collectibles.

In this guide, records, books, and magazines are listed separately, while the designation "memorabilia" refers more narrowly to things like toys, jewelry, clothing, and miscellaneous items which featured the Beatles pictures or names.

NEMS/SELTAEB NEMS (North End Music Stores) was originally Brian Epstein's Liverpool family business, and the name he gave to his first company, NEMS Enterprises Ltd. NEMS gave out licenses to hundreds of companies to manufacture Beatles memorabilia. While hundreds of other items were made without NEMS' approval, those marked NEMS are especially sought after. *SELTAEB* was another licensing name used in the U.S. for NEMS sanctioned items.

NOVELTIES/BREAK-INS Refers to records which are based on some Beatles theme, a take-off on the group, or an "answer" record. All of these were cash-ins on the newsworthiness of the Beatles. They differ from Beatles-related records in that they are not cover versions of Beatles songs (of which there are thousands), but are a category unto themselves. Novelties are usually humorous, or contain a "message" of some sort.

ORIGINAL In the purest sense: something that exists for the first time. A first edition, first pressing, first manufacture. Even a bootleg can be an original, since it never existed in any other previous pressing in that exact form. A collector seeks original items as opposed to counterfeits, reissues, second pressings, replicas, etc.

PEELED/UNPEELED Refers to the "Butcher cover" jacket on the original **Yesterday And Today** LP. An unpeeled version means it still has the second "trunk" cover pasted over the first cover, the picture of the Beatles in butchers' smocks.

A peeled version is one in which this "trunk" cover has been removed (usually by a steaming process) and the "Butcher cover" is now visible.

Both are valuable and vary according to the condition of the jacket and expertness of the "peel job" (or, how well the second cover was steamed off). A bad job may seriously ruin the "Butcher cover" and devalue the entire item.

PICTURE SLEEVE (P.S. or P/S) The paper holder or covering of a 45 rpm record or an EP. In many cases the collecting value lies in the *sleeve* itself. Even without a record, therefore, prices may be the same for sleeves alone as for sleeves with records, as the picture seleve is the rarer item. Most Beatles' singles sold in the millions, however, so that today they are worth only a few dollars by themselves (exceptions other than promos and rare label variations are all noted in the Price Guide). But sleeves were pressed in more limited quantities, and the demand far exceeds the supply available.

PIRATE Refers to recordings which feature material that was previously released, but not in the same form, and is usually unauthorized and illegal. It is not an exact copy but a newly created item: examples: The Tollie EP (there never was an *original* Tollie EP, so this is not a legitimate release from Tollie); **The Savage Beatles, Best Of The Beatles**, both of which rework old material to look like legitimate new Beatles records, which they are not.

PRODUCT A generic term used to refer to all manufactured goods — records, books, memorabilia — associated with the Beatles.

PROMOTIONAL ITEMS (PROMOS) Any item put out officially by legitimate companies to promote new Beatles product. May be any number of different types of items: t-shirts and jackets, buttons, posters, and displays are the most common. More unique promos also exist, such as: sunglasses, combs, sewing kit, frisbee, toys (a toy double-decker bus for **London Town**), etc.

Promos usually refers to promotional records — LPs, EPs, or 45s. Record companies send these to radio stations and the print media in hopes of getting airplay, reviews, and publicity for their new recording. These usually differ from the commercially sold versions, and feature some label changes, or the words "dj copy," "not for sale," or "promotional copy" (on the label or record jacket). Some exceptions are records that are pressed and sent to the media and then withdrawn before they ever are released commercially, for example: *Girl*, or the new "Beatles medly" 45 with the withdrawn interview on the B-side. Some promos are especially valuable and collectable because of a variation which exists only on the promo copy and not the commercial release (e.g., *Penny Lane*, which has an extra trumpet ending on the promo 45 only).

RARE An overused term which dealers give to anything of extra collecting value. A limited number should exist of the item, and the demand should be higher than the supply before an item is really considered *rare*.

It is also used as a synonym for bootlegs, as in "rare record."

REISSUE/REPRESSING Refers to legitimate remakes of an item by the company that holds the current copyright and has the rights to reprint a book, or re-press a record. The reissues (as opposed to first editions or first pressings) are usually not valuable beyond their current selling price, and have little or no current collectors' value. VJ Records, for instance, legitimately repressed the LP **Introducing The Beatles**, among others. The original first pressings are still valuable, but the reissue, still for sale in most record stores, is not worth more than the current store price.

Illegal items are often erroneously called "reissues"; they are really only counterfeits. For some items, such as **Introducing The Beatles**, there exist original first pressings, legitimate reissues, *and* counterfeits.

REPRODUCTION/REPLICA Like the counterfeit, these are remakes of Beatles items which look exactly (or almost) like the original. The terms are usually used in reference to memorabilia items; such copies are distinguished from counterfeits in that they often don't pretend to be the originals themselves. The price is usually the identifying factor. An original Beatles pencil case, which came in a variety of colors, would sell for $40.00 at top market price; a replica, made only in red, would be marked at $9.00 and would exist in quantity.

TEST PRESSING Refers to an exact copy of what will eventually be pressed as a commercial recording. These are more limited than the promo copies and thus more valuable (25--50 percent more than promos). The label will be different from the final promo copy and the official release. May only list title and be an otherwise blank, white label.

WOC/WOL/WOS Abbreviations used in collectors' magazines and by dealers on sales lists to indicate an item is less than Mint and has markings of some sort which devalue it: woc = writing on cover; wol = writing on label; wos = writing on sleeve. Any such notations after an item listed for sale would mean the condition (and corresponding valuation) should be interpreted as VG or less, depending on how prominent the markings are.

The Resource Guide:
An Address List for Collectors

FAN CLUBS/FANZINES

The following is a selective list of U.S. fan clubs which publish their own fanzines and are still currently active. For information on subscription rates/dues, send a self-addressed, stamped envelope to the individual club or publication.

BEATLEFAN
Bill King, Publisher
P.O. Box 33515
Decatur, GA 30033

THE HARRISON ALLIANCE
Patti Murawski, President
67 Cypress St.
Bristol, CT 06010

THE McCARTNEY OBSERVER
Doylene Kindsvater, Editor
220 E. 12th St.
Lacross, KS 67548

WITH A LITTLE HELP
FROM MY FRIENDS
Pat Simmons, Editor
10290 Pleasant Lake No. F21
Cleveland, OH 44130

THE MIKE (McGEAR)
McCARTNEY FAN CLUB
Barbara Paulson, Editor
P.O. Box 164
Genoa, IL 60135

THE WRITE THING
Barbara Fenick, Editor
P.O. Box 18807
Minneapolis, MN 55418

RECORD COLLECTING MAGAZINES

GOLDMINE
P.O. Box 187
Fraser, MI 48026
(Published monthly; subscription: U.S. $20; Canada, $23.)

TROUSER PRESS
212 Fifth Avenue
New York, NY 10010
($15/12 issues; sample issues $1.50.)

BEATLES MONTHLY BOOK
Beat Publications
45 St. Mary's Rd.
Ealing, London
W5 5RQ England
(Published monthly; Airmail U.S. & Canada, $30.)

RECORD COLLECTOR
45 St. Mary's Road
Ealing, London
W5 5RQ England
(Published monthly; Airmail & Canada, $32.)

DEALERS' CATALOGS & SALES LISTS

The following is a list of some dealers who specialize in Beatles related items — records, books, and/or memorabilia. To get on their mailing list, write and send a stamp or two. (The author takes no responsibility for transactions or business practices, as we cannot police all dealers and their activities. Buy carefully.)

RICK RANN BEATLELIST
P.O. Box 877
Oak Park, IL 60303

TONY DAWKINS
"Greenacres," Hawkwell
Hockley, Essex
SS5 4DZ, England

TICKET TO RYDE
P.O. Box 3393
Lacey, WA 98503

OLYMPIC ENTERPRISES
Box 91153
Los Angeles, CA 90009

THE REAL FIFTH BEATLE
P.O. Box 29523
Los Angeles, CA 90029

FRANCK LEENHEER/RECORDS
Smidstraat 70
2231 Rijnsburg
Holland

RETAIL OUTLETS THAT SPECIALIZE IN BEATLES

LET IT BE RECORDS
2434 Judah St.
San Francisco, CA 94122

THE RECORD HUNTER
233 Robina Pl.
Philadelphia, PA 19116

BLUE MEANIE RECORDS
1207 N. 2nd St.
El Cajon, CA 92021

FOLLIES
135 Kings Road
At Antiquarius
London SW3, England

MUSIQUE BOUTIQUE/
  PICCADILLY MUSIC
70 Shaftesbury Ave.
London, W1, England
(Dealers list also)

QUEENS COMICS
1962 Queens St. E.
Toronto M4L 1H8
Canada

RECORD RUNNER
5 Cornelia St.
New York, NY 10014

SPEAKEASY ANTIQUES
799 Broadway
New York, NY 10003

CAVERN MECCA
18 Mathew St., Merseyside,
Liverpool L2 6RE, England
(Also Beatles Museum & Information Centre)

OVERSEAS CLUBS

When writing to the following clubs/fanzines, send two international reply coupons (available at any post office) and ask for subscription information.

BEATLES UNLIMITED
P.O. Box 259-2400
AG Alphen aan de Rijn
Holland

WINGS FUN CLUB
P.O. Box 4UP
London W1, 4UP England
(U.S. rates $7.50 a year)

CLUB DES 4 DE LIVERPOOL
43, bis Boulevard Henri IV
75004 Paris, France
(Written in French, but
  marvelous pictures)

COME TOGETHER
31, William St.
Kettering, Northants
NN16 9RS England

CONVENTIONS/ROCK SHOWS/RECORD MEETS

BEATLEFEST
National Headquarters
P.O. Box 436
Westwood, NJ 07675

ROCKAGES
P.O. Box 69
Bayside, NY 11361

RECORD COLLECTORS CON-
  VENTIONS
Stuart Shapiro
23077 Greenfield, Suite 159
Southfield, MI 48075

Collecting The Beatles
Questionnaire

If you have been unable to find a Price Guide listing for an item you have seen or which is in your collection, please let us know. Even if your price information is dated or unavailable, your description will contribute towards the creation of a worldwide inventory of existing Beatles collectibles. Please make photocopies of this questionnaire to use in submitting your information.

TYPE OF COLLECTIBLE

Consult the twelve categories of the Price Guide to aid you in classifying the collectible you are describing (e.g., promo record, memorabilia, bootleg, solo single, etc.).

_____

DESCRIPTION

Include here any information on country of origin, manufacturer's name, date on the merchandise, type of external packaging, physical dimensions, color(s), itemization of smaller details (number of pages for publications, etc.).

_____

_____

_____

_____

(continue on separate sheet)

LOCATION

Where is the item (personal collection, a friend's collection, on public display) and who should be contacted in order to examine it?

_____

_____

PURCHASE INFORMATION

When and where was the item obtained, what was the price paid at the time, what condition is it in (according to the definitions in this book), how many are in your possession or how many others were observed when you purchased or saw the item? Are you interested in selling?

_____

_____

_____

PHOTOGRAPHS & COPIES

To aid in supplying complete and exact discographic or bibliographic details, would it be possible for you to make a copy of such things as record labels, picture sleeves, record jackets, the first few preliminary pages of books, magazines, etc., using a photo-copying machine (please do not proceed with this unless requested, to avoid needless expense)?

Can you supply a photograph of the item, or will you allow it to be photographed if this can be otherwise arranged?

_____

COLLECTING ADVICE

Any collecting tips or pointers you'd care to share with other collectors (e.g., recommendations about dealers, useful publications, bad buying experiences, advice on protecting and preserving collectibles, identifying counterfeits, collecting terms or practices not covered in this book)?

_____

_____

_____

_____

_____

_____

_____

CHANGES, ADDITIONS & CORRECTIONS

Found any mistakes in this book? Any comments on format, manner of presentation, improving ease of use? Anything you'd like covered in more detail in a supplement or new edition of this book?

_____

_____

_____

_____

_____

_____

_____

CONTRIBUTOR IDENTIFICATION

Your name _____

Street address _____

City/State/ZIP _____

Country (other than U.S.) _____

Thanks for your help! Your contributions will serve not only to improve future editions of this book, but will illuminate the entire Beatles collecting scene.

BARB FENICK
c/o Pierian Press
P.O. Box 1808
Ann Arbor, MI 48106
U.S.A.